The World's Religions after September 11

The World's Religions after September 11

Volume 4
Spirituality

EDITED BY
ARVIND SHARMA

PRAEGER PERSPECTIVES

PRAEGER

Westport, Connecticut
London

Library of Congress Cataloging-in-Publication Data

The world's religions after September 11 / edited by Arvind Sharma.
p. cm.
Includes bibliographical references and index.
ISBN 978-0-275-99621-5 (set : alk. paper) — ISBN 978-0-275-99623-9 (vol. 1 : alk. paper) — ISBN 978-0-275-99625-3 (vol. 2 : alk. paper) — ISBN 978-0-275-99627-7 (vol. 3 : alk. paper) — ISBN 978-0-275-99629-1 (vol. 4 : alk. paper)
1. Religions. 2. War—Religious aspects. 3. Human rights—Religious aspects. 4. Religions—Relations. 5. Spirituality. I. Sharma, Arvind.
BL87.W66 2009
200—dc22 2008018572

British Library Cataloguing in Publication Data is available.

Library of Congress Catalog Card Number: 2008018572
ISBN: 978-0-275-99621-5 (set)
978-0-275-99623-9 (vol. 1)
978-0-275-99625-3 (vol. 2)
978-0-275-99627-7 (vol. 3)
978-0-275-99629-1 (vol. 4)

First published in 2009

Praeger Publishers, 88 Post Road West, Westport, CT 06881
An imprint of Greenwood Publishing Group, Inc.
www.praeger.com

Printed in the United States of America

The paper used in this book complies with the Permanent Paper Standard issued by the National Information Standards Organization (Z39.48-1984).

10 9 8 7 6 5 4 3 2 1

Contents

Introduction

Arvind Sharma

These selections from the presentations made at the Global Congress on World's Religions after September 11, which met in Montreal from September 11–15, 2006, brings together chapters that bear on the theme of religion and spirituality.

The volume is divided into six parts. Parts one through four address the specific themes of Hindu spirituality (Part I), Christian spirituality (Part II), spirituality and new religious movements (Part III), and feminist spirituality (Part IV). The rest of the volume then covers more general themes. Part V deals with religion, spirituality, science, and the environment, while the sixth and final part presents the various specific proposals that have been made for ensuring peace and progress in the world that possess a pronounced spiritual dimension.

In several recent U.S. surveys, in which the questions were phrased in terms of religion and spirituality, respondents revealed a negative attitude toward religion and a positive attitude toward spirituality.[1] This has doubtless much to do with the negative associations the word "religion" may conjure up, such as "organized religion," denominationalism, or violence. The word spirituality is free from such associations, while preserving a religious orientation toward the ultimate reality. The material presented within these pages is of particular interest in terms of the contrasting reactions provoked by the two terms—religion and spirituality. Religion may or may not be on its way out, but spirituality is definitively in, and the volume offers a glimpse of how things begin to appear when viewed through the lens of spirituality rather than religion.

NOTE

1. In a 1999 U.S. survey that asked whether the respondent thinks of spirituality more in a personal and individual sense or more in terms of organized religion and church doctrine, almost three-quarters opted for the "personal and individual" response. (See George H. Gallup Jr., "Americans' Spiritual Searches Turn Inward," http://www.gallup.com/poll/7759/Americans-Spiritual-Searches-Turn-Inward.aspx.)

Part I

Hindu Spirituality

CHAPTER 1

The Future of Mankind: The Bhagavadgītā Doctrine

T. N. Achuta Rao

Humanity is at the crossroads. The horrible incident of September 11, 2001, that reduced the World Trade Center to rubble stirred the conscience of people all over the world. It calls for a new approach to our religions, our religious faiths and beliefs, our scientific and technological achievements, and our goals. Suddenly we feel lost in wilderness and need a proper guide—the Bhagavadgītā. The world is divided into power blocks, including groups of developing and developed nations, and nations based on various religious faiths. There is mutual distrust, ill will, strife, terrorism, and war among nations, particularly in the Middle East. The world is divided on the basis of religious faith and economic disparity, there is competition among nations to possess nuclear arsenals, and one of the main concerns today is to find ways and means of preventing nuclear war.

This chapter addresses what underlies these crucial problems facing us all and tries to find an appropriate solution. The underlying problem of division is so crucial that the very existence of humankind depends on it. In addition, human beings are the most delicate animals on earth and are constantly faced with the dilemmas of good and bad, right and wrong, happiness and misery—and no one is sure what it all means. Man faces the imminent threat of total extinction any time at the press of a button. Even without that threat, humanity's very existence has become problematic because of hunger, malnutrition, scarcity of water, scarcity of food, and disease. The very structure of the human body is always susceptible to infectious diseases such as AIDS and viral fevers (the dengue, Asian flu, etc.) of unknown origin—in addition to the ever-present problems of diabetes, cancer, and diseases of the heart and kidney. These are very real problems that need urgent remedies and solutions of a different type than the ones science and technology can provide. The more the science and technology advance, the more day-to-day life becomes expensive and complicated.

The three major components to man are the body, mind, and soul. Science and technology can provide answers to the questions pertaining to the human body to some extent, but only in an incomplete way. The two other major aspects relate to the functions of mind and senses, and to the spirit or the soul. Many problems remain to be addressed in these more abstract fields.

The answer to the question of human survival lies in spirituality, which is not an easy approach to follow in a materialistic world. However, it is essential to make an earnest effort in this direction. The Bhagavadgītā could be considered the most appropriate guide for humankind at this time, and its relevance is discussed below.

THE BHAGAVADGĪTĀ

The Bhagavadgītā, popularly known as the Gītā, is well known all over the world because its translation is available in various languages. It contains the *udhgīta:* the utterances of Śrī Kṛṣṇa. According to the ancient Hindu scriptures, the people who migrated from the Nordic regions south to the valley of the Indus River, known as the River Sindhu, followed this tradition, and the text dates back to ancient times. In fact, it is stated in these ancient writings that the Lord delivered sermons and commandments to human beings about the secrets of his creation and the ways to help human beings survive on this planet, living along with other creatures. The secret of success, peace, and happiness was first revealed to Manu, the first man to appear on earth. Again, this secret was revealed to Arjuna on the battlefield of Kurukṣetra (near Delhi, India) and again was repeated to him after the war, at the end of Dvāpara Yuga; it was again told in brief to Uddhava, an ardent devotee of Śrī Kṛṣṇa. Thus, time and again the secret of happiness has been revealed to us by no less a person than the Lord. It is not surprising that such a revelation should have occurred since even today an enlightened person may receive revelations of this kind if he or she lives a life of austerity; is of absolute purity in mind, thoughts, and deeds; and is devoted to transcendental meditation.

Whatever the Lord has said has been heard by man—the ancient Seer, the Ṛṣi or the Sage—and he has preserved the Lord's words intact, strictly adhering to the rules and regulations of the Vedic grammar and phonetics in all its perfection; these words have been transmitted with devotion, knowledge, and firm faith to future generations. These sermons or commandments are known as *śruti* (what is heard) and *smṛti* (what is remembered), and they hold good even to this day. The preaching of the Lord is still practiced in India by a sect called the Bhāgavatas, the ardent devotees of Bhagavān Śrī Kṛṣṇa. They are a small proportion of the world population known as the Vaiṣṇavaites. They follow the ancient scriptures such as the Vedas, the Upaniṣads, the Brahmasūtras, and the Purāṇas including the Bhāgavata, Mahābhārata, Rāmāyaṇa, and the Bhagavadgītā. The Bhagavadgītā is the best among these since it is sum and substance all the scriptures, and it is also the most respected word of the Lord.

Among the ancient scriptures, three scriptures stand out as the prominent foundation trinity of scriptures—the *prasthānathrayī*—on which Hindu philosophy is based. These are the *Upaniṣads*, the *Brahmasūtras*, and the Bhagavadgītā. But the basis for all these is the ṚgVeda. The ṚgVeda is also the words of the creator Lord Brahmā; those uttered to his first son, Atharvan, came to be known as the Atharva Veda. These were later subdivided into four distinct parts: the ṚgVeda, the Sāma Veda, the Yajur Veda and the Atharva Veda. However, the ṚgVeda Saṁhitā (totality of Knowledge), also called *apauruṣeya* (unwritten by man) is a beautiful record of supreme Knowledge. These scriptures contain the knowledge of the entire universe in brief, and they stand as eternal Truth (*sat*). Such knowledge (*jñāna*) brings Bliss. Brahman, or the ultimate reality, is therefore called *saccidānada* for short.

The Bhagavadgītā deals with most pertinent question of war fought to establish righteousness, not war fought to obtain peace as present-day advocates of war describe it. Today, wars are being fought against unknown enemies in unfamiliar countries, involving the madness of killing innocent people. But in the Bhagavadgītā, Śrī Kṛṣṇa advocates war to fight injustice and even goes to the extent of adopting unfair means to establish righteousness (dharma). He asks the unwilling warrior Arjuna to take up arms against injustice and asks him not to think of kith and kin when it comes to establishing righteousness. He fears or favors no one when it comes to establishing truth and justice. "Truth only will reign supreme" (Satyam eva jayate) is the Upaniṣadic doctrine. Truth is Brahman/Brahm/ Supreme Consciousness.

Here, it is pertinent to ask whether war that involves killing, bloodshed, and loss of property, and that brings misery and poverty, is worthwhile when people are already suffering from hunger, disease, misery, and poverty. The answer to this question is as follows: who dies in war or who wins it is not the issue. The issue is the eradication of injustice (adharma) and the removal of people who adopt unfair means to achieve their goals. War is considered a necessary evil. All these utterances, however, pertain to the physical aspects that are of no concern to a spiritual seeker, one who wants to establish supreme order everywhere and to bring peace and prosperity, as well as emancipation or liberation (*mukti*) to the entire population of the world. Although the latter brings an everlasting solution to mankind, the former will only bring about an immediate and temporary solution. As Śrī Kṛṣṇa said at the end of the Dvāpara Yuga before departing from the earth, it is not possible to eradicate evil, since good and evil exist in the mind as the product of ignorance; duality is the quality of the universe, and that exists in the minds of the people, too. But a person of true knowledge and enlightenment can usher in equity and justice wherever he goes, by his mere presence, provided he adheres to the principles enunciated in the Bhagavadgītā. As Confucius has said, even if one person is transformed, there will be one less scoundrel in this world. Thus, our aim is to transform the entire population and make this earth a better place in which to live. It is the quality of the people that ultimately matters in civilization.

Bhagavadgītā teaches the secret of attaining to enlightenment through adherence to truth (*satyam*), self-less service (*niḥsvārtha sevā*), love (*prema*) and sacrifice (*tyāga*). The ancient Hindu way of life was one of austerity that followed the principles of universal brotherhood (*vasudhaiva kuṭumbakam*). This is confirmed by the *śānti* mantra from Upaniṣad texts. The proper approach to the problems of the world is through the practice of transcendental meditation and purification of the soul through pure thoughts, good words, and good deeds; thus, cleansing body, mind, and soul is the most important thing. This aspect is considered again at the end of this chapter. Bhagavadgītā is the guide to sensible living. It teaches Yoga to achieve purity in life through selfless action (*niṣkāma karma*); it is action without the motive of profit for the self, but rather action for common good. This is exactly the opposite of the principles of modern business practices where profit is the sole motive.

THE FUTURE OF MANKIND

The entire problem concerning world peace, security, and the welfare of mankind, should be addressed in totality (*saṁhitā*) in a way that brings together the body, mind, and soul to work harmoniously and in unison. Hence, a holistic approach is required. Any other attempt to find a social, cultural, or a political solution to human problems will not yield the desired results. This holistic approach is discussed below.

There is already a loose political organization called the United Nations, with its associated cultural organization, UNESCO. There is a UN Security Council to watch over global security aspects. The extent to which these organizations have addressed the human problems and the results they have attained so far are inconclusive, and terrible problems remain. How long will the innocent continue to suffer? Can we not find a solution to these problems now? The solution lies in the principle of live and let live. Let there be peace everywhere; let each country enjoy its sovereign power without any foreign interference so that vested interests are kept away from trouble spots. The principles of Natural Law and dharma (righteousness) should prevail.

THE DOCTRINES OF THE BHAGAVADGĪTĀ

The doctrines enunciated in the Bhagavadgītā are very clear. First, it implores everyone to work in a selfless manner for the welfare of society, for the common good. The principle involved here is that of sacrifice on the basis of the Vedic ritual of fire sacrifice *yajña* (Yajur Veda). The Lord offers himself as the *āhuti* sacrifice in the form of a horse (*aśva*) as in Śvetāśvatara Upaniṣad. The sun offers itself as the sacrificial offering (*āhuti*): it burns to provide light, heat, and life to the world. The moon is the food to sun; the plants offer themselves as food to man and beasts, and so on. Every object in this material world is for enjoyment and consumption, and each one sacrifices itself for the benefit of the other and thereby attains liberation (*mukti*). According to this principle of sacrifice (*yajña*), the correct path is to sacrifice individual interest for family interest, sacrifice family interest for community interest, and in the same way, sacrifice community interest for the sake of the state or the national interest. It is clear that universal peace depends on the sacrifice on the part of nations even when their vested interests are concerned. Hence, we have the principle of *vasudhaiva kuṭumabakam*, which means that the world is one large family (*vishva-kuṭumba*), and that all men, women, and children are children of God, living with a common interest in sacrifice and survival.

The ancient wisdom implores us that we should respect nature. All living creatures, including plants and birds, are included in this one large, extended family. The mantra is: *prithvivye namaḥ, vanaspataye namaḥ*. The principle of *vasudhaiva kuṭumbakam* is the noblest principle to usher in world peace. There is no room for any selfish interest here, be it religious or economic in nature. The supreme goal is the common good of all.

It should be clarified here when it comes to religious faith, one should not mistake religious faith for spirituality. Religious faith is sheer ignorance, and spirituality is the knowledge of the soul (ātman). Everybody should be concerned more about salvation through knowledge of the soul, ātma jñāna, and not about God, who is everywhere but is nowhere to be found. Clear knowledge about all these abstract subjects comes from purity of mind, thoughts, words, and deeds. There is no place for dogmatism or fundamentalism or groupism here. Religious faith is a purely personal affair. It is a personal communication between the Almighty and the person's soul, in the privacy of one's inner heart. Any outward display of religious faith is based on ignorance about God and is an insult to God. To realize God needs an inner eye. It is the inward-focused senses and mind that receive revelations. Absence of all external activities is the basic rule in religious faith and liberation. In view of this, Lord Śrī Kṛṣṇa advocates *bhakti mārga* and *jñāna mārga*. The proper way to emancipation is through total dedication to public service without any selfish or family interest. The fundamental principle may be formulated as follows: service to mankind is service to God.

The second important doctrine enunciated in the Gītā is that everyone should fight injustice wherever and whenever it occurs. When Śrī Kṛṣṇa says that he will descend to earth whenever unrighteousness (adharma) gains the upper hand, what he means is that everyone (since God resides in the cavity of everyone's heart) should realize the presence of the supreme spirit and fight injustice. This sends a clear signal to all concerned not to indulge in violence, or adopt unfair means to promote one's own selfish interest even in the name of God and religious faith. Everyone should find his own God in his or her heart, and not search for it in any public places such as the temples, churches, mosques, or pagodas.

The Ṛg Veda says that the Lord resides in the cavity of the heart (*hṛdaya*). The Upanishads reiterate this, and the Bhagavadgītā makes it very clear that the Lord exists in the myriad eyes and limbs of living creatures. It says that the Lord sees through the eyes of the beholder, and there is only the Lord everywhere in different names, forms, and functions—and none else. This point is further elaborated in Ishavaysa Upaniṣad as *iṣāvāsyam idam sarvam*. So, before one makes a decision in matters of war, adopts revolutionary methods, takes extreme steps toward destruction, or adopts terrorist ways to achieve goals, one should think about the real meaning and purpose of salvation. Nothing else other than salvation should be the goal. This view deserves to be endorsed unanimously. Let there be peace everywhere on earth.

It has been made very clear that this concept of God, religion, and religious faith should be clearly understood not only in a rational way but in a spiritual way as well. The latter is very important. God is nothing but one's own pure consciousness; God needs no external support for his existence through priests and prophets or preachers. Everyone should mind his or her own business, the business (busy-ness) of his soul, without disturbing the faith of others in this regard. If one turns inward and finds God in the cavity of his or her own heart, one has found salvation. If one finds God in every eye one beholds, one has attained perfection; and if one attains the knowledge of the soul (ātmā), namely that it is eternal, unborn, and immortal, and if one also knows that the Lord created man in his own image, that everything is an illusion (*māyā*), and that we are all a mirror reflection (*pratibimba*) of the Supreme Being and nothing else, then one becomes a *jñānī*. Whoever has realized this truth has attained complete knowledge. He has attained Universal Consciousness (*vishva prajñā*). This level of consciousness helps one see things as they are, in their true nature. It gives complete knowledge (*pūrṇa prajñā*), which redeems us from the cycle of rebirths whether one believes in it or not. It is this level of consciousness that is required in our rulers. It is, however, not forthcoming unless these national leaders become spiritually awakened and tap their hidden resources. Rather, they operate at the *mūlādhāra* level of lower self, which is full of lust, attachment, greed, and selfishness.

The simplest way to develop spirituality is to think of a supreme power that rules the destiny of this world. Just as the sun gets its power from this one single source, the power of Parabrahman rests nowhere else but within the heart of every organic and inorganic substance as miniscule energy, consciousness, or *prajñā*. By constantly chanting of the name of the Lord, *dhyānam, japam,* and attaining to the state of transcendental ecstasy (*samādhi*), anybody can raise oneself to this level. It is difficult but not impossible. A little time reserved for contemplation (*dhāraṇā*) every day will help achieve this transcendental state easily and quickly. At this stage of consciousness, the world looks beautiful; one forgets about one's own selfish interests and strives for the welfare of the society at large. This is the secret. Here, in the Bhagavadgītā, Śrī Kṛṣṇa and Arjuna stand respectively for the spiritually attained person as the supreme consciousness and for the individual mind confused by dualities. The very battlefield of Kurukṣetra is the human body and mind, riddled with dualities, doubts, ego, hunger for power, and selfishness. The battle is between the good and the bad, likes and dislikes, love and hate, the beautiful and the ugly—all positive and negative forces personified. Man is torn between these two opposites. At times, many people lose their balance, torn by this conflict, and find it difficult to cope with the world. Some even take such extreme steps, such as committing suicide or engaging in terrorist activities either under wrong influence or through sheer ignorance. The right solution given in the Gītā is to rise above all these dualities, see things as they are, and realize oneness (*ekatvam*), thereby attaining Unity Consciousness.

HOW TO ATTAIN UNITY CONSCIOUSNESS?

Normally, people in all walks of life function in a routine manner at the level of their lower selves, which exhibits attachment, greed, selfishness, anger, fear, jealousy, hatred, likes, and dislikes, and do not hesitate to practice unfair means to achieve their selfish ends. They are full of ego, and they fail to understand and cooperate with their fellow beings unless it is pleasurable and profitable to them. This attitude is responsible for all the maladies of the present-day world, where each person vies with others in trying to maximize profits and corner the resources of the world.

On the other hand, there are a few divine souls who operate at higher levels of consciousness. They are full of love and respect for their fellow beings, and exhibit divine qualities such as compassion, sympathy, and consideration. They strive relentlessly for the welfare of the society at large, and serve others with devotion selflessly without fear, favor, or profit.

These levels of consciousness, broadly speaking, may be identified as follows:

1. The lower self. It starts from *mūlādhāra* at the end of the spinal cord and rises above, up to *maṇipūraka* near the navel via *svādhiṣṭhāna*, which comes in

between. These plexuses are the seats of qualities displaying a mixture of *tamas* and *rajas*, which explains the behavior mentioned above.

2. The higher self. It starts from the plexus *anāhata*, near the heart, and goes up to the *sahasrāra* plexus over the head via *viśuddha* (near the throat) and the *ājñā* plexus (at the point between the eye brows). It also consists of the third eye that looks inward. These are the levels of divine qualities that ultimately bring knowledge of Brahman (Brahma-Prajñā) and supreme Bliss (Brhamānanda).
3. The highest self. A spiritual seeker should be able to reach the *sahasrār* plexus level of consciousness from the *mūlādhāra* by *sādhanā* following Haṭha Yoga or Kuṇḍalīṇī Yoga. But it is important to synthesize the *sapta vyāhṛtis,* such as *the bhū*, *bhuvaḥ, svaḥ, mahaḥ, janaḥ, tapaḥ,* and *satyam,* along with the seven levels of awareness, along with the Gāyatrī japam and Prāṇāyāma. Progress here is gradual progress, depending on the purity of the person in all aspects of his physical, mental, and spiritual life.

Only such persons who can achieve this level of consciousness can lead the world.

There are well-laid paths of Yoga to attain these higher levels of consciousness, and one cannot attain higher levels without spiritual practices (*sādhanā*). Bhagavadgītā is a text book of Yoga, where Lord Śrī Kṛṣṇa teaches Yoga to Arjuna, as, for instance, in the chapter on Yogavidyā.

There is no need to go into further details here. Suffice it to say that it is essential for man to think and act at higher levels of consciousness. All the corrupt practices can be attributed to a man's thoughts and actions at a lower level of consciousness. Thinking and acting at a lower level of consciousness also breeds corruption. Slums and dirty surroundings are to be found wherever people operate at lower levels of consciousness. People may occupy any position in society in the economic, social, political, or even religious fields, but their actions will result in total destruction of society if they do not raise their levels of consciousness. Doing so also helps people obtain divine intuitional knowledge at higher levels of consciousness.

Thus Bhagavadgītā is the storehouse of knowledge and wisdom, and it is useful for persons of any age; it also serves for all ages to come. It is the only hope for mankind to survive all natural and cultural tragedies.

It is heartening to note that India leads the world in this aspect, and more than 10 million persons have become realized souls, giving the world their spiritual knowledge and experience, and another 10 million persons are on their way to spiritual attainment. However, it must be cautioned here that not all people who pose as spiritualists are really realized souls, and many pose as gurus while lacking spiritual attainments. It is not hard to find such black sheep in the spiritual congregations.

CONCLUSION

Philosophically speaking, the future of mankind rests in the hands of the Lord Almighty, since only his will prevails. There is no escape for the mortals but to surrender their individual will to the supreme Will of the Lord (Śrī Hari Icchā). Śrī Kṛṣṇa implores everyone to surrender to him and to his will unconditionally, and he promises to deliver *mukti* (emancipation) to whoever approaches him with wisdom (*viveka*), knowledge (*vicāra*) and renunciation of worldly pleasures (*vairāgya*). It may not be possible for everyone to reach these heights at one stretch, or in one or two lives. However, there is ample scope for everybody to reach higher and higher levels of consciousness and attain supreme Bliss. This objective world of dualities does not simply exist, for all practical purposes, to such realized souls (*jñānīs*). There are numerous instances where such yogis live happily despite all the commotion in the world, contributing their mite to the betterment of the world. They can use their spiritual powers to change the hearts of people who matter. They can create a new world where people have no ill will or strife, war or misery, hunger or disease; otherwise, how can the present Kali Yuga usher in the Satya Yug, that is, the Kṛta Yuga?

Now, the task before us is to accelerate the rate of spiritual process, raise the tempo of practices, increase the number of spiritual seekers to the maximum possible, and thereby make this world a better place. Spiritual seekers are those who seek nothing in this world of objects but supreme Bliss of solitude, selfless service, and total surrender to the will of the supreme force. The world will change with a change of heart in people. It is the natural law. Everyone should strive to attain the higher level of consciousness from that of the animal level to that of man, and the human and the divine within the lifespan of a hundred years, if one is lucky to live to that mark.

But the problem remains. When the lower creatures are elevated to higher forms of life, such as through the process advocated by Darwin in his theory of evolution, the creatures of lower levels of consciousness also continue to exist. But this problem can be solved by governing the lower creatures and making even the people of lower levels of consciousness obey dharma (righteousness).

There are the teachings of great saints—Shri Ramana Maharshi, Shri Aurobindo, Shri Ramakrishna, Shri Swami Rama, Shri Yogananada, Mahesh Yogi, Maata Amrita, and Aanandamayi—whose thoughts and work lead us now in this critical period. There are many spiritually attained persons who are not even seen in public, but who remain incognito and transmit their spiritual vibrations for the welfare of the people all over the world. These are the eternal sources of wisdom, the light of Asia. Their teachings are to be imbibed, and their principles are to be practiced.

The Bhagavadgītā, as a unifying force, will play a significant role in shaping the future. It is already evident that such a change is possible with the practice of the principles of the Bhagavadgītā. It can transform people and help them raise their level of perception and consciousness. But it requires total dedication, steadfastness, and sincere effort to attain perfection and enlightenment. Only an enlightened soul can reform others. It is not so with the present-day preachers who use their mystic experiences to enrich themselves and forget about the main goal. Such people cannot transform other people. Only a few great souls, such as the Mahavīra, the Buddha, and Jesus Christ, have been able to bring some solace to disturbed souls. All others have either disappeared or divided people on the basis of faith and religion instead of unifying people.

The doctrines of Bhagavadgītā are nothing but the doctrines enunciated in the Upaniṣads. The Vedas are the basis of all divine knowledge, and the Brahmasūtras help one to understand Brahma-jñāna and bring about Unity Consciousness. But the Bhagavadgītā contains all these and much more, including the Yogasūtras (formulas) and the secret path of liberation.

CHAPTER 2

Dharma, the Cosmic Thread

Laj Utreja

BACKGROUND

The word "religion" is used to describe an institutionalized system of religious principles, beliefs, practices, and attitudes as well as the service and worship of God or the supernatural. Correspondingly, a religion is a part of the whole composed of several such systems, not capable of independently sustaining the whole. On the other hand, the generally accepted meaning of dharma is one's duty in fulfilling certain customs or laws, irrespective of the law or custom. Since dharma relates to tradition on an individual level and is based on the family—order in society or station in life—rather than on a community of people, it includes the whole and is thus universal. Dharma is inclusive of all religious principles, the natural occupation of all human beings. Sāmānya Dharma, a derivative of Sanātana Dharma, further offers a code of conduct in human behavior: "Do not do unto others that you wouldn't want to be done unto you." Sāmānya Dharma, therefore, offers a principle of universal inclusiveness and effectiveness. In following Sāmānya Dharma, we acknowledge equal treatment of all, recognizing that the source of all of us is the same.

DHARMA AND *SVADHARMA*

Between the end conditions of birth and death, a human being maneuvers through family, social, and political constraints as boundary conditions. During this journey, every human being pursues certain endeavors that generally fall under the following four categories: fulfillment of obligations and responsibilities of each stage in life (*brahmacarya, gṛhastha, vānaprastha, sannyāsa*) and order of society (*brāhmaṇa, kṣatriya, vaiśya, śūdra*); accumulation and possession of material wealth for security; enjoyment for the pleasure and gratification of the senses; and freedom from wants and worldly responsibilities in favor of spiritual knowledge. Vedic tradition categorizes these pursuits as Dharma, *artha, kāma,* and *mokṣa.* There is no human activity that does not fall in one of the four categories mentioned above. Human beings travel the journey of life in the pursuit of these goals consistent with their nature, called *svadharma.* Correspondingly, all human activities, including religious activities, are performed based on *svadharma. Svadharma,* however, may not be consistent with the family, social, and political constraints.

The adjustment needed between *svadharma* and the constraints of family, social, and political conditions is called dharma. The adjustment is the very *ācāra* and *vyavahāra* of the individual with his environment (family, society, or the world at large) in a social or political situation of conflict, which maintains the integrity of the individual and his environment. Therefore, in the extreme conditions of a polarized world of haves and have-nots, and the powerful and powerless, because we need to share our resources in global trade to fulfill our common need for food, water, and energy, dharma offers the single most effective choice for global peace and a sustainable society. Consequently, there is no better choice of word or action than dharma to guarantee appropriate human conduct as a starting or ending point for any pursuit.

DHARMA AS THE COSMIC THREAD

The concept of dharma lies in *ṛta,* the law and order of the manifested world and its progression as it follows a course of events. *Ṛta* stems from Sanātana Dharma and is therefore eternal as well. The starting point of *ṛta,* tradition, is the cause. Going back to the beginnings, the very first cause has to be the causeless cause, God. Lord Krishna states in the Bhagavadgītā:

> *mattaḥ parataraṁ nānyat kiñcidasti dhanañjaya*
> *mayi sarvam idaṁ protaṁ sūtre maṇigaṇa iva*
> There is nothing else besides Me, Arjuna. The whole universe is here strung on Me just like the cotton beads are formed of knots on a cotton thread.[1]

Every result has a cause. Going back to the beginnings takes us to the primal cause. There is nothing prior to the primal cause. Therefore, there is no one besides God as the primal cause. Our world, comprising space and the objects therein, such as the sun, planets, earth, plants, animals, and living beings; time and the events therein, such as solar and planetary motion, plate tectonics, volcanic eruptions, and lightening; and mind and the thoughts therein, such as mundane thoughts, spiritual thoughts, circumstances, and situations, is constantly changing. The essence is because of that which the world is, and we witness the changes therein as they pervade the world. The world has no separate existence from God, just as air has no separate existence from space. Just as air springs from space, dwells in space, and merges in space, in the same manner, the world is born of God, resides in God, and finally resolves in God. And when there is nothing else besides God, what more is needed to be known after one knows about God?

All activities and effects thereof have their basis in their cause. In fact, cause itself seems to be the activity or effect. Therefore, once the cause is known, the effect loses its basis and merges in the cause. Ultimately, one realizes that there is no cause other than God. The Lord states that the whole world of cotton beads is strung by him as cotton thread; that is, he pervades the world. Just as there is nothing besides cotton in the cotton beads, in the same manner, there is nothing besides God in the world. Although the cotton beads look different from the cotton thread, the cotton they are made from is the same. In the same manner, all beings in the world—with their different names, shapes, and colors—look different, but pervading them is the same essence, and that essence is God. In other words, the nature of the cotton beads and the cotton thread is the same as that of cotton. However, when a person sees the world with the world consciousness, he sees the world and not God. But when that person becomes aware of the essence of God in all, then the essence and his manifestation become one essence, the God essence. That is why the Lord calls himself the primal cause.

Lord Krishna has further made it clear in Chapter X of the Bhagavadgītā that He is the source of all creation and everything in the world moves because of Him. He is the light in the sun and the moon, the primal sound in the Vedas, the gentle touch of the air, the brilliance in fire, and taste in water. He is the purest odor of the earth, the life force in all beings, the austerity and the achievement in human beings. He is the eternal seed of all beings, the intelligence in the intelligent and the glory in the glorious men. He is the impassioned might of the powerful and the virtue in human beings. All forms of life, activity, and inertia have their existence in him, but he is imperishable whereas they change and perish.

ORDER AND PRESERVATION

Sanātana Dharma offers order for the manifested universe for its maintenance and preservation. Consequently, conformity to Sanātana Dharma is order or virtue, and disobedience of Sanātana Dharma is disorder or evil. The application of *ṛta* in human conduct in the various stages of human life and stations in a society is dharma. Correspondingly, dharma represents practical approaches for adopting Sanātana Dharma in different family traditions, business transactions, trade, and practices under all social and political conditions. Dharma is dynamic, inclusive, and evolving.

Sanātana Dharma was revealed to the ancient Seers as a result of their *tapaḥ* (persistent meditation about the reality). Sanātana Dharma is therefore beyond a law regulating individual actions. It is the very expression of God. Adherence to the divine principle is *purushārtha,* the purpose of life. Sanātana Dharma is revealed by God, propagated by God, and protected by God himself. Sanātana Dharma gives us knowledge about Brahman (the reality) as well as *ātman* (the soul). Sanātana Dharma refers to *jñāna* (knowledge about the reality to fulfill the spiritual needs of human beings) and karma (rituals and actions suitable and prescribed for self-realization). The Vedas, Upaniṣads, and the Bhagavadgītā are the source scriptures that provide us with the knowledge of the reality, *jagat* (the manifestation), and *jīvātmā* (the soul).

Sanātana Dharma is universal from the standpoint of its origin. It is not a particular prophet-centric faith; it is a God-centric *jñāna* and karma. It has no beginning, and therefore it will certainly have no end. It was never created, and therefore it cannot be destroyed. Correspondingly, Sanātana Dharma knows no racial, religious, or ritualistic borders, and transcends all space, time, and minds. Sanātana is eternal, and dharma is that which sustains. Therefore, Sanātana Dharma comprises all actions, thoughts, and practices that promote the physical and mental happiness in the world, as well as the harmony of an individual with the environment, and ensure God realization. The eternal precepts of Sanātana Dharma are good at all times and under all situations. Every human being on this earth is an ordering of Sanātana Dharma by virtue of being so. Universality of Sanātana Dharma lies in allowing a person to choose and do what is right by one's own free will.

Manifestation is ingrained with certain *ṛta* for example, the sun radiates its light and heat to make life possible on earth; the earth spins around its axis and rotates around the sun to create days and nights and seasons; the moon processes and rotates around the earth to affect the weather. In that sense, all cosmic and natural phenomena follow *ṛta* and therefore are consistent with dharma of that phenomenon. In following the natural order lies one's greatest duty, because the order provides the support for the progression that follows. Performance of duty is the ultimate sacrifice of a manifestation for the sole benefit of the succeeding manifestation. In the absence of ātman (the intelligent cause), Sanātana Dharma infuses each expression in the manifested universe with dharma of its order as *jñāna.* Devoid of ātman, *jagat* maintains *ṛta* and dharma of its order.

The ultimate expression in manifestation is jīva (human beings) with *jīvātmā* (the entity capable of expressing itself in the space-time continuum) at their very core. *Ṛta* includes the cause and the effect thereof, and in that sense, it includes history up to the present. In keeping up with the *ṛta* of the preceding manifestation, it becomes the dharma of human beings to perform duty for the service of the rest of the manifestation (for example, the environment, including other human beings, plants, and animals). In other words, all human actions consistent with dharma have their basis in *ṛta,* or Sanātana Dharma. To reiterate: the ultimate cause is God emanating Sanātana Dharma that provides *ṛta* for the phenomena and dharma for the jīva (individual human being). Sanātana Dharma, therefore, pervades *ṛta* and dharma and connects jīva (with ātman) to Brahman (the universal soul).

ATTACHMENT AND CONFLICTS

All expressions of manifestation, devoid of ātman, conduct their karma consistent with dharma. However, the presence of ātman in human beings, during their interaction with the environment, allows two different things to happen: *rāga* and *dveṣa* (natural liking and disliking) and *moha* (attachment) for the objects of the world (spouse, progeny, home, wealth, status, name, fame, etc.). Both *rāga* and *dveṣa,* per se, constitute *svadharma* and do not lead to any problems, but *moha* leads to *ichhā* (desire) to possess the object of liking and discard the object of disliking, giving rise to lust, anger, greed, delusion, hatred, jealousy, pride, and malice.

Ṛta includes the past order but does not exclude the current progress. Therefore, any evolving *ṛta,* rule, or order for the maintenance of a group of human beings in any order (*brāhmaṇa, kṣatriya, vaiśya,* and *śūdra*), is dharma. Each family has *ṛta* (traditions, religious and other); each group has *ṛta* (certain rules and charters based on religious and other traditions); each city has *ṛta* (certain ordnances based on religious and other laws); and each country has *ṛta,* (laws and a constitution based on religious and other laws) for people to live in harmony with each other. The boundary conditions of family traditions, group rules, city laws, and country constitution as applied to social situations and political conditions, however, may not be consistent with *svadharma*. Therefore, intentional and deliberate efforts in adjusting *svadharma* for human beings to live in harmony with their environment (other people with different family traditions, other cities with different laws, and other countries with different constitutions) for peaceful and harmonious coexistence is dharma.

RELIGION AND DHARMA

Religion is defined as the service and worship of God or the supernatural, commitment or devotion to religious faith or observance, and a personalized set or institutionalized system of religious attitudes, beliefs, and practices. Dharma is inclusive of all religious principles and therefore is nothing more than one's natural occupation. Religion is a sphere of human activity, whereas dharma is a way of life and a conscious choice to live in harmony with the rest of the manifestation. Religion is a system of beliefs for a group of people, whereas dharma sustains the entire manifestation. Dharma in a family constitutes following the family traditions; dharma in a group constitutes following the rules and charters of the group; dharma in a city constitutes following the city ordinances and laws; and dharma in a country constitutes following the laws and constitution of the country. Religion, if enforced, is divisive and restrictive in its relationship to all segments of a society. It offers restricted modes of worship of a divinity known and understood by a variety of names. Dharma unites all by offering a way of life accepting all viewpoints about the divine.

Dharma is a Sanskrit word with no equivalent in English. It is derived from the Sanskrit root *dhṛ* (to hold), and therefore, dharma stands for that which upholds existence of a thing. That is, the essential nature of a thing without which a thing cannot hold on to its existence. To understand the deeper meaning of dharma, we have to study the ancient texts of Bhārata (India). Only then will one begin to get some understanding. Dharma is an ideal to strive for, an ideal for all humanity. Dharma is a universal ethic, which evolved over time as eternal truth, and one that should govern every human endeavor resulting in the universal good. Dharma is the foundation for the welfare of humanity; it is the truth that is stable for all time. When dharma is not upheld, the world is afflicted by anger, greed, hatred, and fear, and undergoes stormy revolutions.

The dynamics of dharma are always in tune with the social pulse and offer a conscious choice for an individual to live in harmony with the rest of the environment. Law and order, duty, righteous conduct, religious principles, engagement and enjoyment in religion, the code of ethics, justice, compassion, truthfulness, discipline, social merit, cleanliness, and one's natural occupation all comprise dharma in the space-time continuum. It is by living a life of dharma that each element of the universe, human beings and their environment, is connected with every other element and provides ways and means to live together in harmony for collective growth. Therefore, in today's polarized world of the haves and have-nots, and the powerful and powerless, since we must share our resources in global trade to fulfill our common need for food, water, and energy, dharma offers the single most effective choice for global peace and a sustainable society.

It is difficult to define dharma, because every action and principle that supports all life is dharma. It is the very way of life for the highest good. In the Śāntiparva portion of Mahābhārata, there is a statement about dharma:

> *. . . dharmaḥ sudurlabhaḥ*
> *duṣkaraḥ pratisaṅkhyātum tatkenātra vyavasyati*
> *prabhavārthāya bhūtānām dharmapravanam kṛtam*
> *yaḥ syātprabhavasaṁyuktaḥ sa dharma iti niṣcayaḥ*
> It is most difficult to define dharma. Dharma has been explained to be that which helps the upliftment of living beings. Therefore, that which ensures the welfare of living beings is surely dharma. The ancient Seers have declared that which sustains is dharma.[2]

People are protected by the law, so long as they follow the law. There is a statement in Manusmṛti, *Dharmo rakṣati rakṣitaḥ* ("If you protect dharma, it protects you"). Dharma is that which supports the existence of an object. For one human being, it is *svadharma;* for a group and the city, it is the group law, bylaws, or charter; for a nation, it is the constitution; and for the world, it is Sanātana Dharma, the basis of dharma. Just as a thread that goes through different beads and holds them together creates one rosary, so does dharma hold together people of different faiths, races, and cultures together as humankind. Just as the beads come apart and cease to be a rosary when the physical thread holding them together breaks, so do human beings come apart and cease to be humankind if the invisible thread of dharma holding them together breaks. The only way to maintain the integrity of a necklace is if the thread of dharma is kept strong. Correspondingly, it is only by following dharma that proper maintenance of the human race can be assured. It behooves all of us as responsible members of the human race to recognize this and maintain the integrity of this necklace of human beings.

Dharma is preservation principle ingrained in our biological and psychological makeup since we first appeared on earth. It is expressed in our respect for law and order. Our sense of responsibility stems from this knowledge of the preservation principle. It is our collective responsibility to protect dharma that protects the rule of law for harmonious living. In our growing human society, with its complex social, political, and economic systems, we need to exercise dharma to elect good leaders of high integrity and character. It becomes the dharma of leaders to protect the rights of all citizens and create an environment that promotes human values. The policies must allow evenhanded treatment of all parties in commercial trade by rooting out corruption and developing equitable monetary and fiscal policies. The citizens can then freely pursue their needs for security, pleasure, and spiritual growth, and excel in their respective fields of endeavor.

The intent of dharma is to bring good to all concerned in a group. It does so by offering a satisfactory alternative to an established order adjusted to accommodate a change brought into the order because of a family circumstance, social situation, or political condition. At any given space-time condition, an individual belongs to a stage in life and an order of society with a corresponding dharma. The four stages of life and the four orders of society are as relevant today as they were when conceived in the Vedic times.

The first stage is *brahmacarya* (student life). In this stage, a person learns about God, develops skills to earn a living, and comes to understand duties. Dharma of this stage is learning without distractions by practicing self-control and discipline. The second stage is *gṛhastha* (family life). In this stage, a person works for a living and raises a family. Three of the *purushārthas* (human endeavors) of dharma, *artha,* and *kāma* are pursued in this stage. This is the most important and demanding stage in human life. It is in a family that two people from different families and backgrounds decide to live together by choice. Dharma of this stage is to develop mutual love through trust and understanding. Dharma for this stage also calls for spiritual pursuits of service to others, charity, and devotional practices.

The third stage is *vānaprastha* (retirement). After family responsibilities are over, this stage prepares one to slow down from the active pursuits of security and pleasure. Dharma for this stage is to reduce wants and begin to live a simpler life. The fourth stage is *sannyāsa* (preparation for spiritual pursuit). In this stage, a person pursues the ultimate objective of one's life: freedom from bondage. Dharma for this stage is to develop a mind free of desires and attachments to family, wealth, name, and fame.

The four orders of a society are *brāhmaṇas* (the intellectuals and the learned ones in the scriptures), *kṣatriyas* (rulers, administrators, and warriors), *vaiśyas* (business people in science, technology, medicine, agriculture, and trade), and *śūdras* (laborers). *Brāhmaṇas* are highly learned individuals who pursue moral values and ethical principles for the benefit of mankind. Their significant trait is the spread of values by example. *Kṣatriyas* display qualities of leadership, administration, heroism, and courage in all undertakings. Their main *purushārtha* is to protect the virtuous and punish the evil within the society, and defend the society or the country from external aggression. *Kṣatriyas* pursue tasks that are good and auspicious for the society.

By nature and learned skills, *vaiśyas* are inclined to produce food, conduct business, make commerce flow, and develop communication links for the society or the country with the global economy. *Vaiśyas* display the quality of accord with all. Their greatest contributions may be to spread education and healthcare by opening schools and hospitals. But the created wealth must be used for the promotion of worthy causes. These means fostering virtue and righteousness. A *śūdra* promotes cleanliness and order in the life of the other orders, not deviating from the path of dharma. *Śūdras* are always earnest to serve and attend to the needs of all, such as cleaning, washing, or running errands, so that the society functions in an orderly manner.

In this way, the whole society works by the cooperative effort of these four orders. Each human being participates in the well-being of society according to his own *svadharma* (nature and training), with corresponding rules. Such a social order was designed for maintaining dharma (order) for the entire society, the prerequisite being that each member does his dharma (duty) based on his stage in life and order in society. The wealth of the society continues to grow and is distributed in a manner commensurate with the responsibility associated with the order and agreeable to all. If each society adheres to its dharma, the welfare of the world will undoubtedly be assured.

DHARMA AS A WAY OF LIFE

Within each stage of life and order of society, any interaction between a human being and the environment (including other human beings, objects, and events) is governed by the person's *ācāra* and *vyavahāra.* Both *ācāra* and *vyavahāra* are nothing more than rendering of duty consistent with dharma to support and sustain the society. The Manusmṛti states that those who destroy dharma are destroyed by it. It also says *Tasmaad dharmo na hantavyo mā no dharmo hatovadhīt* ("Therefore dharma should not be destroyed so that we may not be destroyed as a consequence thereof"). If some members of a society are either treated unfairly or refuse to perform their duties because of family circumstances, social situations, or political conditions, adharma (disorder) sets in. Unless dharmic actions (order, equitable rule of law, justice) are employed to correct the situation, the welfare and security of the world is endangered. The dictates of *ācāra* and *vyavahār* in day-to-day life come from Manusmṛti and Mahābhārata:

> *Ahiṃsā satyamasteyam śaucamindriyanigrahaḥ, etaṁ sāmāsikam dharmam chaturvarṇyebravīnmanuḥ*
> Nonviolence, truthfulness, not stealing, purity and control of senses are, in brief, the common dharma for all the *varṇas.*[3]
> *Akrodhaḥ satyavacanam saṁvibhāgaḥ kṣmā tathā Prajanāḥ sveṣu dāreṣu śaucamadroha eva ca Ārjavaṁ bhṛtyabharaṇam navaite sārvavārṇikāḥ*
> Not to be angry, truthfulness, sharing wealth with others, forgiveness, having children from one's wife alone, purity, absence of enmity, straightforwardness, and taking care of dependent people are the nine rules of the dharma for people of all *varṇas.*[4]

It is the duty of *brāhmaṇas* to infuse every profession and occupation with dharma (ethical and moral values). And it is the duty of the members in the other three orders to perform their duties based on *svadharma.* Failing this, instability sets in, resulting in disorder, discontent, misery, poverty, and ruin. Even in today's complex societies, when the environmental pressures compel one to have one profession today and another tomorrow, or reverse gender roles at home, the dictates of dharma offer the only conscious choice to live in harmony with the rest of manifestation.

It is said that dharma stands on four legs of *satya* (truth with meditation), *dayā* (compassion with sacrifice), *tapaḥ* (discipline, austerity, and intense practice), and *dāna* (charity and sharing with the underprivileged). Depending upon the state of affairs and the developing culture, a society may stand on one or all legs of dharma. One may ask what must be the way of life: it has to be living in dharma. It is to live ethically, harmoniously, and with stability. People from everywhere refer to various duties, rights, and obligations, but this is not living in *satya,* the highest dharma. Duties, rights, and obligations are only the means, interpretations, and regulations of the family, and the societies make them complicated. Ultimately, *satya* resolves *svadharma* into the *ācāra* and *vyavahāra* of the two forces of creation: male principle and female principle. Taking the *purushadharma* (dharma for the male) and *śtrīdharma* (dharma for the female) takes the ambiguities and interpretations away from the duties, rights, and obligations. Let us consider the application of dharma to some important current issues.

THE POWERFUL AND THE POWERLESS

The modern-day democracies have a system of checks and balances within their constitutions. Constitutional law is no different from the establishment of dharma. However, dharma is ensured only when there are provisions in the constitution restraining the exercise of supremacy by any one of the divisions of the government. The only way to prevent the abuse of power is if no ambiguous and independent interpretations are made by any of the divisions of the government. Otherwise, the government cannot ensure equal protection to the subjects without discrimination. The only way to ensure that a nation will not become polarized into the two groups of haves and have-nots and/or the powerful and the powerless is if the government conforms to justice. This is possible if dharma is the supreme law of the state, where the elected leaders and subjects alike are ruled by the same law, and responsibility is afforded based on one's *svadharma.*

The elected heads of the states and other leaders must abide by dharma. It is only when they live in dharma and rule by dharma that people will live in dharma also. Therefore, it is the highest responsibility of the people to elect only those people who possess the highest moral and ethical values. Only then can all citizens expect equal justice. According to Manusmṛti, "Just as the mother Earth gives an equal support to all living beings, a king must give support to his subject without discrimination."[5]

In the great epic Rāmāyana, Lord Rāma was the ideal king. *Rāma Rājya* (an ideal system of government governed by a constitution that was dharma) provided each citizen a framework to fulfill their highest potential in their pursuits of dharma, *artha,* and *kāma.* Lord Rāma embodied dharma by the performance of his responsibilities and in his *vyavahār.* He was an ideal son, an ideal husband, and an ideal ruler. That is why Lord Rāma is the ideal person to aspire to for every student, son, husband, and ruler. Many rulers have aspired to emulate Lord Rāma and to establish *Rāma Rājya* for their governments in rendering social justice and in regulating the affairs of the state, but human failings have kept them from fulfilling their objectives.

WARS, GLOBAL TRADE, AND DHARMA

History is replete with stories of wars for ideology, faith, territorial disputes, and control of resources. Wars fought for fairness, justice, and protection of equitable rights are dharma. One cannot kill the ātman, so killing *śarīra* (the body that is perishable) for a bigger cause, such as the family, society, country, or humanity, is dharma. Today, there are two major forces at play: the forces of terrorism deployed against the powerful to disrupt their normal lifestyle and global trade, and the forces of powerful countries trying to enforce ideology as well as law and order based on that ideology. What is at stake is our common need for clean air, potable water, oil for transportation, and power. Global scarcity of water and oil and/or their distribution has increased the risk of global conflicts, especially among the poorer nations and disenfranchised people. Political violence often erupts from border disputes or because of scarce natural resources or shortages in needed commodities. It is dharma only that directs the conflicting parties to sit side by side to establish a specific law and order to satisfy the needs for each group.

Although the intent of global trade is to increase the productivity of developing countries and increase competition that will result in lowering costs, in the interim, it has resulted in polarizing the trading countries into the rich and the poor, and making the gap bigger than ever before. Workers in the laboring communities and countries are being exposed to a degraded environment, and the poor countries have had to devalue their currencies to compete. Dharma enters into the global trade through *vaiśya dharma* that sets the terms for the greatest good for all trading partners. *Vaiśya dharma* calls for appropriate policies for those workers who are adversely affected among the trading partners. *Vaiśya dharma* encourages free trade for consumer goods among trading communities just as in supermarkets or flea markets, where a common person can trade at different levels of buying capacity.

CONCLUSION

It is clear that dharma supports the society, maintains the social order, and assures the well-being and progress of the society. Dharma makes it possible for every human being to consciously make the laws of the group, city, and the country his or hers, making it easy for everyone to follow the *ṛta.*

Dharma is not restricted to any particular society or nation. Dharma expresses itself in all walks of life and in all human endeavors at any stage in life or order of society. Dharma applies to *svadharma* (the individual) and as well as to *rājyadharma* (in ruling a nation). Dharma is an ordering principle that is independent of one's faith, methods of worship, or what is understood by the term "religion"; dharma provides freedom in the chosen path for seeking the reality.

Dharma has no prejudice or partiality; it is imbued with truth and justice. So, man has to adhere to dharma, and he has to see that he never goes against it. It is wrong to deviate from it. The path of dharma requires that all human beings must give up hatred toward each other and cultivate mutual concord and amity. Through concord and amity alone the world will grow, day by day, into a place of happiness. If dharma is well established, the world will be free from disquiet, indiscipline, disorder, and injustice. It is the responsibility of every nation to uphold and protect dharma. In our common need for food, water, and energy in international trade, the only law to abide by is dharma.

An action along the lines of dharma can only be good for all. Therefore, justice, righteousness, morality, and virtue are the various forms of dharma expressed as *mānāvādharma* (dharma for the human race). Practical dharma, or *acharadharma* (human behavior and conduct), relates to the physical needs and problems of human beings at the temporal level. Therefore, dharma governing human endeavors is the obvious starting point for such an exercise. Dharma is the cosmic thread made into the beads of the different social orders, including religious faiths, and the cotton essence in all being is God.

NOTES

1. *Bhagavadgītā*, VII.7.
2. *Mahābhārata*, 109.9–11.
3. *Manusmṛti*, 10.63.
4. Śāntiparva of *Mahābhārata*, 6–8.
5. *Manusmṛti*, 9.311.

SUGGESTED READINGS

Goyandka, Jayadayal. *Srimad Bhagavad Gita* (Gorakhpur: Gita Press, 1986).
Jois, Rama. *Dharmarajya or True Government According to Dharma*, http://pages.intnet.mu/ramsurat/Textesdivers/dharmarajya.html.
Kalyanaraman, Srinivasan. *Universal Ordering Principle from Vedic to Modern Times* (Sarasvati Research Centre, 2006).
Nirvedananda, Swami. *Hinduism at a Glance* (Calcutta: Advaita Ashrama, Ramakrishna Mission Calcutta Students' Home, 1984).
Radhakrishnan, Sarvepalli, and Charles A. Moore, *A Sourcebook in Indian Philosophy* (Princeton, NJ: Princeton University Press, 1957).
Sai Baba, Sathya. *Dharma Vahini* (Prasanthi Nilayam, India: Sri Sathya Sai Baba Books and Publications Trust, n.d.).
Saraswati, Swami Prakashnand. *The True History and the Religion of India* (Austin, TX: Barsana Dham, 2003).
Sharma, Arvind. "An Indic Contribution Towards an Understanding of the Word 'Religion' and the Concept of Religious Freedom," http://www.infinityfoundation.com/indic_colloq/papers/paper_sharma2.pdf.
Utreja, Laj. *Who Are We?* (Bloomington, IN: AuthorHouse, 2006).

CHAPTER 3

Religion: Nature, Aim, and Function

B. R. Shantha Kumari

Advaita declares that the individual soul is no other than Brahman (*jivo brahmaiva na aparaḥ*), and Christianity and Islam hold that human beings are the children of God, the Father—the Supreme Reality. But in spite of one's inherited spiritual nature, a human being seems to be a strange creature—one who is always not what one actually is, and is what one is actually not. Thus, a human being considered as a social animal is actually a fallen angel, who exhibits the nature of an animal by living life at the instinctive level, but is a human being at the rational level as well as a divine being at the intuitive level. Thus man is a strange creature who is not. According to Indian philosophy, to restore man to the primal divine status by eliminating the beastly, competing lower self—which alienates one from one's own real self and others in the family, society, and nature—through the cultivation of the edifying, altruistic higher self—which enables one to intuit the unity underlying the universe at large—is the aim of all religious schools of Indian philosophy.

Although originally intended to bind people, religion today has become a deadly, divisive weapon. Consequently, there is enough religion to make us hate each other but none to make us love one another. This is so because words such as "God," "love," "life," and "religion," appear very simple but are actually very abstract and difficult to understand. The understanding and conception of these words differs not only from person to person, but also contextually changes for the same person at different times. The word "religion" has two meanings. In the narrow sense, it means theism, which emphasizes faith in a personal God—Allah, Jesus, Rama, Krishna, and so on. In the wider sense, it means liberation/salvation/union with one's personal God. This chapter explores the nature, aim, and function of religion, according to Indian philosophy.

Excessive materialistic progress (scientific and technological) accompanied simultaneously by a shocking insensitivity to moral values and spiritual impoverishment are the causes of all problems plaguing the world today. Irresponsible statesmen, unethical scientists, indifferent citizens, incorrigible politicians, uncompromising fanatics, inhuman terrorists, and immoral media are all interested only in aggravating the prevailing chaos and prolonging the problems of humankind and nature—the casualties. This disastrous situation can be remedied only by a proper orientation of each person through the values and the truths of inner life as formulated and prescribed by the mystics of India. The future of humanity and the universe depends on a sincere application of the qualities associated with the mystic traditions of India that emphasize discovering one's own self, through which everything else is attained and accomplished. What is required, according to Prof. Balasubramanian, is, on the theoretical level, a hermeneutics of retrieval, or *wiederholung,* and on the practical level, the pursuit of a rigorous discipline that makes one an inner man by helping one go inward to intuit the self through the mystic experience of Reality.

NATURE

Religion is very often identified with emotions, feelings, instincts, cults, rituals, beliefs, and faith. These views are right in what they affirm and wrong in what they deny. Religion implies a metaphysical view of the world, and it is different from philosophy. The methodology of philosophy is reason, whereas the methodology of religion is faith. If there is no questioning in philosophy, this results in dogmatism, and if there is questioning in religion, this results in heresy. Religious beliefs prevail because (1) our ancestors believed them, (2) we have proofs for those beliefs that have been passed down from ancient times, and (3) it is forbidden to question their authenticity.

Three constituents can be identified in any religion, although some religions emphasize some aspects more than the others.[1] They are

1. Philosophy—which depicts the scope of that religion, its basic principles, goal, and the means for attaining it. Because of the absence of one universal philosophy, each religion claims by using different techniques of coercion and violence that it is the only true religion, and that those who do not follow it are doomed to suffer. This attitude generates fanaticism and intolerance toward other religions. And fanaticism is one of the most dangerous current problems threatening social harmony and global peace.
2. Mythology—which includes legends about the lives of men or supernatural beings. All religions have their own mythologies that conflict and contradict the mythologies of other religions, which are condemned as superstitious belief. Examples abound: cow and idol worship of Hinduism; the aversion to the pig in Islam; the belief that God came down to earth in the form of a dove for Christianity, and so on. These details are history to the believers and mythology to the nonbelievers.
3. Rituals—which encompass forms, ceremonies, varied physical attitudes, food, flowers, incense, and other phenomena appealing to the senses. The rituals of one religion are superstitions for another religion; for example, a Síva *liṅga* is looked down upon as a phallus, and the Christian sacrament is considered to be the cannibalism of savages because it involves eating a killed man's flesh and drinking his blood to imbibe his good qualities.

Two important aspects can be identified in any religion: (1) the permanent/core/essential aspect—the mystic experience—and (2) changing, nonessential aspects—customs, names, symbols, and forms over which all religious battles are fought. When we compare religions, we find that in their essentials all religions are in agreement, and their disagreement is only with reference to their nonessentials. For example, all religions postulate perfection variously called God, Reality, Brahman, Truth, Jesus, Allah, Īśvara, and so on; all religions emphasize the practice of virtues and austerities promoting control over the body, mind, and senses for attaining God/Truth. For example, fasting is common to Hinduism, Islam, and Christianity. But how the purity and perfection are to be attained through spiritual exercises and religious techniques differs from religion to religion with reference to time, place, and context. Ethical rules regulate wayward human conduct; they are conventional, and society has every right to amend them to conform to its changing requirements. Ethical rules regulate human conduct, and their relevance is contextual to the society that formulates them. Morality is conventional, and society has every right to alter or amend it according to its changing requirements.

The transcendental Reality is without name and form and can be conceived of in different forms/incarnations/avataras—Krishna, Rama, Jesus, and so on—just as fire has no form, but it assumes the form of the burning wood/charcoal consumed by it. The universalism of Hinduism is proclaimed in the words of Krishna as follows: "In whatever way men approach me, the supreme spirit, even so do I accept them. Whatever path they chose leads to me alone."[2] A person starts a spiritual journey from where he or she is, and an ideal (*iṣṭa*) that is best suited for one's feeling and will is chosen. The finer one's mind, the greater is its capacity for higher forms of worship, until the mind is gradually drawn to meditation and intuition of Reality. Thus, because of differences in mental makeup, people are drawn to different ways of worship. To cater to the varying mentalities, scriptures prescribe different paths for the people who are in different stages of spiritual evolution. For the ritualistic, worship of God in an idol is the means; for the devotee, prayer is the means. Subtler than these is meditation; and the most edifying is constantly being absorbed in the Lord.

One's conception and understanding of God are determined by one's need and attitude, but the individual is rarely aware that one's approach to God is influenced by his or her need. Varying conceptions of God are entertained by different individuals and by the same individual at different times. To the one seeking affection, God is love; to the sinner, God is the redeemer; to the afflicted, God is the dispeller of misery; to the frustrated, God is the benefactor of wishes; to the enquirer, God is the goal of the quest. A body-conscious dualist, who looks at God as a person, different and separate from oneself, considers him- or herself as a servant, child, friend, or lover of God.

All religious experience brings a seeker closer to God. Initially, a seeker approaching God through different attitudes (servant, child, friend, lover) thinks that he or she is separate from God and all other phenomena—conscious and non-conscious—but after a mystic experience realizes that the self is different from one's body, mind, and senses, and that it is the same Reality that is inherent is all phenomena. During the initial stages of one's spiritual journey, the mind of poor understanding is fond of symbols, saints, and forms until the ineffable, formless, transcendental Reality is substituted in their place. If this is not done, worship of idols becomes mere idolatry. The Sanskrit word *liṅga* and the Latin word *symbol/symbolom* both mean a mark/sign through which we infer something. A symbol is a gross sign indicating the invisible through a visible, sensory representative phenomenon. A symbol serves as a reminder of Reality through the association of ideas. According to Swami Vivekananda, "We worship the god through the idol."[3]

Symbols can be (1) personal (e.g., idols, images of deities) or impersonal (e.g., sound, light, fire); (2) external (e.g., sun, moon, idols) or internal (e.g., *cakras*); (3) geometric (e.g., *yantras*) or anthropomorphic/human (e.g., idols, images).[4] A human relationship (servant, son, friend, lover, etc.) is symbolic irrespective of whether an image is used or not. Personality is symbolic, and if we overlook this aspect, we deviate from truth. Shankara seeks pardon for three faults he committed—although God is all pervasive, we think of him as dwelling in Kāśī; God is nameless, but we call him as Śiva, Rāma, and so on; God is without form, but we worship him in the form of a Sivaliṅga.

God is a symbol in which religion cognizes the Absolute. Philosophers may disagree about God—the Absolute—and uphold that God as the holy one who is worshipped is different from the Absolute, which is the Reality demonstrated by logic and reason. But religious/mystic experience has confirmed that the two are really one. The form gradually merges with the formless when spiritual childhood attains mystic maturity. The spiritual longing for liberation is intensified through systematic moral purification, prayer, meditation, and other religious exercises. Once the stage of realization is reached, the soul cannot be restricted to its physical body. Therefore, it condescends to mingle with the ordinary and other devotees, and enjoy the love of God. God retains in them the ego of knowledge and the ego of devotion so that they may teach the world the Truth as his messengers and chosen prophets.

AIM

All religions evolve through the personal insights of their founding prophets. But Hinduism is neither a "founded" religion, nor is it centered around historical events. Its distinctive feature is its emphasis on the inner life of the soul. To know, realize, and convert Reality into a lived experience in one's own physical body, and to transform sensory, mediate knowledge into immediate experience for living a divine life are the aims of all spiritual knowledge in India. The Vedas, embodying ancient wisdom complied by the Indian Seers, are the outcome not of logical reasoning or systematic philosophy but of spiritual intuition. When we say that the Vedas are the final authority, it refers to facts discovered and experienced by the Seers. The difference between what is heard (*śruti*) and what is remembered (*smṛti*) is the difference between abiding intuition and changing interpretations.

A scientist explores the material world; a psychologist analyzes the conscious and unconscious realms of the mind; a parapsychologist, through extraordinary perception in discovering new realms of the mind, demonstrates how the mind can transcend obstructions in time and space and foresee future events. But a spiritual seeker is anxious to directly intuit the infinite Reality that permeates and penetrates every phenomenon—conscious and non-conscious. Material life is preoccupied with the well-being of the body; mental life is concerned with the well-being of the mind; but spiritual life comprehends the body, mind, and soul, harmonizing their aims, functions, and development so that the soul can reveal its innate divinity spontaneously. A person becomes illumined to be a light unto himself or herself, and thereby enlightens the world.

Differences in experience, conscious behavior, and response of the same individual at different times, or different individuals simultaneously to one and the same phenomenon, according to Indian philosophy, are the result of latent mental impressions (*vāsanās*) that determine one's nature and personality; for example, gold and women kindle greed and lust in a greedy and lusty man, and indifference in a monk. In bondage, the daily life of the *jīva* arises from four kinds of impure subconscious mental impressions. They are (1) *loka-vāsanā*, which causes concern for social opinion by generating dislike for disrepute and desire for name and fame; (2) *śāstra-vāsanā*, which causes the ego of erudition in three ways—a person exhibits a passion for study, or is attracted to too many branches of knowledge, or blindly follows scriptural injunctions; (3) *deha-vāsanā*, which produces conceit in the body. Its three effects cause wrong identification of the body with the self, the desire for physical beauty, and the effort to cure physical disorders through impermanent remedies. The above three are impressions of mental desires (*mānasa-vāsānās*). (4) *Viṣaya-vāsanās* are residual impressions resulting from the actual experience of objects. The notions of doer-ship (*kartṛtva*), knower-ship (*jñātṛtva*), enjoyer-ship (*bhoktṛtva*), and plurality responsible for bondage and transmigration are implicit in these subconscious impressions. The latent impressions lying dormant in the mind mature under appropriate conditions, move to the conscious level, and manifest themselves explicitly through emotions exhibited and actions undertaken by an individual. Therefore, these impure impressions that produce a feeling of finitude or individuality must be eliminated, and the mind annihilated in order to terminate bondage and attain liberation.

To rid the fallen jīva of the latent mental impressions generating emotions and passions, likes and dislikes, restricting it and restore it to its divine, blissful status, Indian culture stipulates certain rites (*saṁskāras*) that have to be performed to purify and edify the jīva during its empirical journey from conception in the womb to cremation in the graveyard. The Tantra-vārtika says that *saṁskāras* are those actions and rites that impart fitness in two ways (*yogyatā ca sarvatra dvi-prakārā dośāpanayanena guṇāntaropjananena ca bhavati*): (1) by removing defects/sins (*dośas*) through austerities (*tapas*) and (2) by generating fresh qualities (*guṇas*) through rituals (*saṁskāras*), because if the defects are not eliminated, they prevent the fruit of the sacrifice from accruing to the sacrificer (by making the sacrificer experience his or her own fruits that are opposed to the fruit of the sacrifice).[5] Defining a *saṁskāra* as a peculiar excellence residing either in the body or the soul, resulting from Śāstric rites performed by a person, the Vīramitrodaya says that it is of two kinds: (1) that which makes a person eligible for performing other actions—for example, *upanayana* makes a person eligible for studying the Vedas; and (2) that which eliminates impurity, for example, *jātakarma* removes the impurity resulting from the sperm and the uterus. Since very ancient times, *saṁskāras* have been considered as highly essential for activating the dormant capabilities of a human being for development, and as functioning as external symbols of the internal changes that would make a person fit for social life by conferring a special status on the person undergoing them. The Saṁskāraprakāśa of Mitramiśra prescribes 16 *saṁskāras* that have to be performed during a person's empirical existence. They are (1) first union of the married couple during an auspicious night to facilitate the conception of a healthy male child (*garbhādhāna*); (2) squeezing the juice of the shoot of the fig tree branch into the nostril of a pregnant lady to ensure the birth of a male child (*puṁsavanam*); (3) ritualistic parting of the hair on the head of a pregnant lady with a porcupine quill to ensure the birth of a healthy baby (*sīmantonnayana*); (4) giving the newborn child honey with a golden ring before it is breast fed (*jātakarma*) so that the words spoken later by the child would also be valuable; (5) naming-ceremony (*nāmakaraṇa*); (6) feeding the child with rice and solid food for the first time (*annaprāśanam*); (7) tonsuring the child's head for the first time (*caula*); (8) sacred-thread ceremony (*mauñjī/upanayana*); (9–12) four *vratas;* (13) gifting a cow (*godāna);* (14) ceremonial bath at the guru's place after completion of formal study (*samāvartanam*); (15) marriage (*vivāha*); and (16) death-ceremony (*antyeṣṭi*). The functions of the *saṁskāras* are many: *upanayana* serves spiritual and cultural purposes; *nāmakaraṇa, annaprāśana,* and *niṣkramaṇa* express love for festivities; *garbhādhāna, puṁsavana,* and *sīmantonnayana* have additional mystical and symbolic aspects; and *vivāha* emphasizes self-discipline, self-sacrifice, and mutual cooperation. The *saṁskāras* have a psychological value, too—that of making a person aware of a new role, and the need to observe its rules. Thus, *saṁskāras* channel one's thoughts, purify one's conduct, and make a person aware of the goal of human existence.

The aim of all religion is to tame the ego, which alienates the soul from Reality/God. Thoughts, emotions, and actions influence the stomach, eyes, sex organs, and will power because there is an inseparable relationship between the words, physical organs, and centers of consciousness for thoughts that activate/stimulate the nerve centers. Spirituality is present in all but latent in many. Every saint is a sinner of the past, and every sinner has a saintly future. Purity of the mind, body, and senses is required for its manifestation. Mental impurity and abuse of the physical organs—stomach, genitals, brain, and so on—creates an obstacle and prevents the ascent of spiritual energy. When the lower channels are closed through work, devotion, meditation, and so forth, the higher centers open up until bondage is destroyed, and the mind perceives a new vision of existence and Reality.

The body is like a stringed instrument. Each organ, each nerve center has a music of its own. The Hindu yogis give the analogy of a snake charmer, who holds the snake with music. By playing various tunes, he can make it rise up on end. Similarly, the *Kuṇḍalinī* is aroused until it unites with the supreme Reality. Because of ignorance (*avidyā*), we are unaware of our real nature (*svarūpa-ajñāna*) and are as if we are hypnotized. Through work, worship, mind control, or self-knowledge, we have to dehypnotize ourselves to attain liberation—the goal of religious life. Dogmas, doctrines, scripture, temples, and the like are only secondary details.

As seen in the history of religions, a person can adopt different attitudes toward other religions:[6]

1. Denunciation—an individual considers one's own religion as true and good, and other religions as false and wicked and fit enough to be destroyed.
2. Syncretism—people of different religions stay together and stress their common points rather than their differences.
3. Eclecticism—the good points of other religions are taken into one's own religion, and what is considered bad is rejected.
4. Toleration—a person regards his or her own religion as the best and the truest but does not criticize other religions.
5. Acceptance—there is no negative attitude, and one acknowledges all religions as equally true paths to the same goal.

FUNCTION

The essence of all religions as evidenced in the lives of great mystics and saints is the same—emphasizing purity, strength, and harmony—but the later accretions of creeds and dogmas introduced by ignorant and selfish priests to exploit the gullible for personal gain generate discord. The danger to the world is not because of atheists denouncing God, modern materialism, or rational philosophy, but rather the theists professing to practice religion and protecting it. According to Radhakrishnan, "Every religion has its popes and crusaders, idolatry and heresy hunting. The cards and the game are the same, only the names are different. Men are attacked for affirming what men are denying. Religious piety seems to destroy all moral sanity and sensitive humanism. It is out to destroy other religions, not for the sake of social betterment or world peace, but because such an act is acceptable to one's own jealous God. The more fervent the worship the greater seems to be the tyranny of names. By a fatal logic, the jealous God is supposed to ordain the destruction of those who worship him under other names."[7]

Proclaiming religious doctrines, demonstrating proficiency in scripture, practicing rituals, and exalting orthodoxy above the sanctity of life do not make a person religious or pious—only being compassionate and self-effacing can do so. Being religious does not empower one with an authority to criticize other religions or evaluate another's devotion and spiritual stature. People are judged not by what they say but by what they do.

The aim of any religion is a very important aspect deserving attention. Although the essence of religion is spiritual redemption, the emphasis today is on social reform. Spirituality and piety imply service and fellowship/camaraderie, but cannot be equated with them. The challenge that religion presently has to face is not only disbelief and secularism, but also the invisible threat masquerading as social reform. Much of the so-called social service undertaken by religious institutions is tainted by an undignified sectarian motive of converting their beneficiaries into members of their own religious fold.

We must distinguish between two forms of religion: pseudo-religion and real religion. Nothing is so hostile to religion as other religions. According to

Radhakrishnan, "We have developed a kind of love and patriotism about religion with a code and a flag, and a hostile attitude towards other men's codes and creeds. The free spirits who have the courage to repudiate the doctrine of chosen races and special prophets and plead for a free exercise of thought about god are treated as outcasts."[8] Under these circumstances, it would appear that the world would be a more religious place if all religions were banished from it says Radhakrishnan, echoing the bishop of London's view. As a result, the rational are inclined to believe that the remedy for religious fear, conceit, and hatred is to reject religion itself. Religion today is a branch of statecraft and a plaything of politics. Where religion has not been itself the oppressor promoting ignorance by violence, it seems to lend its authority to the oppressors by apparently endorsing fanaticism and sanctifying people's religious pretensions. The life of the truly religious is life transcending because of life transformation. Genuine religious experience kindles authentic love for God, human beings, and nature. In religious experience, one's self and Reality become one. Mystic experience is the same, but interpretations are different and are determined by one's attitude and exposure to one's own religion and other factors.

The difference between the supreme as the spirit/Reality (Brahman), and as a person/God (Īśvara) is one of standpoint and not of essence between God as he is and God as he seems to us. Brahman is known as Īśvara from the cosmic viewpoint (*saprapañca-dṛṣṭi*), and Īśvara is Brahman from the a-cosmic viewpoint (*niṣprapañca*). The abstract and the impersonal aspect of the supreme is called the Absolute, and the supreme as a self-aware and self-blissful being is called God, but Reality transcends all conceptions and postulations of personality and impersonality. It is called the Absolute to indicate the insufficiency of the language and thought, and is called God to denote that it is basis of all existents and their goal. Religious mysticism often falls into the language of passionate love. During religious experience, its influence is so powerful and overwhelming that one has neither the power nor the desire to analyze it. Only the morally qualified (*adhikārin*) and the fortunate chosen by the supreme Lord can attain it, which is self-established (*svataḥsiddha*), self-evidencing (*svasaṁvedya*), self-luminous (*svaparākaśa*), and a truth-laden experience.

The various religions are like the radii/spokes of the wheel leading to the same center. They come closer to one another as they converge at the center—the mystic experience—in which they all meet. A mystic is one who loves truth for its own sake, has pursued a path, and has perceived the Truth, an intuitive experience that transcends reason and sense perception. The blessed moments of religious experience influence an individual's personal life and so reinforce the person's religious views that nothing can nullify them thereafter.

The chaos prevalent across the globe is the result of the inability of religion to promote a good life, the continuous pressure of new knowledge on traditional beliefs, and the startling success of modern science, especially mathematics, physics, and astronomy. Intellectual snobs think that being religious is being old-fashioned, and that mocking at it is a mark of achievement. A truth is tested by the value of its consequences and its practical utility. In science, experiments are conducted on the basis of the hypothesis even before the hypothesis is tested and proved. Similarly, in religion, too, we must avoid making premature judgments and evaluate religious views not by their objective truth but by their moral and spiritual results.

Social revolutionaries contend that religion blocks the way to all progress, and that it is a superstition that must be rooted out at any cost. Spiritually, a ceremonial religion is good for nothing if it has failed materially to stop the strong from exploiting the weak, and if it psychologically has developed traits that are antisocial, and antiscientific. When we see religious people aligning themselves against common sense and scientific knowledge, against the dictates of humanity and the demands of justice, all in blind obedience to laws whose infallibility is a myth, people get tired of religion and think that it is time to abandon it. What a country wants today is not so much salvation from sin as social betterment that will transform the mass of people who are ill fed, ill clothed, and ill housed into a free community of well-regulated families, living not in luxury but in moderate comfort without fierce or unhealthy competition.

We may not know the ultimate meaning of God, although we may know something about God or what answers to God in Reality through religious experience. The creeds of religion correspond to the theories of science. The theories are symbolic and accepted because they work. Similarly, we have certain experiences that we try to account for through the assumption of God. The idea of God is an interpretation of experience. Speculative theology can conceive of God as a possibility; it is religion that affirms God as a fact.

A philosophy of religion is different from dogmatic theology because it questions the accepted views of religion and grounds its claim on the Reality of varied human experience as a whole. In dogmatic theology, on the other hand, the theologian considers oneself as an expositor of traditional doctrines accepted as revelation, and one's function is restricted to discarding inconsistencies and contradictions in them. One bases one's views on selected facts and discards elements of Reality that are unacceptable to one's framework. Therefore, a theologian is free only within permissible limits to interpret religious doctrines and explain their implications. But one's investigation, explanations, and conclusions have to always confirm one's pet dogmas. Thus, while the methods are optional, in dogmatic theology, one's conclusions are obligatory.

"It is a function of philosophy to provide us with a spiritual rallying centre, a synoptic vision . . . a philosophy which will serve as a spiritual concordant, which will free the spirit of religion from the disintegration of doubt and make the warfare of creeds and sects a thing of the past."[9] A discerning individual must distinguish between what is permanent and what is changing in religious beliefs, and update the permanent through reinterpretations with new knowledge and social needs. In rejecting the a priori roads of speculative theology and the apologetic method of dogmatic theology, one should adopt a scientific view of religious experience, and examine with detachment and impartiality the spiritual inheritance of men of all creeds and of none. Such examination of the claims and contents of the religious experience based on the spiritual history of man points to spiritual idealism, which is opposed to disruptive forces of scientific naturalism on the one hand and religious dogmatism on the other. According to the Advaita-Vedānta, whose epistemology is radically empirical and metaphysics spiritually idealistic, we have to annihilate the ego (*ahaṅkāra*), which is the fount of all personal, social, and global problems. When the alienating ego, preventing edifying influence is annihilated, we can have inter-faith dialogue in the place of religious wars.

NOTES

1. S. Radhakrishnan, *What Religion Is in the Words of Swami Vivekananda*, ed. Swami Vidyatmananda (Kolkata: Advaita Ashrama, 1985), p. 25.

2. *Bhagavadgītā*, 4.2.

3. Swami Vivekananda, *The Complete Works of Swami Vivekananda*, Mayavati Memorial edition (Calcutta: Advaita Ashrama, 1987), Vol. VII, p. 286.

4. Swami Yatiswarananda, *Adventures in Religious Life* (Chennai: Sri Ramakrishna Math, 1985), pp. 147–50.

5. *Tantra-vārtika*, 3.8.9.

6. Yatiswarananda, p. 11.

7. S. Radhakrishnan, *Idealist View of Life* (Chennai: Blackie & Son [India] Ltd., 1979), p. 34.

8. Radhakrishnan, *Idealist View of Life*, p. 34.

9. Radhakrishnan, *Idealist View of Life*, p. 65.

CHAPTER 4

Why Is There So Much Suffering in the World?

Marshall Govindan

HUMAN SUFFERING: WHAT'S NEW ABOUT THAT?

News reports from around the world confront us all with the very difficult question of why is there so much suffering in the world. The phenomenon of widespread suffering is, of course, nothing new. Natural disasters, wars, epidemics, and criminal activity have been around since the beginning. What is new is the way the media, via television in particular, bring the suffering of so many human beings on the other side of the planet right into our living rooms. If nothing else, such a modern phenomenon forces us to focus on this question and attempt to come to find some answers. "If the purpose of human knowledge is the elimination of human suffering, that which eliminates it completely is the highest knowledge," said the great commentator on the Yogasūtras, Swami Hariharananda Aranya.[1] We spend so much precious time acquiring so much trivial knowledge. Let us all pray for wisdom to understand the "why."

Yoga has a great deal to say about the causes of human suffering, and what to do about it, but unlike modern technocratic approaches, which speak of remedies in terms such as "economic development," "legislation," "medical care," and "education," the Yoga siddhas such as Patañjali and Tirumūlar made diagnoses of the human condition at its most fundamental level, and prescriptions as a consequence of those insights. These remain as true today as they did over 2,000 years ago, because our human nature is still the same. That is why it is important for each of us, as students of Yoga, to not only study their teachings, but also to share them with a suffering world.

THE *KLEŚAS* OR AFFLICTIONS

In the Yogasūtras, second Pāda, or chapter, Patañjali tells us about the five causes of suffering, the *kleśas:* "Ignorance, egoism, attachment, aversion and clinging to life are the five afflictions."[2]

"Ignorance" is the primary cause of suffering, and it brings about the others. It refers not to ignorance in general, but specifically to an absence of self-awareness. It is the cause of the confusion between the subject, "I am," and all of the objects of awareness. It hides our inner awareness and creates a false identity: "I am the body, mind, senses, and emotions." In the average person, these five afflictions are constant and sustained. When our well-being or survival is threatened, we typically respond in fear without any reflection. In a subsequent verse, Patañjali tells us, "Ignorance is seeing the impermanent as permanent, the impure as pure, the painful as pleasurable, and the non-Self as the Self."[3]

It is a case of mistaken identity, which causes us to say "I am tired," "I am worried," "I am angry." We approach the truth, however, when we say, "My body is tired" or "My mind is filled with worrisome thoughts." This ignorance of our true identity, the Self, is the fundamental cause of our human suffering. The Self is the eternal Witness, the Seer, a constant, pure One Being, infinite, all pervasive, present in everything. Everything else is temporary and changing. By clinging to what is impermanent, we are bound to suffer, not only when we lose it, but long before, when we succumb to the fear of losing it or her or him. By perceiving the permanent, the Self, pervading everything, as a constant amidst a sea of change, one finds an abode of peace and Self-realization.

"Egoism is the identification, as it were, of the powers of the Seer (*Puruṣa*) with that of the instrument of seeing (body-mind)."[4] Egoism is the habit of identifying with what we are not, that is, the body, the mind, the emotions, and sensations. This error is produced by our basic ignorance as to who we truly are. It is not an individual defect but a universal human trait, or temporary flaw in our design, by which consciousness has become individuated within each living entity and contracted, so to speak, within each individual. It not only contracts around the body but around every individual thought and sense perception. "I see," "I think," "I believe," "I hear," says the ego. This principle of nature, the individuation of consciousness, can only be overcome by a gradual expansion of our awareness, resulting from the cultivation of detachment and discernment: *vairāgya* and *viveka,* two of the most important activities of the *yogin*. Rather than thinking "I am suffering," we begin to rise above the egoistic perspective by becoming a witness to the suffering, and then by doing whatever is necessary to either alleviate it, banish it, or cultivate its opposite.

"Attachment is the clinging to pleasure."[5] Because of the individuation of consciousness, and its false identification with a particular body and set of thoughts and memories, we are attracted to various pleasant experiences in our environment. Attachment, like fear, springs from the imagination, (*vikalpa*) and occurs when we confuse the internal experience of bliss (*ānanda*) with a set of outer circumstances or factors, and we call this association pleasure (*sukham*). We imagine that pleasure depends upon these external circumstances or factors. When they are no longer there, we experience attachment, the delusion that the inner joy cannot return unless we again possess external factors. Attachment involves both clinging (*anuśaya*) and suffering (*dukham*). In reality, bliss is self-existent, unconditional, and independent of external circumstances or factors. One need only be aware to experience it. And practice letting go of attachment.

"Aversion is clinging to suffering."[6] In the same way, we are repulsed by various experiences in our environment. These are relative terms, and what is painful for one may be pleasant for another person. There is a third possible response however: detachment (*vairāgya*), which Patañjali recommends as the most important means to go beyond the duality of pleasure and pain. Changing an outer circumstance is often not possible, at least immediately. We should first focus our will on clearing and deepening our consciousness to avoid reacting with aversion. Then aspire for an outer change, for a more harmonious situation. Accept any work that is given to you in the spirit of Karma Yoga, as a spiritual training, to purify you of attachment and aversion. Perform all actions selflessly, skillfully, and patiently, recognizing that you are not the "doer." Cultivate equanimity as you perform actions, and with regard to the results.

"Clinging to life (which) is self-sustaining, arises even in the wise."[7] Every living being has an instinctual drive of self-preservation, which is based upon the fear of death and false identification with the body. We all have had to go through the painful process of death and rebirth so many times that we shrink from having to repeat it. When our life is threatened, our body instinctively reacts with a rush of adrenalin, and our heart and pulse begin to race. We cry out in fear. However, by reflecting deeply upon our true identity, the immortal Self, we free ourselves from all such *kleśas* or afflictions.

"These (afflictions in their) subtle (form) are destroyed by tracing (their) cause(s) back to (their) origin."[8] On a subtle level, these afflictions exist as subconscious impressions or *saṁskāras,* and can be eliminated only by the repeated return to our source through the various stages of *samādhi.* Because the subconscious impressions are not accessible to us in ordinary consciousness, or even through meditation, one must eliminate their root, egoism, by repeatedly identifying with our true Self. The little "i" becomes subsumed gradually in the greater "I," and as it does, the subconscious impressions dissolve." In Sūtra I.12, Patañjali tells us the method: by constant practice (*abhyāsa)* and detachment (*vairāgya*), one ceases to identify with the fluctuations arising with consciousness.

"(In the active state) these fluctuations (arising within consciousness) are destroyed by meditation."[9] This indicates that meditation is a necessary prerequisite to *samādhi,* to deal with the habitual movements of the ordinary mind. Meditation is calming, and brings awareness of the above cited afflictions as they manifest in our daily lives. Meditation helps us to weaken them.

KARMA AND THE UNEXPECTED SOURCES OF SUFFERING

When unexpected catastrophes strike, such as the tsunami in South Asia, we also find ourselves wondering, Why did some die, and others were spared? Or closer to home, Why me? What did I do to deserve this? Patañjali and the siddhas have much to say about the nature of karma, which may be defined as the consequences of past thoughts, words, and actions. Because of the existence of the five afflictions discussed above, we accumulate and express karmas. These are of three types:

1. *prārabdha karma:* those presently being expressed and exhausted through this birth;
2. *āgāmi karma:* new karmas being created during this birth;
3. *sañcīta karma:* those waiting to be fulfilled in future births.

The receptacle for all karmas is known as the *karma-āśaya*, "the reservoir, or womb, of karma," or "action-deposit." The karmas wait for an opportunity to come to the surface and to express themselves through the afflictions. One strong karma may call for a particular birth and body to express itself, and other closely related karmas will also be expressed or exhausted through it. This goes on until one attains Self-realization and ceases to create new karmas.

Although each of us has his or her own karma, which conditions each of us to live and react in a particular way, this programming is not absolute. We have free will as to how we will deal with our life circumstances, positively or negatively. If we choose to deal with these negatively, for example, by creating suffering for others, the reactions return to us in more intense or terrible forms. Dealing with circumstances patiently and consciously, and creating happiness for others, gradually neutralizes the karmic consequences.

I am reminded of a report from Asanka Wittachy, who was engaged in refugee relief in Sri Lanka, who wrote,

> In the single afternoon that it took to distribute our meager bounty, I witnessed the basest and the highest qualities that men can aspire to. Whilst ruthless and depraved excuses for human beings used violence and guile to loot and rob the remaining meager possessions of survivors and even the vehicles carrying them food were robbed, others displayed the noblest qualities the human spirit can aspire to.
>
> One such instance was a man standing alone amidst the ruins of his house. I called to him and offered him one of the cooked lunch packets which we were distributing at the time. He looked me in the eyes with sorrow and gratitude and quietly informed me that he had already eaten a piece of bread for breakfast and so he would prefer that we give the packet to another who had not been so fortunate that day.[10]

RESPONDING TO SUFFERING

This brings me to the point of this reflection: what is important about such tragic events is what we learn from them and how we respond. Patañjali tells us, "That which is to be eliminated is future sorrow."[11] Only when we remember the Self can we go beyond the "sorrow yet to come," which in turn "results from our reservoir of karma," for "the Seen (exists) only for the sake of the Self."[12] The purpose of "the Seen . . . is to provide both experience and liberation (to the Self)."[13] Nature provides us with experience and ultimately liberates our consciousness from its bondage of false identification. Eventually we feel we have had enough suffering in the hands of Nature and seek a way out of egoistic confusion. ("I am the body-mind," etc.) To put it more plainly, the purpose of every experience is to provide us with a lesson: to distinguish truth from falsehood, wisdom from ignorance, the permanent from the impermanent, love from attachment, the Self from the body-mind-personality, the Seer or Self, from the Seen. Yoga is a wonderful antidote for our Self-forgetfulness. Once we begin to remember who we truly are, when faced with the suffering in others, we have an opportunity to respond with compassion or to react negatively, such as with judgment or fear. Even if what we can do by our thoughts or actions for another is only a little, compassion (*karuṇā*) toward those who are suffering purifies our mind and emotions, and serenity results. With a mind purified by compassion, our actions become inspired, energized, and aligned with the will of the Divine, resulting in the highest good for all.

So, in the face of human suffering, let our thoughts, words, and actions be moved only by compassion. May compassion pour forth from our hearts.

NOTES

1. Swami Hariharananda Aranya, *Yoga Philosophy of Patanjali*, (Kolkata: University of Calcutta Press, 1981).
2. Marshall Govindan, *Kriya Yoga Sutras of Patanjali and the Siddhas: Translation, Commentary and Practice* (St Etienne de Bolton, QC: Babaji's Kriya Yoga and Publications, 2000), p. 4 (II. 3).
3. Govindan, p. 6 (II.5).
4. Govindan, p. 6 (II.6).
5. Govindan, p. 8 (II.7).
6. Govindan, p. 9 (II.8).
7. Govindan, p. 10 (II.9).
8. Govindan, p. 11 (II.10).
9. Govindan, p. 12 (II.11).
10. Asanka Wittachy, report to author by e-mail, January 2003.
11. Govindan, p. 80 (II.16).
12. Govindan, p. 85 (II.21).
13. Govindan, pp. 82–83 (II.18).

CHAPTER 5

Yoga as a Social Movement

Marshall Govindan

ANCIENT CLASSICAL YOGA

You might be surprised to know that Yoga is considered to be one of the six most important systems of philosophy in India. These are known as "darśanas," or perspectives, and Yoga is considered to be the most practical of these. It is based upon an older system known as Sāṁkhya, and it holds to three principal eternal realities: the Lord, the soul, and the world. It rejects the view that the world is an objective illusion, unlike many Eastern religions; in the language of philosophy, it is theistic, pluralistic, and realistic.

THE YOGA SIDDHAS

Humans have the advantage over other animals of being able to conceive of perfection, to notice their imperfections, and to devise and apply means to bridging the two.

The adepts of Yoga are known as siddhas, or those who have realized perfection, transforming large parts of their human nature. Theirs was not merely a spiritual path but an "integral" Yoga, which sought to realize perfection in all five planes of existence: physical, vital, mental, intellectual, and spiritual. Rather than seeking liberation from this world, they sought to bring perfection, the Divine into it, one person at a time. This is a progressive path that occurs as the adept surrenders his or her entire being at all levels, becoming a saint, then a sage, then a siddha. The siddhas have left a large number of literary works, which our Yoga Research and Education Center has been collecting, preserving, transcribing, and translating for many years.

THE SOCIAL CONCERN OF THE YOGA SIDDHAS

An area of interest in these writings is the "social concern" of the siddhas. The mystic experience of the siddhas has given a new dimension to social service. Their mantra, *Śivāya namā* has a double meaning. On a mystical level, it means: "That Supreme Being, I am." But it has an alternative meaning: *namā* means *tyāga,* or sacrifice, Śiva means bliss, and *āya* means result. That is: "the result of sacrifice is bliss." To them, service and work begin with one's own Self-realization, and the personal sacrifice involved, and then includes "*āṟṟupaṭai,*" which means "showing the path to one and all" irrespective of caste, creed, sex, religion, or nationality. The siddhas wanted everyone to enjoy what they themselves had enjoyed, the supernal bliss of God realization. Their songs and poems are indicators of the path to follow. The methods of Kuṇḍalīnī Yoga that they developed provide the practical means of purifying consciousness out of its habitual, egoistical tendencies. They prescribed ethical precepts, or *yamas,* including what one should not do: get stuck in half measures such as caste, rituals, temple worship, dogma, and other institutional frameworks. Realizing that disease and sickness were big obstacles to perfection, they developed a system of medicine known as Siddha Vaidya, which included Yoga therapy. They spoke directly to the common person, bypassing the religious institutions by teaching in the simple, vernacular language of the people, often in ways that would shock people out of their conventional attitudes. All of this threatened the dominant religious institutions, and so the siddhas were often attacked or ridiculed, and their works were not well preserved.

YOGA: THE PRACTICAL SIDE OF ALL RELIGIONS

For more than 100 years, Indian yogis have been teaching in the West. Their influence has been profound in many fields of science, and even in business, despite the fact that there has been little acknowledgement of this by historians, sociologists, politicians, or the media. Where the influence has been noticed, for example by the leaders of Western religious institutions, it has been usually in the form of alarm. Many Western religious institutions have felt threatened by the teachings of Yoga, fearing a loss of influence or something harmful or un-Christian from an Eastern spiritual practice. This is nothing new. Throughout history, mystics (the Western religious term for yogis) have been looked upon with suspicion, even fear, because of ignorance. Yoga is the practical side of all religions. It includes the spiritual practices that enable one to realize the truths of one's chosen religious beliefs. Yoga goes beyond belief to personal experience as a result of its powerful mind-body methods.

As many as 20 million people in North America, by some estimates, are now practicing Yoga; although 90 percent of these practice it only as a physical exercise, this does not mean that the influence of Yoga is limited only to the fields of health or physical fitness. If one continues to practice Yoga, the effects begin to include the nervous system and the mind, and consequently, there is an expansion of consciousness into the spiritual dimension. This occurs as a natural and spontaneous consequence. What begins as a physical need, or a means to control the effects of stress, eventually becomes a very personal spiritual path. A spiritual path leads one to increasing levels of awareness, and therefore to personal freedom from the round of habitual tendencies fostered by our social conditioning.

FROM EGOISM TO SELF-REALIZATION

As our consciousness expands, we become witnesses to our lives, and we rise above the perspective of the ego. "I am a man, a professional, black, white, or Asian," or "I am tired, hungry, angry," says the ego. "I am That I am" the awakened yogi realizes: nothing special. The Witness is not the part of you that is reading these words, nor is it the part of you that is thinking about what I am saying. It is the silent awareness that is watching every movement of the mind and senses. Like the light in a room, it is that which is behind every form and change. It is the one constant reality of your life, your true Self, beyond names and forms. It is pure consciousness, Yoga teaches. Its realization replaces the confusion of egoism, the habit of identifying with what we are not: thoughts, emotions, memories, habits, sensations. The social implications of such a change in consciousness are profound and wide ranging. Not only does the yogi become a source of peace and well-being for those who enjoy his or her company, but also a dynamo of energy, guided by unusual clarity and insight. Such a person can and will act as a powerful agent for the Good, solving the problems of this world in a spirit of compassion and wisdom.

THE YAMAS OF YOGA LEAD TO THE REALIZATION OF THE ULTIMATE SOCIAL STATE

"No man is an island," said John Donne, the English poet, and this applies to the mystic or yogi. In Classical Yoga, the first limb, the *yamas,* or restraints, govern the yogi's social behavior:

1. *Ahiṁsā,* or non-harming in thoughts, words, and actions. Thinking ill of others only reinforces whatever negative quality one perceives, not only in others but in the person making the judgment. *Ahiṁsā* includes speaking only after reflection, and only what is helpful and uplifting. Right action will follow right thought and speech. *Ahiṁsā* may include protecting others from harm.
2. *Satya,* or truthfulness, includes speaking only what is true, and the avoidance of lying, exaggeration, deceit, and hypocrisy. Otherwise, we deceive ourselves and postpone our own purification. Use words to bless others. The truth of things is quickly revealed. This brings clarity to our minds and relationships.
3. *Asteya,* or non-stealing. Stealing engulfs our consciousness in darkness and reinforces egoistic tendencies and closes our hearts.
4. *Brahmacarya,* or chastity. This is conscious and healthy control of sexual energy, not only physically but especially on the mental and emotional planes. It includes avoidance of fantasizing, which is a great source of distraction and frustration, and consequently is an obstacle to Self-realization.
5. *Aparigraha,* or greedlessness, includes not fantasizing over material possessions or desires, which is a distraction from one's inner source of joy and awareness.

These restraints are observed not to satisfy some moral principles, but because their observance is both a prerequisite for, and an expression of, the enlightened state. By observing them, one comes to experience that there is no "other," but only One: the ultimate social state.

The determined observance of these restraints by a number of dedicated yogis can and will have a profound impact upon society. In any social interchange, whether it is with family members, work colleagues, clients, supervisors, or strangers, there is an interchange of energy. That energy may be infused with love and compassion, which is profoundly yogic by definition, or infused with anger, greed, impatience, competition, or antipathy. We feed one another with our love and compassion, helping one another to be who we truly are—conscious, universal beings—or we poison one another with our egoistic tendencies. On the contrary, the determined observance of our egoistic tendencies, for example, by the extremists in the Israeli-Palestinian conflict and in Northern Ireland during the Catholic-Protestant conflict, produces only unending sorrow.

YOGA VERSUS THE MODERN CULTURE OF MATERIALISM AND INDIVIDUALISM

Yoga is a social movement, for it seeks to awaken and to transform one human being at a time from the ordinary egoistic state. Our modern pluralistic culture is largely inspired by the principles of individualism, materialism, and consumerism, which amount to a recipe for egoism. To the extent that one practices Yoga, beginning with the restraints, or *yamas* (cited above), and observances, the *niyamas* (purity, contentment, self-study, intense practice, and devotion to the Lord), one is engaged in a kind of guerrilla war against the prevailing culture. The word "culture" is derived from the Latin word *culte,* which means "worship." So, in our modern culture, most members of society worship or value, above all, those things that are material, which can be consumed and which enhance their feeling of being special. Modern Western culture has largely succeeded in transforming the public's initial perception of Yoga as something which will serve its own values: to look good, to be special, or to experience something new and special.

A true yogi, on the other hand, aspires for or worships, above all, the Lord, the Absolute Reality, and this is found within, in the spiritual plane of existence, initially, until in the enlightened state, one begins to perceive it as imminent in everything. The yogi does not consider himself or herself to be anything special, and does not even see himself as the "doer." The yogi recognizes the hand of the Supreme Being, guiding and empowering at every stage.

THE YOGA COMMUNITY: DEVELOPING COMPASSION

While it is the responsibility of each practitioner to raise himself or herself up (by his or her own efforts), there is an undeniable aid that is provided between members of the Yoga. When a person is discouraged or confused, the presence of fellow yogis will usually serve to heal or inspire. While this exchange is most clearly seen in the exchange of vital energy between two people, a kind word or thought on the mental plane, a bit of advice on the intellectual plane, or a smile and expression of joy on the spiritual plane may be enough to remove the discouragement or confusion. It is therefore essential that all practitioners of Yoga not isolate themselves. By sharing their love and compassion, they learn to integrate their spiritual realizations at all levels of existence.

YOGA: THE GREATEST DEFENSE AGAINST TERRORISM AND THE DARK SIDE OF HUMAN NATURE

We live in a period of history wherein the interdependence of everyone on the planet has never been so great. A social crisis, whether a flu epidemic or an act of suicide in one part of the world, instantly can affect the economy and political stability of a society on the other side of the planet. This reality requires nothing less than the discipline of Yoga by millions of inspired practitioners. The media has become the greatest tool of those who would seek to terrorize society. The greatest defense against terrorism is Yoga, for it strikes at its source the fear that permits terrorism to be effective. Fear is imagination of the possibility of suffering. It is the feeling of separation, that I am merely a body, or I am these thoughts. In Yoga, one experiences profoundly one's unity with everything. This is a change of consciousness rather than of opinion or belief. "I am That," says the yogi, not "I am a Hindu, Christian, male, female." And "You are That, too." Overcoming fear requires mental discipline, the practice of detachment, and the calm, clear thinking that Yoga inspires. Not only is it an antidote against fear, but against all elements of the dark side of human nature. The societal effect of one yogi's positive thinking or blessing is much more powerful than the dispersed negative thinking of a thousand ordinary people.

May Yoga practitioners all come to recognize the power they have to bring peace and enlightened solutions to the world's diverse problems, in every moment and in every situation.

CHAPTER 6

Yoga as a Spiritual Movement

Subhas R. Tiwari

There can be no harmony within or peace in the world until we eradicate the mentality of violence. For this we have got to repair the fragile collective psyche and make the commitment to inner harmony our first priority.

—Swamini Mayatatitananda Saraswati, Wise Earth Monastery

THE CONCEPT OF PEACE IS ENCAPSULATED IN THE DEFINITION OF YOGA

Yoga at its heart aims at attaining inner calmness, a place from which all of one's actions would manifest. Whether we accept the definition of Yoga offered in Bhagavadgītā—*yogaḥ karmasu kauśalam,* yoga is skill in action/behavior—or Patañjali's *yogaś citta-vṛtti-nirodhaḥ*-yoga is the cessation of the disruptions of the mind—or the layperson's view that Yoga helps in attaining a better night's sleep, the underlying concept of peace becomes evident.[1] It also implies that the experience is at the individual level. Yoga psychology is premised on the logic that unless we as individuals cultivate a sense of "dynamic silence," the reference point for our behavior is not likely to be anchored in a wellspring of peace, but instead operates from a place of unsettledness and distortions, and hence wrong cognition. This reference point has to always originate at the level of self. We must make every effort to effect change in the individual self before even considering changes on a societal or global scale: the experience that is Yoga must first be experienced from within. A famous quotation from Mahatma Gandhi, "that we must become the change we wish to see" actually reflects this central philosophy of Yoga.

Peace is not just the absence of violence (*hiṁsā*); it is the conscious and ceaseless nurturance and promotion of non-hurting at mental, emotional, and physical levels. When physical violence is expressed, it is preceded by the expression of violence at a non-physical level of the individual who is perpetrating it. Whether at an individual, community, societal, or global level, peace in Yoga is the result of continuous, conscious effort (*abhyāsa*), which is intended to effect and redirect changes at the thought level. In Yoga this is referred to as *citta śuddhi*, purification of the internal instruments of perception. The yogic Seers recognized the urgency of learning to maintain a fine balance between the individual and society, and therefore introduced the fundamental tenets upon which Yoga is premised: the *yamas* and *niyamas*. These are the codes of conduct and observances by which the individual must abide as a member of society. They require the person to cultivate an early awareness of values and actions through adherence to such principles as *ahiṁsā*, non-hurting; *satyam*, truth as a force; *aparigrahaḥ*, curbing greed; and *santoṣaṇ*, contentment (the *yamas* and *niyamas* will be dealt with in more detail later).

At a broader level, Hindu thought has never interpreted its grasp of Truth as possessing a monopoly of that essential truth, or even more significantly, as a negation of the truth held by other spiritual traditions. Professor K. L. Seshagiri Rao, in his lecture titled "Hindu Perspectives on the Religious Heritage of Humanity" stated that "Vedic teaching helps us to appreciate and understand faith in its various forms and allows them to grow and flourish side by side, without condemning or denigrating any particular form of faith or worship."[2]

PEACE POLITICIZED

Peace is perhaps the most elusive of human aspirations. In the ṚgVeda (1.89.1), we find these verses that implore the Vedic culture to "let noble thoughts come to us from all directions," followed by the words, "ennoble the world by sharing good things." I believe that our sages understood the psychology of peace from a different perspective: although it has been sought after by every civilization, it is perhaps never fully attained. The presence of peace reflects the absence of tension or lack of equilibrium, whether at individual or societal levels. The reverse also holds true. These are opposing forces that operate in a kind of dialectic relationship. Yoga understands this concept of polarity, and its primary objective seeks to introduce and maintain balance between these forces.

Peace as defined historically and presently exclusively places it in the realm of the political. Its currency in foreign policy statements and international relations has fashioned a particular connotation of the concept of peace. Peace is politicized and, according to this model, represents the absence of wars (more so than conflicts) between ethnic groups, religious blocs, or nation-states, and in the current global scenario, between groups considered terrorists and groups considered legitimate. Peace, therefore, is viewed as something external to be promoted, achieved, regulated, or otherwise imposed as is often witnessed in many corners of the world. This paradigm is fraught with problems because it reinforces an adversarial process, one that is polarized and characterized by an imposer and an imposed. In addition, the idea of this top-down approach involving force is inherently contradictory and not likely to generate good will.

Such a paradigm of peace almost invariably assures its colossal and persistent failures, not only to peace ever being germinated as a true force, but it also negates the very principles upon which peace can be cultivated, primarily because it removes the burden of responsibility from the individual and places it collectively on groups. We find ourselves as individuals conditioned to easily surrender and relegate our responsibilities to the narratives of a group, community, organization, or society. Although in an autocratic society, individual choices and freedoms are readily sacrificed, I believe that in our democratic systems, we convince ourselves that we always possess certain inherent rights, and we are prepared to fiercely defend them. At the same time, however, we either voluntarily surrender other equally important values, or witness them being surreptitiously eroded. For example, we are willing to blindly support and accept peace surrogates acting on our behalf, falling victims to the idea that peace starts on the outside, and that someone else can promote it on my behalf. It is a cardinal abdication of responsibility to the self. In the end, I surrender my voice to the agency of our political leadership that, I have convinced myself, speaks on my behalf and reflects my sincere desires for peace. There exists an irony here. In an autocratic society, very few of its citizenry ever believes that its leadership reflects its voices, which were never surrendered in the first place; in a democracy, though, the voice reflected at the leadership level is in reality a consciously surrendered one. However, even when peace is advocated by our leadership, it is a brand that is too often politicized and rarely honestly brokered. How does one speak with a surrendered voice?

Peace, while sometimes defined as pacifism, is itself very dynamic and requires persons of peace to be equally dynamic. One therefore cannot be a witness to peace and at the same time not actively seek to cultivate it. It is a conflicted place for one to situate oneself. When I surrender my voice, I may be choosing to believe that I am a peace witness. That may very well serve to bolster my moral conscience, but it does little to contribute to the cultivation of peace. The peace warriors of history have never adopted silence of voice and actions as their instruments, even though they spoke from a place of profound silence.

This chapter asserts that peace is an inherent, core value embedded within the philosophy and practice of Yoga. Peace is not merely an objective or goal to be achieved; rather, peace is an attitude to be cultivated from an internal environment. In fact, the critical reference point begins not in the external realm but very deep within each individual being. The internal instruments of perception, the *antaḥkarana,* must reflect the true light of the inner spirit, one whose nature is itself peaceful and abides in profound peace, *śānti.* In order to attain this depth of peace, the instruments would have to be reconditioned and purified. When we are seeking harmonious relationships, usually in the external world, and when those internal instruments of perception are not resonating with the true nature of our inner spirit, that peace sought and arrived at is at best superficial and temporal, hence not surprisingly a state that leads to disappointments and disruptions. The presence of disharmony among different groups or nation-states, I believe, is really fostered by the collective absence of peace at the individual level. In the following Sūtra, *tadā draṣṭuḥ svarūpe'-vasthānam,* Patañjali states that when one is established in the self, referring to the absence of the ripples, or the *vṛttis,* of the mind, one experiences deep silence and peace of mind.[3] Similarly, in Bhagavadgītā's *samatvaṁ yoga ucyate,* Yoga is equipoise; we find reference to this centered place.[4] If my senses are tugged between poles of likes and dislikes, *rāga* and *dveṣa,* then any sense of equipoise, a sense of being at peace with myself, is compromised because the cause of the lack of balance is attributed to an external medium, one to which my desires for outcomes are affixed. The external realm as we understand it is not resonating with peace as an inherent characteristic. Many of us need not look beyond our city boundaries to witness this.

Some of the synonyms for peace are pacifism, harmony, and reconciliation, but really these are preconditions to peace. Pacifism, for example, is interpreted to mean opposition to the use of force under any circumstances. While this interpretation is true, it is nonetheless limited. One would not find this word in the language of peace negotiations since pacifism really has found itself outside the dynamics of the conflict resolution game played out in the international forum. It is considered ineffective and naïve because historically we have come to accept violent opposition as a valid means to resolve conflict situations among the many nations of the world.[5] However, in spite of the enormous loss of lives and repeated failures of this approach, nation-states and groups rely on it as if it were the prescribed code of response. Pacifism has failed to establish itself as an effective instrument of peacemaking because those supporting violent opposition as the effective weapon of peace have managed to convince themselves and others that this is the only viable alternative. However, more importantly, pacifism has failed many of its own proponents if only because the latter also adopted it as an external instrument of peace promotion. Pacifism, at its center, must psychologically stem from the deeper spiritual core of the human person. It is not an automatic response to an event, nor is it an engagement. Professor Stanley Hauerwas, in an article several years ago titled "Taking Time for Peace: The Ethical Significance of the Trivial," wrote that "peace is not a static state, but an activity that requires constant attention and care."[6] Cultivating such an outlook means cultivating the outlook of a peace warrior: one whose total consciousness and awareness revolves around fostering and maintaining the delicate balance of actively promoting peace, while at the same time ardently adhering to the principles of *ahiṁsā,* even in the face of hostility and opposition.

Mahatma Gandhi was such a peace warrior; he demonstrated the effectiveness of that approach in his struggles to unyoke India from colonial rule. *Ahiṁsā* arose from a deep place of conviction, somewhat independent of the external forces, many times hostile and life threatening. We witness countless examples of societies, equally diverse as India, which are still trapped in the throes of violence and ethnic divisiveness half a century after declaring their political independence. We will see that, in Yoga, honing one's attention, one's awareness is critical to developing and practicing intense one-pointedness of attitude and vision. This is called *ekāgratā,* transcending the quixotic and agitated mind. This was one of the yogic principles cultivated and embodied by the Mahatma. Another was *tapaḥ,* or austerity, each time he engaged in a hunger strike. It was readily interpreted as an act of defiance to the external forces against which he waged his struggles. That was the manifested political behavior. However, there is another side to this act that is rarely understood: denying oneself food as sustenance of the body, while subjecting the body and mind to suffering and discomfort, was also an act of *pratyāhāra,* withdrawing the desire and the senses from food, the object. It was an inner expression of spiritual sacrifice. This act, harsh at one level, allowed him to reconnect to that centered space of equipoise from which he emerged every time ever more resolute in his resistance. The successful practice of *pratyāhāra* gives one complete control over the senses. In the Bhagavadgītā, Lord Krishna tells us that "when one withdraws one's senses from the sense-objects, like the tortoise which withdraws on all sides its limbs, then the person's wisdom (*prajñā*) becomes steady."[7]

Similarly, in Yogasūtras we find the following verse: "You are no longer their slaves. You become their master."[8]

Successful peace warriors such as the Mahatma adhered to the philosophy of Yoga, which behooves the individual to imbibe and embody its teachings at deeper levels. Yoga therefore obliges each individual to cultivate and articulate themes of peace not as policies to be imposed, but as principles to be embodied and practiced at the level of personal self.

Many areas of the world have descended into horrific conflicts that revolve around opposing religious "truths" and expectations, with the Middle East a clear case. Warring sides assume inflexible postures and are prepared to decimate each other regardless of the consequences, even though victory for either side does not appear assured or ever possible. In an article on the conflict between Muslims in the Middle East and Israel, author Charles Selengut cites the following salient themes underlying that conflict: the role of "cognitive dissonance," "religious and theological reinterpretation," and "the reconstruction of reality."[9]

Viewing this scenario from a yogic perspective, one witnesses a mental posture that is inflexible, commitment to a religious truth that aims at obliterating the other at any cost, and "a state where two elements of belief or 'fact' turn out to be contradictory or inconsistent."[10] The purpose of Yoga is to adopt a flexible mental posture, to practice withdrawal (in this scenario, at multiple levels), to adhere to the universal truth that accepts all of humanity as "valid," and to develop the awareness of a unified consciousness, all of which oppose cognitive dissonance.

YOGA IS INNER BALANCE

Yoga, no doubt, has grown to occupy a unique place among the world's spiritual traditions; its wide appeal and acceptance across many cultures around the world makes it truly universal. Whether it is for acquiring health and beauty, or to realize one's spiritual nature, at its core Yoga cultivates inner peace, balance and well-being. It behooves the sincere student to cultivate and practice values that foster tolerance for self and others, to accept the oneness of being of all peoples. A spiritual tradition that exhorts its practitioner to rely on direct experience, *pratyakṣa bhāvanā,* as part of the process of transcending limited awareness both prods and precipitates the process of self-inquiry. Only when the awareness resonates with the deeper self is one's true purpose of life understood; that is, understanding resonates from a place of deep silence, unconstrained and undistorted. The afflictions of the mind are removed. The consequent actions of the individual then stem from a place of inner peace and equipoise, as stated in Bhagavadgītā. Such behavior, whether at individual or societal levels, (micro or macro) is not motivated by irrational or selfish desires, but instead by a sincere desire to promote harmonious relationships because of the deeper insights of one's place in the universe, gained from the spiritual practice of Yoga. We will see later that the tendencies shackling the mind, which constantly impinge on our awareness, the *vṛttis*, and which precipitate a state of unease, afflictions, must be removed.

The Sanskrit word for peace is *śānti,* which is recited three times at the end of every Vedic prayer. It is an attempt to propitiate the forces that can cause distress, which can manifest from three possible levels: *ādhibhautika, ādhidaivika,* and *ādhyātmika.* The first seeks relief from the threats of external agents, such as other individuals and creatures as well as inanimate objects. The second propitiates to divine, supernatural phenomena and spirit worlds. The third seeks peace from the intrinsic forces, pertaining to one's self and spirit, which can cause mental and physical illnesses and distress. This view of one's world, in addition to recognizing the dynamic forces that can easily upset our sense of harmony, also recognizes the individual's place vis-à-vis the larger cosmos. It also demonstrates the depths of understanding by our sages of the intricate workings of the cosmos, the elusive nature of the concept of peace, and our own tendencies to easily descend into disharmony with self and others. This view is universal within Hinduism and posited by Sāṁkhya philosophy. However, although we recognize that there exist certain forces external to us, for example, supernatural phenomena, which can cause sufferings, we would also note that one of the causes of sufferings is attributed to fellow humans.

CAUSE OF SUFFERING IN YOGA

In Yoga the primary cause of suffering is attributed to ignorance of not being able to draw a distinction between the consciousness principle, *Puruṣa,* the Self, and the material, unconscious principle, *Prakṛti,* and its *guṇas,* the three aspects or properties that characterize all of nature.[11] Although *Puruṣa* by its nature is free from afflictions, it experiences suffering as a result of falsely identifying with the modes of the mind (*guṇas*). As the consciousness principle, it is void of any ability to act and experience on its own; therefore, it relies on the vehicle of *Prakṛti* and its instruments of perceptions and actions. Soon, *Puruṣa* begins to identify with the senses as it was, and thinks that it is experiencing pleasures and pains (modifications of the mind) as experienced by *Prakṛti.* Consequently, one begins to feel that one is suffering. The sense of afflictions is rooted in this primary ignorance of not knowing my true nature, that I am really above all modifications of the mind.[12]

Earlier, I referred to the *vṛttis* that beset the mind; these really have their bases in the afflictions, or *kleśas.* Patañjali, drawing from the Upaniṣads, tells us that there are five *kleśas,* and as was stated above, they have their origins in the wellspring of ignorance, *avidyā.* That is, ignorance of the essential nature of reality that provides fertile ground for the others to manifest, those being the sense of ego, *asmitā;* attachment and aversion, *rāga* and *dveṣa;* followed by fear of death, *abhiniveśa.* They are said to be present in either potential or active form. Swami Hariharananda Aranya comments that "the common feature of all the afflictions is erroneous cognition which is a source of pain," that when *kleśas* prevail, "the afflictive modifications grow."[13]

Sage Gheraṇḍa, a Haṭha yogi, commenting on one of the *kleśas,* ego, in the Gheraṇḍa Saṁhitā (1804), states that "there are no fetters like those of illusion (Māyā), no strength like that which comes from discipline (Yoga), there is no friend higher than knowledge (Jñāna), and no greater enemy that Egoism (Ahaṁkāra)."[14]

Kleśas result in a sense of dis-ease at deeper mental and spiritual levels of a person. Patañjali instructs that in order to eradicate them, one must first practice Kriyā Yoga, and prescribes *tapaḥ,* austerity, and *svadhyāya,* study of the self and scriptures.[15] Kriyā Yoga here refers to the external limbs, the *bahiraṅgas,* of Aṣṭāṅga Yoga.

A traditional universal peace invocation is found in the Kaṭha Upaniṣad, one of the older Upaniṣads. It belongs to the Krishna Yajur Veda and is considered part of the revelatory, or *śruti,* knowledge tradition. It implores the participant to invoke a sense of togetherness and peace. This prayer is traditionally recited by all at the start of any learning engagement, typically between a teacher and students, inspiring a sense of harmony at an early age. It reads as follows:

> *Om Sahanā vavatu, saha-nau bhuñaktu*
> *Saha vīryaṁ karvāvhai*
> *Tejasvi-nā-vadhi-tamastu*
> *Mā vid-viṣāva-hai*
> *Om Śāntiḥ, Śāntiḥ, Śāntiḥ.*
> May He Protect us all, May He nourish us
> May we work together with enhanced vigor
> May our learning be enlightening and fruitful
> May we not dislike one another
> Peace, Peace, Peace

TRUTH PRINCIPLES

The inner balance sought in Yoga can only be experienced when the fundamental personal and social codes of conduct, the *yamas* and *niyamas,* are fully imbibed. The *yamas,* or restraints, are *ahiṁsā, satya, asteya, brahmacarya*, and *aparigraha,* which are counterbalanced by the observances, the *niyamas.* These are *śaucha, santoṣa, tapaḥ, svadhyāya,* and *Īśvara praṇidhāna.* These together form the first two levels of the eight limbs of Patañjali's Yogasūtras. The *yamas* oblige the individual to cultivate non-harming, *ahiṁsā;* maintain truth and honesty, *satya* and *asteya,* as a force; and practice sexual abstinence, *brahmacarya*, and non-greed, *aparigraha.* In the *niyamas,* the individual has to develop mental and physical purity, *śauca,* and contentment, *santoṣa;* engage in austerity, *tapaḥ,* as well as self-study and study of scriptures, *svādhyāya;* and finally surrender to a higher consciousness or God principle, *Īśvara praṇidhāna.*

The ancient yogis recognized that in order for individuals to function and relate to society—and vice-versa—in a harmonious way, each person has to cultivate the above principles. However, even though on the surface some of these do not appear to bear relevance to peace, they are powerful behavior regulators and form part of the arsenal that would condition all the emotional and psychophysiological aspects of the person. They redirect one's behavior at a deep level of awareness, which leads to balance and harmony both within and without.

The wisdom in the Yoga tradition also extends across diverse cultures because its innate nature accepts and promotes several universally accepted truth-principles: It does not seek to superimpose, conquer, distort, deny, minimize, convert, or co-opt.

These paradigms would be antithetical to the very nature of Yoga, and against the truth-principles of the *yamas* upon which it thrives; they would even instigate and promote conflicts instead of harmony, the essential nature of our being. We need only look at the ethnic and religious strife, or the foreign policy approaches adopted by several nations, individually and as blocs, in order to grasp the chaos that they precipitate in various corners of the world.

We need also look at religious conversions as entrenched policies of one of our major faith traditions, and how that contributes and results in non-peace.

Conversion runs counter to *ahiṁsā, satyam,* and *asteya,* core truth principles of Yoga. It also reflects the pursuit of greed and lack of contentment, direct opposites to *aparigraha* and *santoṣa* respectively. Additionally, the absence of sincerity underlying this approach runs counter to *śauca,* purity of the mental arena. Force as a weapon, whether overt or covert, is also seriously relied upon. However, force in Yoga is a language of another kind; it is a discipline intended to exert control, as in restraint *(yamas),* and at the same time nurture and train the unruly nature of the sense impulses and desires through the practice of austerity, *tapaḥ.* That is, mental discipline precedes and determines our behaviors at all other levels. In Kaṭha Upaniṣad, Yama, Lord of Death, explains it this way:

> The steady control of the senses and the mind is the Yoga of concentration. One must be ever mindful of this Yoga since it is difficult to acquire and easy to lose.[16]

The root word of *yama* is *yam,* which means to exercise control or discipline, not as an external projection or extension of force, but rather as an internal awareness and restraint practice. That is, reigning in the raging senses and modifying my actions to reflect a centered, internal reference point for my behavior. This requires constant, mindful attentiveness to my internal environment, and therefore also requires constant effort on my part. That is why Patañjali in the Yogasūtras emphasizes the discipline of practice as a practice in itself, *abhyāsa.*[17] It is essential to modify and govern our internal environment, and allow the truth principles to ascend to the surface. We saw in the life of Mahatma Gandhi the embodiment of the principles of *ahiṁsā* and *satya* as a reflection of a lifetime of *abhyāsa.* Other practices would engage the other limbs of Patañjali Yoga, such as postures, *āsanas,* intended to remove physical disturbances; breath practices, Prāṇāyāma, connecting body and mind; withdrawal of the senses, *pratyāhāra;* and the practice of concentration, *dhāraṇā,* and meditation, *dhyāna.*

That force in Yoga is indeed a language of another kind and is also evident in the use of the term *nirodha,* often poorly translated as suppression. We see that in the very second Sūtra of the first chapter, Patañjali's definition of Yoga as *yogaś citta-vṛtti-nirodhaḥ,* Yoga is the cessation (silencing) of the ripples of the mind. In order for this state to be attained, the individual is required to engage in practicing all the limbs mentioned above until the pyschoneuro-eco dynamics of the individual are reconditioned. Consequent to conditioning the physical body through postures and breath practices, one begins to understand the obsessive tendencies of the senses to dwell on sense objects (largely in the external environment), and hence the need to withdraw them. The person's awareness begins to traverse from the external to the internal realm. This marks the journey from the *bahir* to *antar* awareness, and also signals the transitional axis point of the change in one's consciousness. The next limb of concentration, *dhyāna,* continues to be deepened in preparation for meditation.

MEDITATION OR *DHYĀNAM*

Experienced Yoga practitioners have long known that the meditative mind is profoundly serene and reflects a highly integrated state of awareness. This awareness is centered within one's consciousness, which is moving from differentiation to nondifferentiation, from non-neutral to neutral, from agitated to restful, and all of which pour into a global, total state of transcended unity and awareness. It is a place above all else where all conflicts are destroyed. The Maitrī Upaniṣad describes it as "that which is non-thought, which stands in the midst of thought, the unthinkable, the hidden, the highest, let a man merge his thought there. Then will this living being be (free) without any support. . . . For by the serenity of thought, one destroys deeds, good and evil, with the serene self abiding in itself, he enjoys eternal happiness."[18]

This journey of one's awareness reflects the progressive evolution of mind through the various states moving from the dull and negative, called *mūḍha* citta, through the disturbed, indecisive, and conflicted states, *kṣipta* and *vikṣipta,* and finally coming to a mental state that is focused and one-pointed, *ekāgra.* Consciousness is becoming unified and facilitates the eventual arrest of the modifications of mind, resulting in the state of *nirodha.* This reflects Patañjali's definition of Yoga.

In Bhagavadgītā Chapter 6, on the Path of Meditation, this quiescent mind is compared to the unflickering flame of a lamp held in a sheltered place.[19] We are also told that the state in which thought is restrained by the practice of concentration is one in which one sees oneself, one rests content in oneself.[20] This state, called *samādhi,* is one of unified consciousness, of non-dual awareness, in which it is believed that one's awareness merges into that of the Divine Self, the ātman.[21] When the individual abides in this arena of consciousness, the individual's being is spiritualized and begins to relate to other beings from this place of serenity, acceptance, and non-judgment. "Eternal peace belongs to those who perceive God existing within everybody as Atma," states the Kaṭha Upaniṣad.[22]

The meditative mind allows one to perceive the whole world as one family; *vasudhaiva kuṭumbakam* is a familiar expression that expresses this sentiment among many Hindus. The one whose self is disciplined by Yoga sees himself as dwelling in every other being and every being in him.[23] When this kind of global awareness is cultivated, how then does one bear malice toward and perpetrate conflict on another? This transcended state of awareness is also called *turīya,* or the fourth state of consciousness. Dr. Vinod Deshmukh, in two recent articles, analyzed this state from the perspective of modern neuroscience and commented that "during meditation, when situational conflicts, desires and needs are resolved, and when there is no need to attend to anything specific, one can return to a naturally restful state of undistracted, nonspecific (*nirguṇa*) awareness, with no sense of ego or authorship. Such spontaneous, self-absorptive, non-dual state of being is known as *Turīya*."[24] We would recall that ego, or *asmitā*, is one of the *kleśas* and a cause of suffering. Yoga provides a method of eradicating the *kleśas*, and that is meditation.

A recent study on the effects on the brain as a result of meditation reveals some very poignant findings. The left frontal cortex of the brain, for example, which nurtures emotions such as love and compassion, a sense of relating to the universe with positive attitude, or *bhāvanā*, and reduced anxiety and happiness, appears to be directly activated by meditation. What is even more impressive is the fact that changes in the brain persist several weeks after meditation.[25] Scientists are beginning to conclude that repeated meditation practices lead to permanent reconfiguration/rewiring of our brain structure. The yogis understood this positive reshaping of the total personality, not from a neuroscientific basis, but from a place of higher intuition and from observing personality changes in themselves and others engaged in such practices. Neuroscientists and researchers engaged in research are in many ways beginning to understand that repeated practice of meditation alters deeply ingrained physical and emotional patterns. It affords each of us the unique opportunity to develop inner harmony. More importantly, it inspires our actions not from a fragmented, compartmentalized reference point—that would merely contribute to the cognitive dissonance already characterizing many aspects of our behavior—but from a place that breeds tolerance and the understanding that I am part of the larger matrix of humanity. Our tendencies to dwell on our differences, be they cultural or religious, are largely an extension of this fragmented understanding of ourselves in relation to others; our understanding is sufficiently infused with parochial appendages, mainly brought about by colonial and religious influences, and permits the insertion of filters through which we view others and take action. Essentially, this fragmented understanding emanates from a place of limitations: a mind shackled by indecisions and conflicts, *mūḍha* and *kṣipta* states of awareness.

The introduction of *dhyānam* in Yoga obliges one to focus one's attention in a concentrated way (the practice of *dhāraṇā*), with the intention of removing negative tendencies of the mind while sharpening one's alertness and introducing mindful awareness. This gives rise to a special knowledge, called *prajñā*, from which a dynamic consciousness arises and overwhelms all other knowledge shaped by our limitations. Yogasūtra points out that when this special insight arises (in *samādhi*), it overrides the flow of prior impressions that have colored one's mental dispositions ("*tajjaḥ samskaro' nyasaṁkārapratibandhī*").[26]

UNITY IN DIVERSITY

Yoga operates on the "unity in diversity" principle and therefore is not culturally blind. The word Yoga itself is derived from *yuj*, meaning to join as in bonding, uniting, or integrating; in spiritual terms, this refers to the union between the individual self and its limited consciousness with the cosmic, universal consciousness, the higher self. At a practical level, the individual who deeply experiences Yoga gains balance and harmony of body, emotions, mind, and spirit, and hence relates to the world, as we see above, not from a fragmented perspective, but instead from a reference point of wholeness and centered consciousness. Again, the Mahatma's life provides an apt illustration. The concept of a uniting principle, when examined closely, essentially points to uniting beyond those areas that are naturally alike. Those principles that are already similar will naturally gravitate toward each other; however, the emphasis is also on uniting that which is diverse and opposed—the pleasure-pain conflict *rāga* and *dveṣa,* for example, or the internal and external, or the micro- and macro-cosmic dynamics—and therefore striving toward harmony on multiple and diverse levels. This is where consciousness of the individual, Yoga-reconditioned, begins to truly manifest the behaviors that are necessary preconditions or seeds of more lasting peace for all. These preconditions would include universal love, sense of sister and brotherhood, tolerance, acceptance, and restraints.

BHAKTI YOGA, THE YOGA OF DEVOTION

One of the four paths of Yoga propounded in Bhagavadgītā is that of devotion, or *bhakti.* This is not so much a path as it is the path which underlies all the other paths, whether it is the path of meditation or selfless service, Karma Yoga, or the path of knowledge, Jñāna Yoga. Unless there is an emotional dedication, unless the heart is engaged, one will not practice meditation or study the self or scriptures with any kind of commitment. Bhakti Yoga requires the person to be fully engaged—head, heart, and body—and execute all behaviors in the name of the Supreme Being. Here, the individual accepts that the sole purpose of the human body is for the practice of spiritual practice, *sādhanā.* Again we see that Yoga is the primary instrument that engages and conditions the individual's mental and emotional frame.

Peace must first flow from the inner wellspring of our individual being in order for it to prosper in the world. Yoga continues to sow such seeds of peace because, by its very nature, it engenders harmony. It has to emanate from a positive space: the person experiencing Yoga cultivates a positive disposition and learns to constantly rise above negativity and pessimism, and to strive toward being creative and constructive. The true purpose of Yoga then sincerely seeks the mutual physical, psychological, and spiritual growth and balance of all, because only when our consciousness dips into the spiritual realm will the oneness of all be realized, a harmony of cultures.

NOTES

1. Patañjali is credited with codifying Yoga in 196 aphorisms (Sūtra) known as the Yogasūtras. He is believed to have lived around 200–300 BCE.

2. K. L. Seshagiri Rao, "Hindu Perspectives on the Religious Heritage of Humanity," (keynote address at World Association for Vedic Studies conference, Houston, TX, July 9, 2006).

3. *Yogasūtra,* 1:3.

4. *Bhagavadgītā,* 2:48.

5. Ronald C. Arnett, "Conflict Viewed from the Peace Tradition," *Brethren Life and Thought* (September 23, 1978), pp. 94–95.

6. Stanley Hauerwas, "Taking Time for Peace: The Ethical Significance of the Trivial," *Religion & Intellectual Life* (September 1986), p. 92.

7. *Bhagavadgītā*, 2:58.
8. *Yogasūtra*, 2:55.
9. Charles Selengut, "Sacred Visions, Cognitive Dissonance and the Middle East Conflict," *Dialogue & Alliance* 17.2 (Fall/Winter 2003–04).
10. Selengut, "Sacred Visions."
11. *Yogasūtra*, 2:6.
12. *Yogasūtra*, 2:24.
13. Swami Hariharananda Aranya, *Yoga Philosophy of Patanjali with Bhaswati* (New Delhi: University of Calcutta, 2000), p.116.
14. *The Gheranda Samitha*, trans. Rai Bahadur Srisa Chandra Vasu (New Delhi: Munshiram Manoharalal, 2003), verse 4.
15. *Yogasūtra*, 2:1.
16. *Kaṭha Upaniṣad*, 2:3:11.
17. *Yogasūtra*, 1:12-14.
18. Maitri Upanīṣad, verses 18–20.
19. *Bhagavadgītā*, 6:19.
20. *Bhagavadgītā*, 6:20.
21. Ātman refers to the Absolute Reality or Brahman Reality. In Vedic literature, it is sometimes used interchangeably with *Puruṣa*, although its use in reference to Classical Yoga is often more limited.
22. *Kaṭha Upaniṣad*, 5:13.
23. *Bhagavadgītā*, 6:29.
24. Vinod D. Deshmukh, "Neuroscience of Meditation," *Scientific World Journal* 6 (2006), pp. 2239–53; Deshmukh, "Turiya: The Fourth State of Consciousness and the Step Model of Self-consciousness," *Journal of the Interdisciplinary Crossroads* 1.3 (2004), pp. 551–60.
25. R. J. Davidson, J. Kabat-Zinn, J. Schumacher, M. Rosenkranz, D. Muller, S. F. Santorelli, F. Urbanowski, A. Harrington, K. Bonus, J. F. Sheridan, "Alterations in Brain and Immune Function Produced by Mindfulness Meditation," *Psychosomatic Medicine* 65.4 (2003), pp. 564–70.
26. *Yogasūtra*, 1:50.

Part II

Christian Spirituality

CHAPTER 7

The Cave: Teaching Religion Students to Rethink Exclusivism and Embrace Tolerance

Rob Sellers

This chapter is largely autobiographical and, admittedly, quite straightforward. Certainly there are topics more esoteric, multifaceted, and challenging. Perhaps no subject, however, is more important for successful interreligious relationships than examining the matter of how people's attitudes enable or obstruct community. In the small city in the United States where I teach religion at a Baptist university, I've encountered this problem again and again. I offer, then, an analogy of a cave—not Plato's cave, but one excavated from my life as a missionary, crisscrossed with suggestive theological connections, yet menaced by the possibility of deep sinkholes and complex labyrinths in the unexplored territory underground.

MY LIFE AS A MISSIONARY

For almost twenty-five years, my wife and I lived in Java, Indonesia, where we worked as Christian missionaries sponsored by a Baptist agency in the United States. I must admit that when we arrived in Jakarta in 1975, I knew very little about the Animism, folk religions, Hinduism, Buddhism, and Islam that millions of Indonesians practiced. Although my seminary education had been rigorous and my ministry experience varied and highly practical, nothing I'd experienced had prepared me adequately for living in such a multi-layered and pluralistic setting as Java. Sadly, even our mission agency's four-month training program had included only a few days of introductory lectures on the world's religions, contrasted with several week-long sessions on evangelism and church-planting techniques.

Moreover, I arrived in Indonesia as a Christian exclusivist. I hadn't made an informed, intentional decision to be an "exclusivist" and wasn't even aware of the term, much less its meaning. But I was an exclusivist by default, having been taught by my Southern Baptist upbringing to think—in language that was rarely questioned—about the "lost" people around the world who needed to be "saved."

My first exposure to Asia had occurred immediately after my college graduation in 1967, when I spent eleven weeks as a short-term volunteer in the Philippines. I had been sent as a "summer missionary," assigned to help lead a series of small evangelistic meetings throughout Luzon, Mindanao, and the Visayas. Those weeks were amazing! As the time approached when I would leave the Philippines, I knew that some day, somehow, I would return to live in Asia.

Interestingly, it wasn't a preaching service or witnessing experience that summer that particularly struck me, even though those events consumed most of my schedule. What stirred my passion was being shown how the poorest of Manila's poor were trying to exist. "People live there on what the locals call 'Smokey Mountain,' the garbage heaps of Manila," my missionary host said, pointing from our air-conditioned car toward the tiny shacks constructed from wet cardboard, warped sheets of plywood, broken roof tiles, plastic string, and whatever else of any value had been salvaged from someone's trash. "This is the dumping place for all of Manila's garbage," he explained, "collected from more than 6 million homes!" I didn't doubt it. The hot July breeze carried the rancid smell of decay and mold, and the mountain of smoldering, rotting refuse spread out before us as far as we could see. "Having nowhere else to settle," he continued, "these people live here, on the trash heaps. They survive on whatever they can scavenge. From the time their children can crawl, they play in that garbage, search through it for 'treasures,' even eat discarded food found in that filthy mess! Have you ever seen anything like this in your life?" I shook my head in disbelief. It seemed so far away from the Manila Intercontinental Hotel, where we had stopped that very noon for an American meal at the poolside patio restaurant. The contrast pressed on my chest like a barbell too heavy to lift. I gasped for air—but it wasn't just the stale smell of Smokey Mountain that made my eyes water: it was an undeniable tug of compassion and a dawning awareness that "Good News"—if it be genuinely liberating—must announce that basic necessities such as food, shelter, clothing, and health care are for everyone!

Fewer than ten years later, I was back in Asia—this time in Indonesia and married to a wonderful woman who shared my love for international travel, my commitment to cross-cultural friendships, my zeal about responding to a world of need, and my faith in Jesus Christ. We were excited as we landed at Kemayoran Airport in Jakarta, eager to begin our new life on one of the world's most fascinating islands.

We had been appointed by our mission board to be "youth and student evangelists." Quite frankly, the designation never really fit my perceived calling from God, my sense of self-identity, my skills, nor my interests. It certainly wasn't that I didn't care for Indonesians—I loved Indonesian people! I thought their country was beautiful, their culture intriguing, and their demeanor gracious and winsome. I thoroughly enjoyed being with youth and students—in our home, at the market, on the playing field—talking together, laughing about my language mistakes, exchanging stories, becoming friends. What was problematic for me was the label "evangelist." That was a role that didn't match who I was.

As I carried out my assigned missionary responsibilities, I was often working with fellow Christians. But at random moments of the day and in unplanned activities around the city, most of the people I encountered were not Christians. Two impressions about these followers of other faiths began to form in my mind.

One thought concerned how alike we all were. We experienced the same life passages, faced parallel challenges, shared common joys, endured comparable sorrows, harbored similar dreams, and walked analogous pathways. I began to see that they were hoping *their* religious customs would enrich their lives just as I hoped *my* traditions would enhance my life. The other thought that came to me from time to time was how different we all were. I had learned enough about their sacred stories and rituals to recognize that these were not identical with the ones I cherished. But I also could see that so many people gained strength for daily living from their own spiritual journeys. Beyond that elementary discovery, I began to realize that the devotion, self-discipline, and basic goodness of many acquaintances and friends challenged *my* spiritual identity and moral character. It became increasingly difficult for me to accept that such persons needed "saving"—as if they were "wandering," "sinking," "stumbling," "groping," "dying," or carrying out any of the other precarious activities that some Christian evangelists used when describing those who aren't Christians.

During this time in our Javanese sojourn, we were privileged to live in Central Java—surrounded by volcanic mountains, verdant rice fields, historic monuments, ancient temples, a highly refined culture, and a gentle people, whose life struggles and disparate religious rituals were reminding me both of the common experiences of humankind and of the rich particularity of place. Over the years, without consciously choosing it, Indonesia's national motto—"*Bhinekka Tunggal Ika*" [Unity in Diversity]—became a philosophical watchword for me.

This was my state of mind, late in my missionary career, when my immediate supervisor came to Indonesia from the home office to attend an annual mission meeting. He was invited to preach the sermon in our concluding session, a final "challenge" that he addressed to a room filled with career missionaries. His message was "heartfelt" and consistent with how he views the world, but I just didn't get it. He used his time to stir us to renewed urgency and faithfulness in witnessing to Indonesians about our faith. I recall his saying, "When you drive down the streets of your city, do you weep for the people you see on the side of the road who are spiritually lost? If you don't, then you need to ask God to break your heart and make you the kind of person who cries for the lost people of this nation." I remember sitting in my chair and being *very* uncomfortable. But I wasn't under spiritual conviction! In my heart, I was disagreeing with this preacher. I knew that when I traveled along the streets of my city—with its million-plus inhabitants—I did see the crowds of people on the street. I also knew that, seeing them, I didn't weep. I smiled! Watching the sort of people whom I had come to know personally, whose language I loved speaking, whose culture I admired, and whose ideas I was beginning truly to understand made me exceedingly happy, not sorrowful! It was so good to live in Java!

Not long after that meeting, we left Indonesia, and our mission agency, to move back to the United States. We didn't leave because of philosophical or theological differences with our administrators, although I surely felt the tension. Our primary work as seminary educators had been abundantly rewarding for Janie and me. We had made hundreds of Indonesian friends across the years. We were leaving behind a beloved adopted country where we had lived almost half our lives, the place where our children had been born and reared. But we were facing what so many persons who work internationally eventually confront—the debilitating illness of elderly parents back home. Sadly, our adventure in Java had come to a close.

In a stroke of good fortune I choose to interpret as divine providence, we have made a new home in a small West Texas college community—very far from Indonesia. Janie is busy with church and community responsibilities, while I teach in a Baptist school of theology. Admittedly, cross-cultural appreciation and religious tolerance are uncommon values among my students. Most of the undergraduates and even the seminarians I teach have never experienced foreign cultures, nor encountered religions other than their own. Because of factors such as provincial ideas, conservative theology, nationalistic fervor, insulation from diversity, fear of terrorism, unconscious prejudices, or childhood training, they often enter my classes with preconceived notions about cultures and religions. So in a strange way I could have never have predicted, my life as a missionary continues. Now the youth and students I try to get to know are American and Christian. Most of them—like me so many years ago—are exclusivists by default. They've never really thought critically about why they say that Jesus is the "only way," except perhaps that they know the Gospel of John (14:6) has words to that effect. Others have been so successfully enculturated by their conservative churches that they rarely question the language of exclusivism.

One of my goals, as their teacher, is to lead them to rethink exclusivism and to embrace tolerance. But I am still not a good "evangelist." I am no more committed to proselytism in Texas than I was in Java. I will not indoctrinate. I hope to educate. So while some of my students are scandalized by the suspicion that I might be a religious pluralist—and I am the only theology professor at my university for whom a small student group formed to pray for my salvation—I have found a modicum of success through a simple analogy of a cave.

THE CAVE

Suppose you are among strangers who find themselves deep in the earth in a vast cave system, with no experienced guide to lead everyone out to the surface. Suppose, then, that the group decides to split into smaller parties and follow separate passageways to search for a way out of the darkness. Furthermore, suppose that your pathway leads to the light at the mouth of the cave. Although ecstatic over your own salvation, compassion and concern for others will nevertheless compel some of you to rush back down the tunnel calling out, "I've found the light! I've found the light!" Finally, suppose that upon traveling deeper into the cave, you come once again to the large cavern at the bottom, where you encounter travelers from different groups who just as urgently as you claim that other, opposing pathways are the ones that really lead to safety.

If this is the situation (realizing, of course, that no analogy is entirely perfect), how should we respond? Many of my students, upon hearing this illustration, suggest that we immediately can and must label other paths as "dead-end roads." But I ask them how we can know that those tunnels end at a wall of solid stone? Are we really in a position to pontificate about pathways we ourselves have never walked? Or, rather, is it the case that all we can do is testify with passion about the one path we have traveled—and the light we have seen?

SUGGESTIVE THEOLOGICAL CONNECTIONS

Caves captivate the imagination. Major underground voids like Mammoth Cave in Kentucky, the world's largest system with more than 365 miles of passageways already explored; Toca da Boa Vista in Brazil, the longest known cave in the Southern hemisphere; and Sarawak Chamber in Malaysia, the most massive individual cavern ever discovered, attract thousands of tourists annually. Why are so many people drawn to caves?

Many of them come seeking an adventure unlike anything they've experienced before. Adventure is an important theme in Christian theology that is suggested in the cave analogy. Life itself is adventurous, being marked by unpredictability and uncertainty. Cave exploration requires a willingness to step into the unknown—to "walk by faith, not by sight"—an apt metaphor for faith and the very essence of religious pilgrimage.[1] Following a particular "way" whose "end" is hidden is risky behavior and not for the spiritually faint of heart.

One of the attractions of a cave is its multiple paths. These different passages demand that choices be made. The Bible is familiar with multiple paths that beckon and call forth a response. People make decisions daily, and the choices they make have consequences that can determine the rest of their lives. Not all paths necessarily lead where people would want to go, so they must be careful when they are choosing.

This cave analogy begins deep in the earth and suggests that the way of rescue is an upward trail. Biblical writers conceive of God as living in the heavens, high above the earth. Jesus was carried up into heaven after his resurrection and will come down from heaven in a similar way on the day of his second coming.[2] In one of Jesus' famous stories, a rich man in Hades looks up to Paradise for help.[3] The reference to ascending is clearly metaphorical, but traditional. So, in the words of the ancient proverb, "For the wise the path of life leads upward, in order to avoid Sheol below."[4]

The deepest pits of caves are unbelievably dark, but the mouths of caves are flooded with light. Darkness and light are rich, theological images that can stand alternately for death and life, sin and righteousness, evil and goodness, lies and truth. In the analogy, the desired movement is from a dark to a lighted place. Salvation is found where the light is found. In the Fourth Gospel, Jesus claims: "I am the light of the world. Whoever follows me will never walk in darkness but will have the light of life."[5] As the lost searchers in the cave analogy approach the mouth of the cave, the light pours down the passageway toward them, and they can see the source of their salvation. They round a corner, and suddenly the dark crevices and foreboding spaces around them are illuminated by the wondrous light from the cave mouth. Similarly, in the words of John, "The light shines in the darkness, and the darkness did not overcome it."[6]

Whenever people come out of absolute darkness into the light, their eyes must adjust to the glaring brightness of the sun. Although they can surely see better than they did in the dark, their view is limited until they have been in the light long enough for their vision to clear. Yet, some Christians—having "seen the light"—act as if they can "see" perfectly. So when these rescued ones turn back to the cave as rescuers, some of them will likely insist that they know everything there is to know about the light, or that the light they have encountered is the only light to be found. They may sincerely believe that if they don't warn others and lead them to *their* path, then those persons will be lost forever. This style of evangelism becomes complicated (and sometimes contentious), however, when people from other religious groups claim that *their* ways lead to the light. The analogy of the cave illustrates, then, that one's understanding of "the light" may be blurred and incomplete, so that one should approach others with humility rather than arrogance.[7] It also teaches that one cannot comment on the efficacy of a path one has never personally walked. We can only talk about the path we *have* walked.

Yet, according to Christian scripture, we who have met the Christ "cannot keep from speaking about what we have seen and heard."[8] This, in fact, is what it means to be a "witness"—to give an account of what we have seen and heard, but not to discount the things that we have not seen and not heard. We can speak passionately about the light we have experienced, but we mustn't assume we know the mysteries of the whole cave system!

UNEXPLORED TERRITORY

Some of the world's most famous caves have unexplored passageways. So does my little "cave" analogy. Since it is not a perfect creation, there are some threateningly deep "sinkholes." For example, I don't yet know how best to answer a student who challenges my analogy by saying: "But we aren't in the world (the cave) without resources, groping about on our own. We have divine help. God's Spirit guides us to the Truth." She points out a pretty deep conundrum, and I haven't been able to "touch bottom" in that sinkhole yet.

Another danger in my cave comes from complex "labyrinths." A student may posit something like this: "Well, we could just follow the markers that were put there to lead us out of the cave. After all, we have God's Word! It's like those little signs along the cave paths that point the way to the light, or like the map of the cave system we were given at the ranger station (church) before we got into trouble in the cave (world). Where is the Bible in your analogy, anyway?" The issues he raises from this perspective are complex indeed, with many spurs and tunnels to explore, and my route through the labyrinth usually doesn't entice him to follow.

In conclusion, I would love to report that my analogy has helped turn back the tide of Christian exclusivism in West Texas. I would be thrilled to say that for the last eight years "the cave" has just about eliminated religious intolerance at my university. I would also love to tell you that West Texas is as beautiful as New Zealand, and that I'm turning thirty on my next birthday. Alas, none of these things is true. What is the truth is that I occasionally do connect with a student through this analogy, but often I don't. What is also true is that I will not quit trying to help my students—whom I'm beginning to love almost as much as I did my Indonesian friends—reexamine their attitudes toward others. It bothers me when I sense they are moving along a passageway—exclusivism—that I once walked, unthinkingly, and that I now find wanting. I would love for them to move in that other Christian direction, one that I believe would illumine and enlighten them—the path of generosity, compassion, and openness.

NOTES

1. See 2 Corinthians 5:7; Hebrews 11:1; Hebrews 11:8. These and all other biblical references are taken from *The New Oxford Annotated Bible: New Revised Standard Version with the Apocrypha* (New York: Oxford University Press, 2001).
2. Luke 24:51; cf. Acts 1:11.
3. Luke 16:23.
4. Luke 16:23.
5. John 8:12.
6. John 1:5.
7. Cf. 1 Corinthians 13:12.
8. Acts 4:20.

CHAPTER 8

This Magdalene Moment

Joanna Manning

Justice and equality for women and the marginalized, the earth, and all its religions, plus the fire of an integration of the feminine and the erotic into Christian spirituality and a new respect for religious pluralism: that's what the current "Magdalene moment" in history is about, and it is very relevant to a discussion of the role of religion in a post-9/11 world.

One of the earliest symbols associated with Mary Magdalene in art is the egg. Many religious icons portray her holding an egg. The egg is the Easter symbol of resurrection, fertility, new life. But I think there is also another meaning. Once the growing chick inside the shell has used up all the nourishment of the egg, it has to break out of the shell. The old shells of religious structures, of religious institutions that came into being in contexts of hyperpatriarchy, no longer nourish the human spirit. The shell is now suffocating and will be death dealing if the new spirituality does not break out. The current Magdalene moment is about breaking out of these old shells and taking a risk to venture out into the new, the unknown. As Jesus himself indicated, you can't put the new wine into old wineskins.

Jane Schaberg is the author of a book published in 2002 called *The Resurrection of Mary Magdalene.*[1] Schaberg contends that there have been two models of Christianity in the West, and they're now both in deep trouble. The Petrine model of Christianity is the Roman Catholic Church—now wracked by revelations of clergy sexual abuse and experiencing a steep decline in membership among the young. The Pauline model is the reformed Protestant tradition—now splintering over issues such as homosexuality and contending with the rise of the so-called Religious Right in the United States. Schaberg calls for a new "Magdalene Christianity," which would reestablish the prophetic leadership of women that was suppressed early in Christian history and recognize that Mary Magdalene, at least as much as Peter or Paul, played a crucial role in transmitting the message of Jesus. Schaberg calls Mary Magdalene "the creator of the Church's Easter faith." The time is right for Mary to be resurrected.

And she is being resurrected in popular culture, as we've seen from the phenomenal success of Daniel Brown's *The Da Vinci Code.* Of course, it's a novel. It's a fast-paced story. But I think the reason for its popularity is because it has touched a nerve in the zeitgeist of our age—it has opened a quest for a new meaning, a longing for the sacred. At the end of the book, the main character, Langdon, comes to a realization that the Holy Grail represents not literally the offspring of Jesus and Mary Magdalene, but the whole of the lost sacred feminine that has been suppressed by the Church for almost 2,000 years. The loss of the feminine is also linked to the loss of the earth as a place where we are at home. Too often religion has led to a distancing from the earth—the "vale of sorrows" as it is named in several traditional Catholic prayers—to the view that our true home lies after death; the siren call to the suicide bomber that heaven awaits him in the hereafter, replete with willing virgins available to assuage his every desire, is an example. The body and the earth have been de-sacralized by Christianity for so long. The recovery of the sacred feminine within the world's religions (and the most ancient have never lost it) and the return to honoring the sacred power of women—somehow intuitively we know that this is what is necessary to heal the troubles of our age.

The study of ancient Christian texts, such as the Gospel of Mary that first came to light in 1896, the scrolls discovered at Nag Hammadi in 1945, and others, is revolutionizing our understanding of early Christianity. The texts of these early Christian writings other than the Gospels show that the companionship of women was highly valued by Jesus. These texts also show that Mary Magdalene played a key role as the close companion of Jesus and as a leader, visionary, and healer within the mixed group of men and women who were his closest associates.

The synchronicity of the time here is extraordinary: the discovery of these texts has coincided with the beginnings of the feminine scholarship of theology and scripture, and this has been exhilarating. Women themselves are now able to reappraise the importance of female leadership within the early church. This has allowed many to hope that this combination of the human experience of women in the twenty-first century and the rediscovery of the ancient practices of women's leadership in the Christian community will support their efforts to open up the structures of Christian communities in our own day to mutual partnerships between men and women at every level. These texts also demonstrate the pluralism that existed in the first two centuries of Christianity and the diversity of interpretations regarding the meaning of Jesus's life and teaching.

After the conversion of the emperor Constantine to Christianity in the early fourth century and the adoption of the Roman imperial government within the church, and as a Roman imperial structure and mentality gradually encroached on the church, Mary Magdalene was first edited out of the Christian tradition and then labeled as a repentant prostitute. And as the early Christian communities spread within the Roman Empire, the mutual leadership of women and men declined under the impact of Roman familial structure, which emphasized the role of the man as paterfamilias and head of household. The church's internal structure took on the same pattern.

But the impact of the 1945 discovery of the suppressed texts has exposed the fact that the deliberate exclusion of women from church leadership represented a departure from the earliest tradition. The initial impetus of the Jesus movement, stemming from Jesus himself, was to value female leadership. The theological position outlined in these early texts lost out in the battle for orthodoxy, which saw the Roman church emerge as the triumphant seat of Western orthodoxy. As a result, the Roman imperial view of the early church won out in the struggle for orthodoxy.

The rediscovery of the early texts has given us an insight into the Christian world of the first few centuries. The rediscovery of the early texts that the Roman group had ruled out of the canon has stirred up subversive memories. Contemporary human experience is bringing these texts alive again. The Magdalene moment in Christianity can enable us to rethink what it means to be a Christian in a pluralistic world: not a world circumscribed by the boundaries of the Roman Empire of old, but one that now spans the whole globe. The models of Christianity that we have now came into existence as a result of being shaped by a context where hierarchical and authoritarian structures were the modus operandi of society. These structures no longer serve the modern world at all well. This egg needs cracking open.

I believe that it is no mere coincidence that this conjunction of modern human experience, especially the experience of women, with the newly discovered ancient texts is taking place at this particular time in history. It is part of the work of the ever-creative Spirit of God to empower men and women of good will inside and outside of religious traditions to wake up and save the planet.

Sometimes I fear that we may have entered into a very dark and hopeless period of history indeed. Religious fundamentalism in both Islam and Christianity threatens to plunge the world into a new age of war. The world is divided not only along religious fault lines but also between the haves and the have-nots within each nation. The earth itself is at risk from continuing excessive greed and consumption. The AIDS epidemic threatens to wipe out millions in Africa—the list goes on. Christian fundamentalism has both a Catholic and a Protestant section. Catholic papal fundamentalists believe in a rigidly hierarchical structure of the church and unquestioning obedience to the Pope, and Protestant biblical fundamentalists extrapolate certain passages from the Bible and interpret them literally without any consideration of their context. Protestant and Catholic fundamentalists in the United States have forged a new alliance because they have discovered much common ground around issues such as gay rights, abstinence-only sex education, women's equality, Christian exclusivism, individual family values, free market capitalism, and contempt for creation-centered environmental values. Many in the Protestant Religious Right hold to the theory of the Rapture: war in the Middle East is part of a series of events that will lead to the Rapture of the God fearing and Armageddon for the rest.

But all that this Religious Right stands for is diametrically opposed to the initial thrust of Christianity, which respected pluralism, diversity, and the leadership of women. I believe that in a multiplicity of diverse churches and movements focused on the service of the poor and marginalized, humanity, and the earth, there is now a new energy rising that cuts across denominational and religious boundaries. The leadership role of women is a key factor in this new dynamic.

In many communities inside and outside the churches, the human race is moving into a new awareness of our interconnectedness with the rest of creation. The realization of human kinship with the natural world, and the dangers that humanity's depredations of the earth pose for the survival of the natural world, is growing. Human consciousness is changing as we become more aware of global warming, species extinction, inequities between rich and poor, and the ravages of runaway consumption in the one-third of the world that is called "rich." An emerging planetary awareness that celebrates unity and searches for the common ground on which we can base the survival of future generations is increasingly compelling.

A new creation story is emerging from the discoveries of the origins of the universe. Beginning with the original burst of energy—some call it the Big Bang—approximately 13 billion years ago, the first stars that exploded and then died out released the material constituents of life that were to evolve into the myriad forms of living organisms in the universe. We now know that everything in this universe hears the imprint of that original flaring forth: that all life is connected by the stardust that floated and scattered from the primal flaring forth of light.

Through eons of evolution, the forces of mutual attraction within the universe resulted in the solar system and planets within their orbits. The origin and survival of life rests on relationality. This new understanding of cosmology calls for an evolution in the human understanding of God and of the relationship of God with humanity and with the earth. I like to call this the greening of spirituality. Medieval history was my first academic interest, and I can remember the glow of excitement I felt when I discovered the writings of the mystics of that period. One of the greatest, Hildegard of Bingen, speaks of the greening of the soul:

> We need a greening of the soul of humanity and of religion.

In the account of the resurrection in the Gospel of John, Jesus and Mary Magdalene meet and embrace in the garden on that first Easter morning. They are the new Adam and the new Eve in the restored Garden of Eden. Within their embrace lies the hope and promise of a new creation, a new mutuality of men and women in the Christian community. The light of that first Easter morning lit up the world with an inner radiance that is present within all of creation, renewing all life. It could do the same today. The recovery of the inner radiance, the fire of love at the heart of creation, is the great work of our age. The reinstatement of women within the heart of Christianity would represent the possibility of a greening of spirituality, a new and dynamic consciousness of the rich life of the universe.

But the greening of the earth and of religion, the preservation of the delicate ecological balance of the earth, is not just a poetic dream. It also demands a deep and difficult conversion of our lives. It means that people like us in more affluent countries, most of which have had significant exposure to Christian tradition, embrace a more frugal, altruistic lifestyle. Such a conversion also would remove one of the most potent contributors to terrorism and war: the poverty of the majority of the world's population and the overweening control of corporate values and interests.

Here again the women around Jesus, led by Mary Magdalene, provide a role model for a recovery of Magdalene economics in Christian households. It was the women disciples who placed their wealth at the service of the common table. They supported Jesus out of their funds and thus organized the new economy of the reign of God preached by Jesus and practiced by his community. In the Acts of the Apostles, the sharing and redistribution of wealth, modeled on the example of the women, became a condition of entry into the Christian community.

The apostolic role of the women followers of Jesus, who placed their economic resources at the disposal of the community, also became a key component in early

Christian tradition. The most ancient Christian tradition around wealth was not about charity: it involved real redistribution of resources. The church was not a place of brokerage between rich and poor, a place where the rich came to give checks or dump used clothing, and the poor came to get stuff. It was an organic community where rich and poor broke bread at the same table. As I read in one book recently, "If we really rediscovered the communal love of the early church then capitalism would not be possible and communism would not be necessary."[2]

The current Magdalene moment calls us to a difficult conversion: to come home to our roots of simple living inherent in the origins of our tradition. This simplicity of life will also call us home to the earth. The earth, the Garden of Eden, the green grove of the Resurrection, is calling us to come home after a period of long exile. We have been exiled from our roots in the earth and cut off from the sacredness of its waters and forests. Patriarchal religion in the West has suppressed the sacred feminine and dishonored the healing power of sex. But now, more and more women and men are waking up from a deep sleep, and we are seeing the world around us again with new eyes. We are cracking the shell of the egg of patriarchal thinking and systems in readiness for a new resurrection. We are realizing the connections between the fate of the earth and our ecological environment with the way we live out our economic, political, sexual, and religious lives.

So what would a Magdalene leadership mean for the world today? The novelist Virginia Woolf once wrote, "As a woman I have no country. As a woman I want no country. As a woman my country is the whole world."[3] Substitute the word spirituality or religion for country, and what do you get? So if my spirituality is the whole world, who then is my God? Is my God only for some and against others? It's time to let go of the petty God of patriarchy. How can God's activity be confined to any one continent, culture, or church? The supreme mystery who is God can no longer be held within the shell of any one religious boundary. "There will be no peace in the world until there is peace among the world's religions" says Hans Küng.[4] Religious pluralism is not just one of the foundations for peace: it is about rediscovering the true nature of God: a God who is for all, not just a God of a privileged few.

There is now a common context of human and ecological suffering that overlaps religious boundaries. The Magdalene moment demands that all religions take as the starting point for their dialogue a solidarity with the suffering earth and its peoples. It was Mary of Magdala and Mary the Mother of Jesus who stood by the cross to accompany the Crucified One on his great journey through the gates of death. It was they who showed the way toward a praxis of solidarity with the suffering. I was reminded of this just last month during the AIDS conference in Toronto, where Stephen Lewis spearheaded the formation of a new international group: grandmothers to grandmothers. With the loss of the middle generation of parents to AIDS, it is the grandmothers of Africa who are standing by the children. It is the brave stand of these women who are sheltering the generation that has lost parents to AIDS that will carry Africa to a new resurrection.

Solidarity with the suffering earth and its peoples opens the door to dialogue among the world's religions: dialogue that is based on solidarity of service, not on gabfests about dogmatic teachings and unanchored truths that float around in a transcendent soup of abstractions.

This shared process directed toward compassion will open up a third space for dialogue—a new threshold, a liminal third space—that is beyond the enclosed areas occupied by competing traditions that have contributed to competition and war, and one which, from a Christian perspective, is a lot like the original ideals of Christianity: "To find an ecumene of peace and solidarity with the suffering and the victims of war and violence."[5] This is the great call of all contemporary religions. The task of the present moment calls for a willingness among all religions to stop competing and proselytizing, and to find common ground in a spirituality of service to the poor and the earth.

God's spirit at work is forcing us to rethink our place in this vast universe, to honor the wonder of creation's diversity, and to embrace it with awe and graciousness instead of exploiting it. There is only one earth. There is just one flesh—the human flesh—that we can wound in war. God's Spirit is at work on the margins inside and outside the churches, empowering women to announce the good news that God has chosen them as witnesses to justice and love in all creation.

This new Magdalene movement has awakened a subversive memory buried within Christian tradition. Another future is possible. The subversive memory of Mary Magdalene could light a fire in many hearts—and this is the year of fire. It will give us the courage to crack open the shell of old ways of thinking. A new eruption of women into spirituality and religion is already happening. But it is fragile. The egg that the Magdalene holds is only just breaking open, and the new life that is emerging, like the newborn chick, is small fragile and undernourished. We need courage like Mary Magdalene's so that we, too, can go out to renew the earth.

NOTES

1. Jane Schaberg, *The Resurrection of Mary Magdalene: Legends, Apocrypha and the Christian Testament* (New York: Continuum, 2002).
2. Shane Claiborne, *The Irresistible Revolution: Living as an Ordinary Radical* (Grand Rapids, MI: Zondervan, 2006), p. 164.
3. Virginia Woolf, *Three Guineas* (London: Harcourt Brace Jovanovich, 1966), p. 109.
4. Hans Küng, "Address to the Parliament of World Religions at the Signing of the Document *Towards a Global Ethic: An Initial Declaration*" (Chicago, 1993).
5. Küng, "Address to the Parliament."

CHAPTER 9

Incarnation as Worldview

Tobie Tondi

I'd like to start with a question: Why are we here? I'm a teacher, and year after year I realize how "dangerous" the profession is . . . for a number of reasons. One reason is this: the first class of any semester probably determines whether or not the course will provide satisfaction for students and for the professor. The first day sets the stage. A bit frightening.

But all is not lost; I have discovered a solution that has worked fairly well. I teach religious studies to undergraduates at a small liberal arts college. I start every course with a day or so on what I call "existential questions." Why are we here, what is the meaning of life, is there life after death, why do innocent children suffer, is there a God and if there is, does God have anything to do with these concerns of ours? These questions intrigue my students just as they have intrigued people for centuries; they intrigue us, too. So I ask: Why are we here?

JESUS: THE CENTRAL FIGURE IN CHRISTIANITY

The belief at the core of Christianity is the identity of the person Jesus. How Christians have come to understand the person of Jesus has been, throughout history, both the source of religion gone wrong and religion as a force for good. Let me explain.

When Christian teaching understands belief in Jesus as the sole route to salvation, then those outside of that circle of belief are automatically doomed. When Christian teaching says Jesus meant to establish a new church that should replace Judaism, there is a problem. I could go on, but you understand the point. I'm sure each tradition could supply examples of a similar kind.

But there's more: When Christians speak of Jesus not only as savior but also as one who is both human and divine, followers of other traditions shake their heads in disbelief. What could the joining of human and divine possibly mean?

I am a teacher, a professor of religious studies, a Catholic systematic theologian. I am also a member of a community of women whose founding principle, the Incarnation, is this core Christian belief—God becoming human. So, for a variety of reasons, both professional and personal, I am constantly on a journey to try to understand this belief, Incarnation, better. When I probe more deeply, I see that the meaning of the Incarnation goes far beyond the historical Jesus—both before Jesus and after Jesus of Nazareth.

I don't mean to minimize the place of Jesus of Nazareth—but for a few moments, let's explore "incarnation" as three moments of the creative and nurturing activity of the Transcendent One: creation, Jesus, and the Kingdom of God. If we expand our understanding of the Incarnation, it is easier to see how incarnation can be, for those who wish, a comprehensive view of the world.

Incarnation can be a lens through which we see all of reality. Incarnation can be a worldview. So, another reason for being here is to probe a religious belief that can go very, very right . . . for all of us—Christians and followers of other traditions, too.

CREATION: THE FIRST MOMENT OF INCARNATION

The Hebrew scriptures provide us with the basic elements of the first moment of the Incarnation: creation. What do we learn from the creation stories in the Book of Genesis?

1. Human persons, different from all of the rest of creation, are made in the image of God.
2. By design and invitation, human persons are to share in God's creative and nurturing activity.
3. It is all good.

These three fundamental elements tell us much about God, about human persons, and about our world. Creation is the first moment of incarnation—God sharing God's self. Incarnation means a continuous nurturing of creation by God, a communication of God's self to God's creatures. It is the nature of the Transcendent One to go beyond. God goes beyond God's self. Humans, too, are transcendent, always searching, always going beyond themselves toward the mystery we call God. St. Augustine says we have restless hearts. Thomas Aquinas says we are on a journey from God that eventually leads back to God.

JESUS: THE SECOND MOMENT OF INCARNATION

In the prologue to the Gospel of John, we read, "No one has ever seen God; it is the Son who is nearest to the father's heart who has made God known."[1] For Christians, Jesus is the special way to understand better who God is; Jesus is the second moment of incarnation. But Jesus is also the way to understand who people can become. Incarnation is as much about human transcendence as it is about divine transcendence.

The Incarnation as we traditionally have defined it in Jesus is a unique, concrete event within this process of divine meeting human or, better said for our purposes, human meeting divine. Jesus is the one in whom God's transcendence and human transcendence meet. This meeting of human and divine in Jesus is the way in which Christians understand the desires of God and the hopes of the human community: humans become more and more in God's image, more and more God-like. Augustine tells us our hearts will be restless until they rest in God.

All fine and good—but back to my students. They would admit that they are searching, and some might even say okay to God's searching for them . . . but when it comes to the theoretical meeting place—the real world—my students are quick to bring me back to reality. "This ain't no Garden of Eden," they say. (Perfect, I think.) And I respond, "Yes, there's a flaw in the program, and there's a lot of work to be done."

What does Jesus have to say about this reign of God, and how is it related to our very needy, broken world? How, in concrete terms, do we join human and divine? How does the Incarnation continue?

THE KINGDOM OF GOD: THE THIRD MOMENT OF INCARNATION

In the Christian scriptures, it is clear that Jesus does not preach about himself; he certainly never mentions the establishment of a church. The core of the preaching of Jesus of Nazareth is the kingdom or reign of God (and I use the terms interchangeably). What does it mean to be in the kingdom of God? Monika Hellwig, a Catholic theologian who died recently, provides us with what I consider to be the best description/definition of the kingdom of God: a kingdom of right relationships . . . not right from wrong, but "right" in the sense of justice and equality: enough food for all, shelter of some kind for all, peace.[2] Our world today is a broken world, one in which we throw food away when most people go to bed hungry, a world in which some people have a number of luxurious homes, and many others sleep in cardboard boxes or bomb shelters.

This does not mean that the reign of God is some version of a perfect world; what it affirms is that human endeavor to bring about right relationships is a vital and essential part of a process of the radical reordering in our world—a reordering of relationships, of the distribution of material goods, of the availability of opportunity.

Human endeavor is *not* the reign or kingdom, but the reign of God will not come about without human effort. In other words, we are in the process of coming to the fullness of the third moment of incarnation: the reign of God.

Why are we all here? The picture is becoming clearer.

We are charged with the building of the kingdom here and now. We are partners with God in its building. Remember: we are made in the image of God, each and every one of us, and we are invited to participate in the continuation of creative, nurturing activity.

Why are we here? The reign of God, building the earth, mending the world: traditions refer to the human-divine project by many different terms—but the project is the same. We may have many diverse sets of creedal statements, but the human/divine project, I believe, is one that is common to us all. We can be incarnation in the world today; we can be God's creative and nurturing presence in the brokenness around us.

How do we do it? Reflecting on Hellwig, right relationships are understood best by Christians from a careful study of the activity of Jesus: feed the hungry, care for the sick, forgive the sinner, and so on. For Christians, Jesus is the exemplar of human activity geared toward the establishment of the reign of God.

SOCIETY OF THE HOLY CHILD JESUS

So, here we are, a group of Sisters of the Holy Child Jesus, a community dedicated to the Incarnation. As you read other chapters, you will find practical examples of the "coming to flesh" of the founding principles of the community.

Why are we here? We are not here to blow our own horns; quite the contrary, incarnation is all about a humble and a hidden life. But hopefully you will see how incarnation can be a worldview; it can give shape and purpose to human activity; it can define that toward which we all labor. Incarnation need not be divisive; incarnation as worldview tells us about who we are, all of us here and all of us not here, as valuable individuals deserving, at the very least, food, water, shelter, education, safety, peace.

Incarnation as worldview tells us about who the Transcendent One is: compassionate, generous, supportive but not confining, present to us in all we experience. Incarnation as worldview tells us about how and why we as humans are connected, and how and why humans and God are related. Incarnation as worldview makes sense of our efforts to build the human community; incarnation grounds our efforts to build a better world in something more lasting.

Like Jesus of Nazareth, we have no intention of preaching about ourselves; there are many groups similar to ours. Our mission as Sisters of the Holy Child is "to help others to believe that God lives and acts in them and in our world and to rejoice in God's presence."

Whatever our ministry (and the works of the members of the community are quite diverse), we try "to help others grow strong in faith and to lead fully human lives." What does it mean to say we try to help others lead fully human lives? Throughout this volume, you will learn more about concrete manifestations, practical ways of living incarnation as worldview.

NOTES

1. John 1:18.
2. Monika Hellwig, "Eschatology," in F. S. Fiorenza and J. P. Galvin, eds., *Systematic Theology: Roman Catholic Perspectives* (Minneapolis: Fortress Press, 1991), pp. 349–371.

CHAPTER 10

Making Known the Reality of the Incarnation in Business Ethics

Helen Costigane

Before I joined the Society of the Holy Child Jesus, I earned my living in the business world, first in marketing and then in accountancy. I worked as an auditor, checking the veracity of the financial statements of different organizations, such as commodity brokers, banks and insurance companies, car dealerships, retail outlets, manufacturing companies, airlines and travel companies, and voluntary organizations.

In doing so, I encountered many good people just trying to do their best and make a living; others I encountered were more problematic, often making the lives of co-workers difficult in many different ways. Often, people were stressed because of unrealistic demands made on them by management; managers were stressed because of the lack of cooperation or effort made by their staff. That period of work was for me a time of enlightenment, insight, and empathy with those involved in the world of business. To quote Charles Dickens from *A Tale of Two Cities*, "it was the best of times, it was the worst of times."

I then got religion in a big way, or rather, it got me, and I joined a community whose mission statement is "to help others grow strong in faith and to lead fully human lives." I began a study of theology that is still ongoing, and then taught Christian ethics, specializing in business ethics, which I teach at undergraduate and postgraduate levels, while still continuing to work as an accountant in the voluntary sector.

When people hear that I'm an accountant and a theologian, I tell them that when it came to a choice between "God" and "Mammon," I couldn't decide, so I chose both. What's more, if I had a pound or dollar for every student who has told me that "business ethics" is a contradiction in terms, I would be very well off indeed. However, these two points raise what for me is a crucial question: if God and Mammon are polar opposites (as it is commonly believed) and if Mammon (however defined) is equated with "business," is it the case that the activity of business is inevitably irredeemable, or is it the case that God is present in the everyday business world?

What we mean by "business" requires some definition. We can speak of an individual business quoted on a Stock Exchange or a family-owned company—in both instances, we might be concerned with issues such as the treatment of employees, suppliers, and customers. Or we might be speaking of the structural system within which individual businesses operate. Here, I am speaking mainly of the first, while acknowledging the importance of the second.

There is no doubt that business activity can be problematic. We have seen many financial scandals, and the fact that so much legislation has had to be put into place (financial and compliance legislation; antidiscrimination and equal opportunities legislation; health and safety regulations; and legislation to protect whistleblowers, consumers, and the environment) gives us an indication of where business has been going wrong. Whether the result of individual iniquity, or the structural pressure put on business sectors and/or individual corporations, there is no doubt that the business world is far from being a garden of Eden; instead, many people—myself included—have considered it to be a war zone or a jungle, where the Golden Rule becomes "do unto others before they do unto you."

At the same time, we are ever more aware of ethical issues in business, both micro and macro. Doing a quick trawl on the Internet (using the Google search engine) reveals that there are 89.6 million entries for "business ethics," 37.3 million for "corporate social responsibility," 31.1 million for "corporate ethics," 15.2 million for "ethical investment," 1.7 million for the "ethics of multinational corporations," and numerous sites for workplace issues such as "whistleblowing" and "discrimination," and for the relationship of business to the environment. Many books have been published on business ethics in recent years, and no respectable management or business course is complete without a module on business ethics. So that's fine; we have become aware of business ethics, and we could conclude that religion has nothing to add in this area. However, I want to propose that religion can be a force for good in the business world, and in the teaching of business ethics. Further, I want to suggest that without the insights of religion, the business world is a more impoverished place. We heard earlier about the meaning of "incarnation," and incarnation as worldview, which tells us about who we are, who we are meant to become, and how we should be in relation to other people in a kingdom of "right relationships." This worldview means that we incarnate the principles of justice, equality, and peace; that we work toward a world where there is fair distribution, the availability of opportunity, and social responsibility.

We could respond by saying that we are already working toward this—many business corporations have adopted principles of social responsibility; there are very significant ethical investment and consumer movements; we have a raft of legislation against discriminatory practices at work; the fair trade movement is growing; and we have become very conscious of the way business in general interacts with the environment, from over packaging to carbon emissions, the use of scarce resources, and the dumping of toxic wastes. Not only that, but we are teaching present and future managers how to make ethical decisions in dilemmas they may face.

However, I want to suggest that religion in general, and "incarnation as worldview" specifically, has two challenges to make to the business community. Recently, I was struck by an excerpt from the Letter of James in the New Testament: "this is the meaning of religion that is pure and unstained before our God and Father: visiting orphans and widows when they are in difficulty, and keeping ourselves unstained by the world" (James 1:27). What, then, is James saying about "religion," and what might it mean in our own day? We could interpret this by saying that the true meaning of religion (in terms of the world of business) is having a concern for all people, particularly those who are unable to participate in economic or business circles. This might be through structural exclusion (such as unfair competition, inequitable trade agreements, or monopolies) or more localized situations of discrimination, lack of opportunity, or social circumstances. How do we incarnate James's view of religion in business? In the challenges we face, there are a number of important issues that arise, and here I am focusing on two of them.

First, are there absolutes? One challenge that we face today, I suggest, is a wrong understanding of "tolerance"—this is the tolerance that is used in a way to imply that all values, beliefs, and claims to truth are equal. From a society where there were absolute standards of right and wrong, we have moved through a period that saw truth as relative to circumstances and consequences, to a postmodernist belief that we create our own truth. On a practical level, then, it can become difficult to run a business where everyone's values are considered equally valid and therefore have to be balanced. It also raises questions about which or whose business "ethic" we teach. So, we need to rediscover and assert a common platform on which to base our ethics, and I think Hans Küng's work on "A Global Ethic" is a good place to begin. Küng's work asserts the need to cultivate a spirit of truthfulness in daily relationships with one another, honest dealing, a sense of moderation instead of unquenchable greed, a culture of solidarity, respect for the individual, and the Golden Rule: "do unto others as you would have them do unto you." Incarnation as worldview says to me that we need some absolutes in ethics, rather than an individualistic balancing of principles against an egocentric self-interest. In that way, we have some hope of incarnating right relationships and justice in business.

The second issue relates to a point I made earlier about the raft of legislation affecting business in many different areas, often drawn up in the wake of certain corporate scandals. I also mentioned corporate social responsibility, and I want to acknowledge that many companies have formulated codes of ethics for their stakeholders in an attempt to inculcate these very principles for action: fairness, integrity, honesty, respect, responsibility, and compassion. However, we can legislate that people do not engage in unfair, unjust, and dishonest practices; that they do not discriminate in hiring and firing; that they treat the environment with respect—and so on. What we cannot do is legislate that people are fair, just, or honest. However, if we are to address the areas I mentioned earlier, it becomes imperative that those who run our businesses and corporations, those who make economic decisions that affect millions, those who are in positions of power and service, are ethical individuals who are fair, just, trustworthy, and who can see beyond the confines of the immediate profit margin and their narrow self-interest. Incarnation as worldview in business, as I see it, means that as business leaders, decision makers, and teachers, we inculcate and develop individual responsibility and the core values already mentioned in ourselves, in those we teach, train, and supervise, and in those with whom we work. In other words, as individuals, we incarnate what it means to be ethical in the world of business, and how we fulfill the demands of true religion as outlined by James.

Coming to grips with these two issues—universal standards and individual ethical growth—and permeating business activity with them represent for me something of the challenge and the promise of incarnation.

Part III

Spirituality and New Religious Movements

CHAPTER 11

CaoDai: A Way to Harmony

Hum D. Bui

Along with materialism, differences in religions have brought conflicts to people resulting in many wars all over the world. The Inland Empire Interfaith group in California has been working to bring religions together in harmony, cooperation, and understanding. In this effort, we would like to introduce CaoDai, a new faith founded in Vietnam in 1926 by the Supreme Being via spiritism, based on the principle that all religions are of one same origin (which is God, although called by various names or no name), having the same teachings based on Love and Justice, and are just diverse manifestations of the same truth.[1]

CaoDai, literally meaning "High Tower" or "Roofless Tower," is used as the name of God. It embraces all religions ranging from what is termed the way of humanity (Confucianism) to the way of genies (geniism, or Shintoism, or the veneration of ancestors), the way of Saints (Judaism, Christianity, Islam), the way of Immortals (Taoism), and the way of Buddhas (Hinduism, Buddhism). Although they have different physical manifestations, all religions have the same ethical teachings based on Love and Justice—Love being unconditional and without desire, and Justice being equated with the Golden Rule: "Do not do to others what you do not want done to you."[2]

In addition to these teachings, there are other similarities among religions; the conception of God is one example.

CaoDai believes that the Supreme Being is from the Hu Vo (the nothingness or cosmic ether). In the cosmic ether appeared a great source of Divine Light called Thai Cuc (Monad) or the Supreme Being. The Monad then created yin and yang energies, the two opposite logos, the interaction of which led to the formation of the universe.[3] The Supreme Being, in giving the following message, confirmed that God's energy had manifested through different prophets in the world:

> Nhien Dang (Dipankara) is Me,
> Sakya Muni the Gautama (Buddha) is Me,
> Thai Thuong Nguon Thi (Lao Tse) is Me,
> Who is CaoDai.

and

Buddha, God; God, Buddha are Me,
Although different, all branches belong to one same trunk (family).
Buddhism, Taoism, Christianity are in my hands;
Because of love, I come to save humanity for the third time.[4]

With the same conception that the Nothingness is the origin of everything, in the Tao Te Ching, Lao Tse says:

There was something nebulous,
Existing before heaven and earth,
Silent, empty, standing alone, altering not,
Moving cyclically without being exhausted,
Which may be called the mother of all under heaven.
I do not know its name; therefore, call it the Tao.[5]

A similar conception that God is the Nothingness is found in Buddhism: "There is an unborn, not become, not made, unmanifest, which is called Brahmakaya or Sunyata, the Void, or the Nothingness."[6]

Sadly, it was because of this conception that Buddhism was misunderstood as not believing in the existence of God.

In the same light, Confucius says that God has done nothing but created everything:

Does Heaven ever speak?
The four seasons come and go,
And all creatures thrive and grow.
Does Heaven ever speak?[7]

Judaism believes that God, or Elohim, is a state of consciousness that pertains neither to perception nor to non-perception; or, in other words, the state of consciousness perceiving Nothingness, which comes from the chaos.[8]

Christianity believes that God is the Word: "In the beginning was the Word and the Word was with God, and the Word was God. All things are made by Him, and without Him was not anything made that was made."[9]

Not only religions but science theorizes that the universe came from the nothingness: "The Big Bang took place about 13 billion years ago. From nothing, a tiny speck of brilliant light appeared. It was infinitely hot. Inside this fireball was all of space. With the creation of space, came the birth of time. The infant universe was searingly hot, brimming with the energy of intense radiation . . ."[10]

Modern science has also conceptualized the void, which, according to field theory, is far from empty, but on the contrary, contains an unlimited number of particles that come into being and vanish without end.[11]

This scientific conception so far has brought science closer to the contradictory Eastern idea of Nothingness, the void, or cosmic ether, which is considered as "the suchness," as stated in the following phrase from the Buddhist Prajñ-Pāramitā-Hṛdaya Sūtra: "Form is emptiness, and emptiness is indeed form. Emptiness is not different from form; form is not different from emptiness. What is form that is emptiness; what is emptiness that is form."[12]

Isn't it wondrous how much religions and even science have in common? If one takes time to study others' religions, one would realize that religions are but one unified truth that has been expressed in different ways. At this moment, in this current world situation, CaoDai's purpose is to remind humanity and all religions that all religions are of the same origin and principle, and are just different manifestations of the same truth.

A thorough study of all religions leads to the conclusion that all religions are one, not in their historical accuracy or separate customs, but in their essential messages:

> All religions come from one common divine source.
> All ethics are essentially contained in the Golden Rule and Love.
> All humanity is one common family.
> Divinity can be experienced and realized in the individual through prayer/mediation.
> Good deeds are rewarded, and evil deeds are punished.

The noble effort of CaoDai is to unite all of humanity through a common vision of the Supreme Being, whatever our minor differences, in order to promote peace and understanding throughout the world. CaoDai does not seek to create a gray world, where all religions are exactly the same, but only to create a more tolerant world, where we can all see each other as sisters and brothers coming from a common divine source, reaching out to a common divine destiny.

If people are open to independently read from and study each other's religions or to contact other religious communities in their areas—to simply build an ongoing dialogue of understanding between them—this likely would be the most powerful weapon against hatred and intolerance, and the most powerful force toward friendship and peaceful coexistence.

In addition, various faith groups could organize meetings where different religions could be discussed, speakers could be invited, videos and music of different traditions could be presented, and understanding between people could be enhanced.

Also, charity projects could be established for communities in which everyone could participate, regardless of their different religious and ethnic origins, so that through love and compassion for the needy, humans would become closer to each other, love would develop between them as a solid bond, and peace would subsequently come to prevail, between individuals at first, and then progressively in local communities and finally, throughout the world.

NOTES

1. Hum D. Bui, *Cao Dai: Faith of Unity* (Fayetteville, AR: Emerald Wave, 2000), pp. 16–18.
2. Bui, pp. 92–99.
3. Bui, pp. 32–33.
4. Bui, p. 39.
5. Gia-Fu Feng and Jane English, *Tao Te Ching* (New York: Vintage, 1997), p. 25.

6. Bhikkhu Bodhi, trans., *The Connected Discourses of the Buddha: A Translation of the Saṃyutta-Nikāya* (Somerville, MA: Wisdom Publications, 2000).

7. Bryan W. Van Norden, Confucius: Analects 17:19. *Confucius and the Analects: New Essays*, p. 73. (Available at http://books.google.com/books?id=nqb0Fa8Umv4C&pg=PA73&lpg=PA73&dq=Does+Heaven+ever+speak%3F&source=web&ots=8CUNBvI5np&sig=bt8DBNBIneBy8wKrVBIBMmt3drc&hl=en#PPA73,M1.)

8. Job 26:7. The Holy Bible. New International Version. (Grand Rapids, MI: Zondervan Bible Publisher, 1983), p. 393.

9. 1 John 1–3. The Holy Bible. New International Version, p. 94.

10. Heather Couper and Nigel Henbest, *Big Bang* (New York: DK Publishing, 1997), p. 10.

11. Fritjof Capra, *The Tao of Physics* (New York: Bantam Book, 1984), p. 209.

12. Capra, pp. 201–2.

CHAPTER 12

Prophecies and Signs of the World Teacher

Tom Pickens

This chapter is about the future, the future of our children and grandchildren. It begins with a brief survey of two diametrically opposing world conditions, one driven by fear and the other by hope. Because of the second condition, this chapter ends with a story of incredible possibility.

SEPTEMBER 11, 2001

The tragedy of 9/11 sent shock waves around the world that caused people everywhere to stop and begin to ask some serious questions. Those questions are largely what the Global Conference on World's Religions is all about. But at the same time, 9/11 also created a focal point of fear—not just fear about terrorism, but about the future, our future. Some say this is the time of crisis foretold in ancient spiritual prophecy. And others say that 9/11 was the wake-up call. Could this be true? If so, then there must be signs—signs of impending crisis and, at the same time, signs of hope.

SIGNS OF IMPENDING GLOBAL CRISIS

> Our world society is presently on a non-sustainable course. . . . The reasons for this are like time bombs with fuses of less than 50 years.[1]

This statement is from Jared Diamond in his recent book, *Collapse,* in which he explains why past civilizations have failed. At the end of the book, he summarizes why societies collapse by listing twelve reasons. All twelve of these apply to our present world situation, and all twelve must be solved within the next fifty years or there will be very serious consequences worldwide. To give you an idea of how serious this really is, I will discuss only one of these problems, the one that will precede all the others.

THE PEAK OF GLOBAL ENERGY SUPPLY

Global energy production from finite deposits of fossil fuels is leading to a dead end for the future of this planet. This is because there is no escape from the inevitable depletion of these resources, and right now global oil and natural gas supplies are already falling behind daily demand, so that everywhere we look, all we see are rising prices for gasoline, heating fuel, natural gas, and electricity. Furthermore, all the currently known sources of renewable and alternate energy do not even come close to the amount of oil and gas now used in the world on a daily basis. In other words, with this problem alone, we are facing a crisis like no other in all of human history simply because the energy needed to keep the global economy running as it now is will soon begin to recede—with no end in sight. In order to understand this better, consider the following facts: Oil and gas production has now reached 123 million barrels per day. At the present rate, the global production of oil and gas can probably meet total world demand until around 2010. After that, global oil and gas production will begin an irreversible decline simply because there are not enough resources on the planet to reverse the trend.[2]

However, in the late 1960s and early 1970s, at about the same time that it was first recognized that depleting global energy supplies would create an unavoidable crisis in the future, certain unexplainable phenomena began to occur throughout the world. These phenomena fell into a fairly diverse range of unexplained events that are usually referred to as miracles. These were and are signs of hope.

Appearances of the Mother of Jesus

From 1968 until 1971, there were daily appearances of the Mother of Jesus that were seen by more than a million people in Zeitun, Egypt. The apparitions were broadcast on Egyptian television, photographed by hundreds of professional photographers, and personally witnessed by Gamal Abdel Nasser, who was the Egyptian president at that time. The appearances at Zeitun were unique in that they were seen daily by people of many different faiths for a very long time; since then, these appearances have continued to the present day, occurring at locations associated with the travels of Mary and Joseph during their lifetimes.[3]

The Hindu Milk Miracle

In September 1995, news swept around the world concerning milk-drinking Hindu statues that were observed first in a temple near Delhi, India. Very soon the phenomena spread throughout the world, where it was witnessed by millions. Never before in history has a simultaneous miracle like this occurred on such a global scale. This rare occurrence happened again on August 20–21, 2006.

Signs of Allah

In 1996 an Islamic woman living in Bolton, England, purchased an eggplant, and when she cut it open, the seed pattern clearly showed the Arabic symbol for *Ya-Allah,* which means "Allah exists." Since then there have been numerous other incidents involving the seed patterns in various kinds of garden vegetables and even in the scale patterns of fish.[4]

The Red Heifer

In 1997 a red heifer, of a variety believed extinct for centuries, was born in Israel to a black-and-white mother and a tan-colored bull. Jewish history speaks of nine red heifers with a tenth to come, and Jewish scholars say that not since 70 CE has a red heifer been born in Israel.

The White Buffalo Calf

Finally, in 1994 a white buffalo calf was born in Wisconsin. According to statistics from the U.S. National Buffalo Association, the likelihood of a white calf birth is approximately one in 6 billion. Yet since 1994, more than nine white buffalo calves have been born in North America. These rare births hold great cultural and spiritual significance for the native tribes of the North American Great Plains.[5]

SO, WHAT MIGHT ALL THIS MEAN?

In every case of the miraculous phenomena just discussed, the primary response of the witnesses has been generally the same: since time immemorial, men have known of, and expected, the coming of a great teacher, an outstanding man of wisdom and revealed truth.

Christians expect the return of the Christ, Jews await the Messiah, Muslims expect the Imam Mahdi, Hindus expect the Kalki Avatar, and Buddhists await the coming of the Fifth Buddha, also known as Maitreya Buddha. North American indigenous tradition forecasts the coming of the White Buffalo Calf Woman, and, of course, there are others.

PROPHECY

The widespread prophecy of the coming of a great teacher is particularly interesting at this time of unprecedented miraculous events in virtually every culture around the world, and it raises some very interesting questions. What if all the major spiritual traditions and cultures of the world are actually forecasting the coming of the very same person? And what if that person were already here? Could this be possible? Well, if world conditions have you deeply concerned and searching for slender threads of hope, then please consider what follows.

THE NAIROBI VISIT

On June 11, 1988, a man suddenly appeared of out nowhere before a vast crowd in Nairobi, Kenya, who were gathered to witness healing prayers. Instantly recognizing the tall, white-robed figure as "Jesus Christ," the crowd fell down, overcome with emotion. The editor of the Swahili edition of the *Kenya Times,* veteran journalist Job Mutungi, witnessed the event and took pictures.[6]

MAITREYA, THE WORLD TEACHER

Benjamin Crème lives in London, England, and has been speaking publicly since the late 1970s about the existence of a great teacher named Maitreya. Mr. Crème's story is currently the only completely hopeful, nonjudgmental, and universal explanation I have found pertaining to the signs of hope we have just covered in this chapter. What follows is what Mr. Crème has been saying for over thirty years.

Maitreya arrived in London in July 1977, where he has lived since then as an ordinary man among men concerned with modern problems—political, economic, and social. During all this time, he has worked behind the scenes in a wide range of activities aimed at stimulating and raising global consciousness, which is essential to the timing of his eventual emergence into public view. He comes not as a religious leader, but as a teacher and educator in the broadest sense, pointing to the way out of the present world crisis. Maitreya's primary goal and reason for being here is to encourage and stimulate humanity to change the world's dominant political and economic order from one that is based upon the increasingly destructive and unsustainable principal of competition to one that is based upon the principle of sharing.

The Principle of Sharing

The idea of sharing as a solution to the world's problems is not new. For example, if a fair and equitable distribution of the world's resources suddenly and magically happened so that adequate food, housing, clothing, education, and health care were universally available to everyone on the planet, who could possibly object? Turmoil and conflict would end, let alone war and terrorism.

However, in the existing climate of dominating world powers, competition, and imposed scarcity, many are afraid that there is now no hope for sharing. The magnitude of the problems and the obvious domination of those who would not welcome such an idea seem overwhelming. Yet, according to Mr. Crème, Maitreya says that a future based on sharing is possible, not only because sufficient resources exist, but also because the people of the world, united and firm, have within themselves the capacity to bring this about—peacefully. Because the alternative is almost too horrible to contemplate, Mr. Crème summarizes it this way:

> Without Sharing there will never be Justice.
> Without Justice there will never be Peace.
> Without Peace there is no Future.[7]

The obvious conclusion to this statement takes us immediately to Maitreya's most urgent priorities.

Maitreya's Priorities

Given a global community of nations finally committed to a future based on the principle of sharing, Maitreya will inspire and urge people and nations to do two things immediately. The first is to feed the starving millions, and the second is to stabilize the global environment that is now being seriously degraded by industrial pollution, deforestation, and global warming.

The world today is like a man just moments before he becomes a critically injured crash victim. When he finally arrives at the emergency room, every available resource must be brought to bear to save the patient. Then, after the patient is stabilized, other long-term recovery efforts can begin. For the people of the world, this means establishing adequate food, housing, clothing, education, and health care as universal human rights. In the case of the environment, this means changes that will take decades, if not generations, to accomplish. But in the end, we'll finally have a healthy planet and the foundations for truly lasting peace.

The World Teacher

Probably one of the most common expectations attached to the coming of a great teacher at a time of unprecedented crisis is that many think that such a person is coming here to save us—from ourselves, it turns out. However, it is not that simple. Instead, Maitreya's presence will establish a focal point of trust in the world that is so profound people cannot help but respond. This does not mean that every response will be positive, but it does mean that we will finally have a clear choice—between the looming darkness just ahead of our present course and something far more hopeful. Maitreya is not here to build a new religion or recruit followers. Instead, he will offer a vibrant new vision of human potential and planetary peace based upon the practices and principles of right living, cooperation, and sharing.

How and When Will Maitreya Emerge?

The emergence of Maitreya into the spotlight of world awareness as the world teacher is a gradual process and will continue to be so. This is because his emergence depends on a growing expectancy and hope that the principle of sharing can truly save the world. In other words, the focus will not be on Maitreya as a savior, but rather as an unprecedented and vocal advocate of the principal of sharing, which will ultimately become our greatest gift to the earth. Therefore, no one knows when the tipping point between the thinking that now dominates the world and the thinking that is beginning to happen right now will take place, but as sure as the sun shines and the rain falls, it will come. And, with it, the most incredible event in all of human history: the discovery of who we truly are in a vast and magical universe and peace on earth—created by us.

NOTES

1. Jared Diamond, *Collapse: How Societies Choose to Fail or Succeed* (New York: Viking, 2005), p. 498.

2. For more information on this topic, see http://www.peakoil.net.

3. After Zeitun there were appearances at Edfu in 1982, Shoubra from 1986–91, Shentana El Hagar in 1997, Assuit from 2000–2001, and finally in Gabal Dranka in 2001.

4. The locations and dates were Senegal: miracle melon (1996); London: Allah eggplant number 2 (1997); Huddersfield, UK: miraculous tomato (1997); Bradford, UK: additional eggplant (1997); United States: the "Allah fish" (1997); Holland: name of Allah on eggs and beans (1997); and India: miracle potato (1997).

5. Pictures of the above, except those pertaining to Zeitun, Egypt, can be seen at http://www.mcn.org/1/Miracles/. The Zeitun pictures can be found at http://members.aol.com/bjw1106/marian7.htm and http://www.apparitions.org/zeitun.html.

6. These pictures may be seen at http://www.shareintl.org/background/miracles/MI_nairobi_pictures.htm. Shortly after this event, Benjamin Crème announced that the man who appeared in Nairobi was Maitreya.

7. The present wording in this statement comes from the ideas and sentiment expressed in a number of books authored by Benjamin Crème, most notably *The Great Approach*, which was first published in June 2001. In June 2007 Mr. Crème published a book titled *The World Teacher for All Humanity*, in which he makes this statement on page 10. All Mr. Crème's books are published by the Share International Foundation in Amersterdam, London, and Los Angeles.

CHAPTER 13

Religion and Spirituality: Our Common Mission

Odette Bélanger (alias Vedhyas Divya)

The future is not ours to tell, but to allow.

—Antoine de Saint-Exupéry[1]

The word "religion" has become taboo, pejorative, except in some specialized milieu. In certain countries, religions play a major role in the affairs of the state, while in others secularity is the prevalent system. Such is the case for Québec, Canada, and France among others. How can we reconcile these different visions? Can a harmonious coming together of the various religions of the world and secularity be brought about?

But first, let us find out what the word "religion" and "religious institution" exactly mean.

CAN ONE DEFINE RELIGION?

Several thinkers throughout the centuries have tried to define religion without success. But, closer to our time, G. Van Der Leeuw proposed to define the religion as "a lived experience of the limit which hides from view . . . a revelation."[2]

However, what is lived and falls within experience directly relates to the human being. Anthropologists who have studied human behavior realize that, independent of any religious institution, human beings do possess a religious nature.

Religions and religious institutions, however, have their own raisons d'être. Just as we need a highway code so as not to drive recklessly and hurt others, so also we need a guidebook for the moral plane. Religions as well as religious institutions are thus there to establish such a code of good conduct, to give points of reference, and to take charge of human beings so that they do not go in all directions, and just wander about and hurt others. Beyond the religious institutions or religions, human beings—and sometimes animals—behave in ways that may be described as religious because they involve ritual practices. Three principal criteria help us understand this religious phenomenon and approach it in a scientific way:

1. There is a story (a discourse).
2. There are practices (rites).
3. There are rules.

If one considers that our behavior of a religious character forms part of our deep nature, whether we are atheistic, agnostic, or merely lay followers, then it becomes possible to suggest that people belonging to the religions of the world, as well as those who have chosen secularity, may be able to live in harmony.

This is especially possible because human beings are also spiritual beings. In other words, even if secular people are not practicing a given religion, they are nonetheless beings that have spirituality, and this should suffice to harmonize the religious and the secular people. All we have to do now is to define what spirituality is.

THE CONCEPT OF SPIRITUALITY

According to the dictionary, the word "spirituality" denotes the character of what is spiritual, and what is "spiritual" means that "which is spirit." The spirit means "breath" or the principle of the immaterial life. Breathing commences at birth and leaves us only when we die, and when a person dies and takes the last breath, one says that the person has returned to the spirit. The Latin *spiritus* refers to the breath as the "thinking principle in general (as opposed to the matter)."[3]

Spirit and matter are thus the two poles of life.

Therefore, independent of all beliefs, we are spiritual beings. Spirituality relates to "the capacity which the human being has to wonder about its existence and on its place in the universe."[4]

Whether one is the follower of a religion or not, it remains a fact that we all seek, in our own ways, to probe the mysteries of the life and death; we want to understand what is greater than us; we seek the essence of the things of life—we seek the essential.

RELIGION AND HUMAN RIGHTS

One way of bringing together the secular and the religious dimensions of life is by promoting the adoption of a Universal Declaration of Human Rights by the World's Religions. I shall now respond to some questions associated with it in the light of the teaching of Aumism, a universal "active and dynamic religion."[5]

Question: Wouldn't it be wise to adopt a Universal Declaration of the Human Rights (and of their duties) against the ideological excesses of religious extremism?

Answer: Yes, especially if the duties are also clearly enumerated. And as the founder of Aumism recommends, one could perhaps add a clause that would define the citizen as "a citizen of the universe respecting the laws of the country where it lives."[6] That would allow a reference to citizens' duties and to one taking the responsibility for one's actions.

Question: "Isn't it time to temporarily suspend proselytism so that the religions find the means of transmitting their messages without giving the impression of imposing them on others"?[7]

Answer: "Living its faith without seeking to impose it on others" is one of the fundamental principles of Aumism.[8] However, we are allowed to question ourselves.

It may be objected that in our modern societies, marketing is present everywhere, and publicity is a part of life. These two means of influencing us are already accepted, which, by acting in a subliminal way, almost force us to buy a product. Why then should one suddenly speak against proselytism, which is how a religion makes itself known?

Similarly, an artist has the right to have enthusiastic followers or fans, and political parties conduct campaigns—so why can't a religion do so without the risk of being treated as a fanatic, unless it be the case that this zeal to seek followers is seen by the rest of the world as a commercial act, and that which is commercial in the world's eyes cannot be authentically religious.

It is this dichotomy in the perception of things that seems to point to an issue. One wants to separate the material from the spiritual, even though there is material in the spiritual and spiritual in the material, rational in the irrational and irrational in the rational, the yin in the yang and the yang in the yin, a male animus in the woman and a female anima in the man. The answer to this issue lies in the realization that proselytization should not involve compulsion but rather allow us to compare various worldviews. Then someone trying to promote one's religion by sometimes using marketing tools to achieve this goal will not seem that disturbing.

Question: Since "religions differ between them" and can "also differ compared to the direction which they give to the word religion" thus affecting "world peace," "couldn't one use a word like that . . . of dharma or dao as a starting point"?

Answer: It is true that the word *dharma* has passed into the French and English languages, and this facilitates its use. Perhaps it can also be said that most religions, if not all, and each one in its own way, count on universal values such as respect, love, and so on, and state the principles of moral and physical conduct, but they are not all free from excess.

Why not use AUM (OM), the Mother Sound of all sounds, universally known, which transcends all the languages, and allows one to ascend toward Love and Light, Wisdom, Tolerance, and Compassion? It constitutes the best form of "asceticism" to pacify the mind of human beings and might be worth considering as a starting point.

Question: Can there be "a convergence between the religions in the world from a practical point of view, in spite of the doctrinal differences"?

Answer: According to His Holiness, the Lord Hamsah Manarah, one should exert control over the mind by developing a culture of positive thoughts, by introspecting one's personality, and by daily assessing oneself before going to sleep, inter alia. In other words, if one wants to transform the world, it is necessary to start by changing oneself. But this has to become a daily practice.

Any person, irrespective of religious or spiritual inclination, can do that, and it would be undoubtedly an excellent and effective way of leading people toward peace, harmony, and serenity.

Question: Do religions "have . . . from within the resources making it possible to transform their relations between sexes beyond appearances, or must they themselves be transformed beyond appearances when they struggle with this question"?

Answer: According to the founder of Aumism, it is because people tend to identify themselves with their transitory personality, with their differences, that this kind of problem arises. When we identify ourselves with the Supreme Self within us and see God in us as well as in others, it is not any more a woman or a man who is in front of us, but an asexual soul, free and seeking the Light. This attitude creates a feeling of unity and erases distinctions.

In Aumism, men and women occupy the same position. There are monks and nuns, priests and priestesses, as well as bishops of both sexes. Both can officiate or give the sacraments. The relations between sexes thus tend toward balance. We have the practice of greeting each other with the hands joined in prayer (*anjali*) while saying OM to express the fact that we recognize the divinity of the other. It seems to me that in this practice, we have an important internal resource and one, moreover, which is easily adopted in everyday life when one comes in contact with any person, irrespective of that person's religion, ideology, or gender. It is a healthy and liberating practice, and it can become universal.

Question: How can we make "sure that the religion is well represented by the media"?

Answer: This point is of capital importance. Indeed, the media directly influence people even when people try to be discriminating. Too often it is the negative aspects of religions—wars, fanaticism, extremism, constraining sects—that we are shown. Interreligious dialogue has been started, but has a long way to go. But to answer in a more concrete way, the researchers and academics should find a place in the media to come to speak about religion, spirituality, and the religious phenomenon as a whole in order to educate the people. Many colleagues are astonished to learn that courses in the scientific study of religions exist that involve religiology, that is, the criteria allowing one to distinguish between what is sacred and what is profane.

It would be indeed a good idea for academics and researchers to speak in the media about faith, true love, charity, and prayer because education constitutes the foundation of society.

CONCLUSION

Religiology occupies a place of pride in the study of human behavior when speaking about religious phenomenon involving experimenting with the sacred. The monk is the outstanding specimen of it, for through his meditative practices he feels connected, becomes One with the Whole, thus providing a living example of *religare*. Women and men of the street—in other words, people in general—also occupy a high place in this scheme through their spiritual exercises, which lead to self-actualization, as Abraham Maslow would say.[9]

I would like to conclude with the words of His Holiness, the Lord Hamsah Manarah, to illustrate what has been just said:

> The only religion to which it is worthwhile to devote all of one's efforts,
> Is that of Love purified of any possessiveness; . . .
> A revolution must occur in our consciences
> With the watchwords:
> Perfecting oneself to make society better.
> Burning away selfishness to foster social harmony.
> Developing a sense of Unity,
> Is to make possible, in this lifetime,
> the conquest of true happiness.[10]

Isn't this small sentence a key for each one of us: "The only religion to which it is worthwhile to devote all of one's efforts,/Is that of Love purified of any possessiveness," whatever our beliefs are or not, our faith, our religions, or spiritualities of membership[11]

Isn't it our common mission?

NOTES

1. Citation taken from http://www.evene.fr/citations/mot.php?mot=prevoir and also on the website of an association for justice and peace: http://www.rmlaiques.org. This citation is probably taken from Saint-Exupéry's book *Le Petit Prince*.

2. G. Van Der Leeuw, *La religion dans son essence et ses manifestations—phénoménologie de la religion* (Paris: Payot, 1955), p. 665.

3. *Nouveau Petit Robert*, version 1.2 (Windows), 1999.

4. "Spiritualité," Wikipedia: http://fr.wikipedia.org/wiki/Spiritualit%C3%A9 (accessed January 9, 2006).

5. L'aumisme: http://www.aumisme.org/fr/aum.htm (accessed August 27, 2006). "L'Aumisme est une religion active et dynamique nous permettant par des moyens simples, concrets, accessibles à tous, de construire ensemble au-delà des races, des classes, des croyances, les nouvelles valeurs de notre humanité."

6. This citation is taken from the *dodecalogue*, an internal document for monks and nuns that sets guidelines for right conduct. A similar example can be found on the Aumism website: "Being Aumist, is developing a feeling of Unity and Universality. It means loving one's country faithfully without forgetting nevertheless to be a citizen of the World and Universe" (http://www.aumisme.org/gb/aum.htm).

7. Quoted material in these questions is directly from the website of the World's Religions after September 11 Congress (http://www.worldsreligionsafter911.com/Description%20Congress%20Programm_EN.htm).

8. Hamsah Manarah, *La doctrine de l'Aumisme—Fondements de l'Âge d'Or* (Baume de Castellane: éditions Le Mandarom, 1990), pp. 50–51.

9. Encyclopédie Microsoft Encarta (2003): "Le psychologue américain Abraham Maslow (1900–1970) a proposé une hiérarchie pyramidale des motivations déterminant le comportement humain, en y rattachant notamment les besoins de sécurité, d'amour et de

sentiment d'appartenance, de compétence, de prestige et de considération, d'accomplissement de soi [actualisation de soi], de curiosité et de compréhension."

10. Hamsah Manarah, *Mémoires d'un Yogi* (out of print), p. 346; also found in HAMSANANDA, S.M., *La doctrine de l'Aumisme—Fondements de l'Âge d'Or*, éditions Le Mandarom (Baume de Castellane, 1990), 611 pages, p. 87.

11. Hamsananda, p. 87.

CHAPTER 14

For an Education to Nonviolence: Religion's Necessary Contribution

Vedhyas Mandaja

Violence, particularly religious violence, is a reminder of this question asked by the Buddha: "If violence is returned by violence, how far will it go?"

Indeed, worldwide divisions confront us. It is urgent that we remedy the educational deficiencies, which are the root causes of violence. Families have a way to make a direct contribution to social peace through children's education. It is a difficult but important responsibility.

In the first part of this chapter we will see how education can encourage respect by restoring a genuine relationship with God.

In the second part, we will review educational attitudes, particularly the importance of setting an example, something that young people really need.[1]

In this chapter, which addresses values common to all the great traditions, we will mention education in Aumism, the religion of the Unity of God's Faces, founded by His Holiness, the Lord Hamsah Manarah, the headquarters of which are in the south of France at the Monastery of Mandarom Shambhasalem.

THE BASES OF EDUCATION ABOUT NONVIOLENCE IN THE RELIGION OF AUMISM

His Holiness the Lord Hamsah Manarah addresses the parents and educators in this way: "Prepare your children to become Knights of Universal Peace. This means: cultivating non-violence, the absence of racism, sympathy towards all nations, respecting all faiths, beliefs and religions, the greatest possible tolerance, and Universal Love."[2]

The foundation for nonviolence in the Teachings of Aumism is the fact that the same divine Principle is at the source of all forms of life, through the Oneness of Creation: "The sound OM pulsates within each and every mineral, plant, animal and human being."[3]

Therefore, violence can only be but the fruit of ignorance.

Respect for All That Lives

The slow evolution of consciousness from the realm of the minerals, to the realm of plants, to the realm of animals, to the realm of humans, who then move on toward divinization, is represented as the "Evolutionary Pyramid of the Realms of Nature." This interdependency between various forms and levels of life implies several ideas.

Respect Toward Nature, Which Is Alive

Aumist parents, like their Jain or Hindu brothers, explain to their children that they are vegetarians because they respect the lives of animals, and they bless their meals on a daily basis.

The children see them repeating the Sound OM for the evolution of all realms of Nature.

Respect Toward Human Beings

- A youngster who knows how to respect himself will also know how to respect others.
- The human body is the Temple of the soul, and the child learns how to preserve it, refusing the use of drugs, for example. (Let us note that suicide is considered as a serious crime against oneself. Prayers are said to help the souls of those who have committed suicide.)
- The child learns respect not only for life, but for the rights of all human beings, whatever their origins or culture.

Sectarian people divide the world into two halves, seeing others as strangers or enemies. But meeting different people, at school for example, allows one to go beyond prejudice. Understanding that misery and injustice are causes of violence in the world allows people to develop sharing and solidarity. Teaching reincarnation, which is known by many Traditions, is an incentive toward tolerance. (In Aumism, after death but before being reincarnated, the soul keeps learning to develop tolerance and love in the "Column of Light").

Avoiding the Spiral of Violence

Education teaches us how to control our own violence.

Learning How to Forgive Is the First Step Toward Nonviolence

If a child has been violent, his parents will help him to forgive himself, thereby avoiding guilt, and teach him to ask for forgiveness, to say he's sorry.

If he is the victim of violence, he will be able to forgive others, thus avoiding the path of revenge.

The objective is that the child gradually learns how "not to do to them what he does not want done to him," the Golden Rule in most religions.
In both cases, prayer is helpful to avoid the spiral of violence.

Developing Inner Strength But Also Love Is a Necessity

A child must be able to defend himself, and gain respect.
One could say, along with Jean-Marie Muller in his *Dictionnaire de la non-violence*, that nonviolence is "the ethical and spiritual attitude of an upright man who recognizes violence as a denial of humanity, and who decides to refuse to subject himself to its dominion."[4] Real nonviolence is not a weakness; it is a force.
A physically, mentally, and spiritually healthy life makes it possible to operate a transmutation of violence and also to surmount obstacles.

- It is possible for a child to work on controlling his own emotions through the practice of Praṇāyāma, Haṭha Yoga, and martial arts.
- Mastering one's mind is fundamental because "man becomes what he thinks."
- It is possible to strengthen oneself through positive affirmations, for example, "I am a center of Strength, Light, and Conscience"; "I am the Supreme Self."
- The child can also repeat the Sound OM, which is helpful in quieting one's mind.

Self-control is a source of happiness for an individual, and a factor of peace in society.

Opening Up One's Mind to the Principle of Unity between Religions

Unity between Religions Is a Factor of Peace

A central feature in several traditions, Unity is particularly significant for Aumism, whose only dogma is the Unity of God's Faces: "God is One, whatever the Name we may give to Him."[5] Thus, religions are different paths leading to the same goal, and religious peace is "Unity while respecting differences."[6]
The Aumist symbol of the Hexamid shows that the rainbow-colored religions converge toward the same Creator, the white light of the Sound OM.
Encouraged by the example of their parents who pray to God with the same love, whatever Name He may be given, children avoid the throes of sectarianism and division. They respect all religions.

Finding Unity with God Is Inseparable from Divine Compassion

The purpose of most religious paths is merging into God, who is Love.
So, sincere followers from all traditions develop more and more nonviolence and fraternity, until achieving, sooner or later, divine Compassion.
The Founder of Aumism, a self-realized Master, said: "Man or woman, if you meet somewhere a foolish being who claims to be my enemy, or who simply behaves as such, tell him that he is within me and that I give him my peace."[7]

Education must therefore teach how to grow in love as a young Knight of Peace, who "develops the sense of Universality. His family is the whole of humanity. He will look at what will draw humans closer to each other rather than divide them. A youngster loves his country faithfully, without forgetting that he is a citizen of the world and of the Universe."[8]

Step by step, a child learns to send thoughts of peace everywhere in the world.

Thus, to build up his existence, a teenager gets an identity, a goal, and the possibility of achieving genuine autonomy, expressed by those fine words of Divine Love: "Become the God you are."[9]

Religion's contribution is important: young people who have not love enough, no self-esteem, and no ideals sometimes look for identity in delinquent behaviors, in violence.

Perhaps a humanistic atheist might say, "According to you, then if I do not believe in God, I cannot educate my child in nonviolence?" Naturally you can! The "principle of humanity," respect for every man according to humanism, is a paramount value if we think that man is of divine essence: one cannot respect God without respecting men and women. There are thus moral values that Aumists and atheists have in common, in striving more and more toward nonviolence.

EDUCATIONAL ATTITUDES AND NONVIOLENCE

Intelligence of the heart is more useful and necessary than wealth or a high social status.

Love and Authority

Maltreatment and frustrations often generate violent behaviors. The experience of an authentic love in childhood helps one to be able to love in turn.

Loving God within the Child Implies:

- Unconditional love, accepting each and every one with their differences
- A positive attitude, reinforcing their self-esteem
- Nonpossessiveness, enabling them to be autonomous

The chance to bring up a child is given to us as the privilege to favor the evolution of a soul.

Fair Authority Is Essential

- Step by step, parents have to help children understand the law of cause and effect: what you sow, you will reap in the future.

It also serves the interests of society where law and order must be respected so that people can live together.

- A well-adapted authority will help us develop the sense of effort: it is necessary to build one's fate by avoiding the pitfalls of juvenile delinquent behavior.

So, by favoring the full blooming of every child, the family favors the social and global peace.

The Example Given by Parents

To Give the Example of Nonviolence Is the Fruit of Working on Oneself

Education is difficult: no family can avoid occasional crises.

To help parents, the Aumist teaching gives useful indications about preparing for a child's birth; the laws governing the child's development; and the importance of praying, meditating, and offering up one's actions to the Divine. It is also helpful for self-transformation: trying hard to break with one's heavy past, to transmute one's own violence, allows one to provide the best possible example.

Giving the Example of Nonviolence Is "Learning How to Be"

It requires coherence between words and deeds.

Nonviolence must be in thought, word, and action. This is the first Teaching of Jainism: *Ahiṁsā* is written on the wheel of the Dharma, and under the symbol, we read in Sanskrit "compassionate living"—live and help to live. This is a code of conduct in daily life.

"You have to be the change which you wish to see in the world," said Gandhi.[10] So, to teach a child how to be, begin by learning how to be, yourself. By forcing the parents to better themselves, the child helps them to evolve, to progress.

In their difficult task, parents can themselves take for models the great Educators of Humanity and show them as examples to the young people, because the direction of the evolution is the same for every child and for the whole humanity.

The Example of Humanity's Great Spiritual Guides Shows the Path of Nonviolence

The power of their example really becomes a demonstration: spiritual Masters themselves have won victories against human obstacles. Through their visible experience, they are able to communicate to us faith in our own victories over ignorance, division, suffering, and death.

The Example of an Authentic Master Is First an Act of Love

Setting an example is rooted in sharing the human experience and condition. The Sages and founders of religions carried out their mission as educators of humankind, which needs to be guided from suffering to peace, from dependency to autonomy, from human being to the Divine Being. In this sense, setting an example is a form of self-abnegation.

In Christianity, when Christ says, "Love each other as I loved you," he refers to an example where he communicated to his followers something of his Being, the strength to give in turn.[11]

For His Holiness, the Lord Hamsah Manarah, "it is necessary to show the path through the example of an impeccable perseverance, by serving the Almighty God present in everyone."[12]

The Example of the Spiritual Great Masters Leads to the Internal God Beyond All Divisions

In these times, as fanaticism and religious divisions are generating war and violence, but also as new hopes are seeing the light of day, it is important to allow the world the epic of Guides who have dedicated their existence to nonviolence, to bringing people, nations, religions, and churches closer together.

The Founder of Aumism dedicated each and every instant of his life to building bridges of tolerance and love between faiths. In accordance with the Teachings of great Sages such as Ramakrishna, Vivekananda, and Sivananda, who initiated him to *sannyāsa,* he returned to the source of each Tradition, meeting great Sages who gave him initiations and initiatic titles, before saying, "I have experienced many techniques of prayers, meditations, visualizations, many sacred languages also, to finally discover that beyond the religious rainbow; there was only one single and unique Divine Diamond."[13]

Therefore, a fundamental point of his Teaching is "become the God you are."[14] This is also found in the heart of many religions. For example, in Hinduism, "You are That"; in Jainism, the goal is to become a perfect soul known as God; Buddha said: "Look within yourself, you are the Buddha"; and Christ stated: "The Kingdom of God is in yourself."[15]

The example of authentic Spiritual Guides, helping to discover unity beyond the differences, shows the path of nonviolence.

CONCLUSION

We'll say that each person, in his own right, can be an example of nonviolence for youngsters.

Meeting people from different religions as well as university researchers during this Global Congress on World's Religions is a nonviolent way of opposing violence and an example for future generations.

In accordance with this opening mind, Aumist education encourages respect for differences: "Accept others along with their differences, says His Holiness the

Lord Hamsah Manarah, because Unity is not the destruction of those who do not think as we do, but indeed the reconciliation of all those who think differently, while uniting their efforts towards a better world."[16]

At the end, if you wish to, this is a short extract from a meditation reminding us that the educative mission of religion is to connect human beings to God and with one another.

> I am one with all the families of men and women and children
> Populating the whole earth . . .
> I reject nobody, I love everyone,
> For I understand that the Earth is a unity of divine Love
> Therefore I need to have solidarity.[17]

NOTES

1. The pronoun "he" has been used for men and women so as not to weigh down the text. It is not a question of discrimination.
2. Hamsah Manarah, *Aumism, the Doctrine of the Golden Age* (La Baume de Castellane: Editions du Mandarom, 1999), p. 252
3. Hamsah Manarah, *La Révolution du monde des vivants et des morts* (La Baume de Castellane: Editions du Mandarom, 1993), p. 198
4. Muller, Jean-Marie, *Dictionnaire de la non-violence* (Gordes: Le Relié, 2005), p. 242. (our translation)
5. Hamsah Manarah, *La Révolution du monde des vivants et des morts* , p. 66.
6. Hamsah Manarah, *Une Loi pour détruire le mal* (La Baume de Castellane: Editions du Mandarom, 1993), p. 427.
7. Hamsah Manarah, *Le Yoga de l'Amour dans la Force* (La Baume de Castellane: Editions du Mandarom, 1990), p. 49.
8. Hamsah Manarah, *Aumism*, p. 252.
9. Hamsah Manarah, *La Réintégration divine par le Yoga: deviens le Dieu que tu es* (Paris: A. Michel, 1978).
10. Gandhi, discours d'août, 1942.
11. *Evangile selon Saint Jean* XIII:25.
12. Hamsah Manarah, *Le Flambeau d'Unité* (La Baume de Castellane: Editions du Mandarom, 1993), p. 271.
13. Hamsah Manarah, *Une Loi pour détruire le Mal*, Introduction.
14. Hamsah Manarah, *Le Flambeau d'Unité,* p. 514.
15. *Evangile selon Saint Luc,* XVII:21.
16. Hamsah Manarah, *Une Loi pour détruire le Mal,* p. 427.
17. Hamsah Manarah, *Le Flambeau d'Unité*, p. 421

SUGGESTED READINGS

Books

Hamsah Manarah. *Aumism, the Doctrine of the Golden Age* (La Baume de Castellane: Editions du Mandarom, 1999).

———. *Le Flambeau d'Unité* (La Baume de Castellane: Editions du Mandarom, 1993).

———. *La Loi d'Evolution des Ames* (La Baume de Castellane: Editions du Mandarom, 1992).

———. *Une Loi pour détruire le Mal* (La Baume de Castellane: Editions du Mandarom, 1993).
———. *La Révolution du monde des vivants et des morts* (La Baume de Castellane: Editions du Mandarom, 1993).
———. *Vers un Age d'Or d'Unité* (La Baume de Castellane: Editions du Mandarom, 1993).
———. *Le Yoga de la vie pratique* (La Baume de Castellane: Editions du Mandarom, 1997).
Herbert, Jean. *l'Enseignement de Sivananda* (Paris: Albin Michel, 1958).
Muller, Jean-Marie. *Dictionnaire de la non-violence* (Gordes: Le Relié, 2005).
Shah, Natubhai. *Jainism: The World of Conquerors,* Vols. 1–2 (Brighton: Sussex Academic Press, 1998).
Vivekananda. *Yogas pratiques* (Paris: Albin Michel, 1998).

Magazines

The Lighthouse Beacon, Vol. 43, 2004.
The Lighthouse Beacon, Vol. 46, 2005.
Sciences humaines H.S. December 2004/February 2005.

Part IV

Feminist Spirituality

CHAPTER 15

The Glory of the Divine Feminine

Her Holiness Sai Maa Lakshmi Devi

The Global Congress on the World's Religions gives us all a golden opportunity to transform our consciousness so we can all live on a common ground, transcending the boundaries of religions and thereby creating a violence-free society, a resentment-free society, with a commitment to serve each other. Thus it provides the basis for forming a nonjudgmental community, based on education and knowledge, allowing for the revival of ancient wisdom and creating an empowerment to be shared. It can be a place where we could care for each other, and move from an individual, family-minded consciousness to a global consciousness to become citizens of this world, for which we have great respect.

Such an individual peace could create a peaceful world, in which we promote love, celebrate life, and divinize our minds. The result is the creation of a one-world family, where identification with a limited religion resulting from our limited minds is dissolved, and where we could discipline our minds, discipline our emotions, dare to look inside, face our challenges, and take ownership of our actions—all of which naturally creates peace, which is an attribute of Spirit, of God, of Natural Law. Religious, pious people have always wished to serve others. During the present shift in planetary consciousness, as people are being challenged in their own religions, they are redefining meaning and purpose as true service to humanity. It is high time for us to realize the meaning of the word freedom: what does it really mean to be free?

The conflict we see in the world first starts from individual conflict. It is a war going on within that is then projected outside. We are not honoring our higher selves, the grandeur within us; we worship the material world. The shift demands that we stop being so selfish toward others, serve others, become full human beings, be of service, feel others' pain and suffering, discover the dignity of human life, and build a strong foundation within in order to serve and protect all life. We should act with maturity, take responsibility, and live with grace and humility.

Lack of knowledge and lack of education, meaning ignorance, create contractions in the mind, whereas knowledge uplifts and liberates us. We have a choice today in the twenty-first century between contraction and liberation. Most religions, in their own ways, speak of "self," the indwelling Power of God, of Life, the Presence, where we contemplate and practice introspection. A change in mind leads to a change in behavior and attitude, and leads to a life of righteousness containing the beginning of Knowledge, of the Light of Wisdom. With the realization that we are all children of the same source, we can treat the other as one's self, also acknowledging the self in the other. The shift in one's awareness is felt as a vibration by others; a feeling of sisterhood and brotherhood, a feeling of knowing one's self, emerges. Are we not all brothers, sisters, Beloveds of the Divine? When we transform ourselves, we are transforming the world. Our transformation, a shift of our own consciousness, a transformation of it, is now an imperative.

What is our dharma? When are we going to be awakened? When will we dare to open our hearts to love our brothers and sisters, to accept each other? An awakening happens with education and knowledge of the higher Self. The awareness of nonviolence lifts our identity to a Self level, a Divinity level. There is only One Spirit, One Light, One God, One Source.

If we remember that we are all from one and the same source, we will naturally create a safer place on this planet, realizing we are all human beings. Then we will honor all human values; we will honor life within each of us and a life of wisdom as a wise one. Technology can be used to serve the world, promote a better life, eradicate poverty, stop domestic violence, and revive the law. It is the Shakti that binds us all as pearls on one thread. Technology can be used with wisdom to reinterpret religion in the twenty-first century, and to breathe new life into religion and revive it. Technology can help our government bring wisdom to our schools, so that our students will become wiser. Each child should know that there are many different religions. We should put before them the global ideal of general knowledge of religion, which is an inseparable part of human life. These young children have a different consciousness and are so awake. Our role is to take the step toward globalized wisdom and if needed reinterpret, revise, or modify philosophical concepts.

Spiritualizing our everyday life will serve as the greatest example. We can be models of compassion, of nobility, an expression of Divine Love, apply the Golden Rule in our daily lives as we grow.

Religious texts, although they have been translated so many, many times, do not often address the feminine aspect of God. Esoteric teachings are very beautiful and respectful of both man and woman, and they seem to understand that both male and female energies go together. They offer a higher level of religious life. There are many references in different traditions of the feminine aspect of God, of life, of Source. The feminine principle was created with the Shakti of life itself. Jesus used to speak of the Mother, the Cosmic Mother, Father Creator. The roles of Jesus's grandmother, Anna, and Mother Mary, remind us of the Law of Forgiveness, that which we carry within each of us. Sophia, principle of feminine wisdom, is one aspect of Shakti. In the creation, there is no evolution without the feminine aspect.

In India the word *Shakti*, the Divine Feminine Principle, encompasses all the feminine aspects of the cosmos. This has not changed since the beginning of the human race. Shakti is the embodiment of the omnipresent, omnipotent, and omniscient that is worshiped, even though adorned in different forms. Shakti is a recognized form of women in Hinduism, even though in some areas of India, women are still badly treated. Meditation, stillness is important to be a better vehicle of that Divine Feminine Principle. As meditation liberates one from inner conflict, it dissolves the "stuff," clears the sense of separation, and brings forgiveness, thereby leading to a better life, better behavior, better relationships, an uplifting of consciousness, and higher frequencies of our energies in the *chakras* of our subtle bodies. The power of meditation also brings unity, love, peace, sacredness, and mindfulness to all. It is urgent that we allow our Divine feminine to reveal herself so that spiritual growth occurs, allowing spiritual integration in everyday life. There is a lot that can be derived from the feminine principle.

What has happened to the feminine in religion? Our role is to cultivate that love and teach others how to respect, understand, and accept other faiths, and how to be awakened to a higher vibration and to the virtue in each human heart. Cultivating the feminine principle in religion leads to a deeper understanding of who we really are, enabling us to articulate the wisdom of responsibility. It contributes to maturity, healthy relationships, caring behavior, commitment, and oneness in our diversity in all aspects of our daily life experience. Peace will prevail when individuals are at peace. The foundation of religion is to be relevant and coherent. Another aspect of religious evolution is to collaborate with different faiths and traditions, interact in interreligious activities, share one's knowledge, and promote discussion and dialogue.

If God possesses both feminine and masculine energy, how could God, as Creator, diminish the dignity of its own creation? Religion is here to sustain society, teach sharing and caring, and share the feeling of oneness, respect, and love of the Creator.

When we consider the fact of birth, what would life be without the feminine? Could there be life? Impossible! If a child does not receive the love of the mother, the brain does not grow. A loved heart has such potential for growth. We need to ask such questions as these: What are we passing to the next generation? How are we educating our children, the custodians of planet Earth? What are our moral values? How can we find a common ground, a togetherness, to uplift human consciousness? How do we kindle the heart of the human race? In most religions we have golden rules, vows that have embodied respect and justice since the beginning of the human family. Such is the dignity and nobility of being human.

Love, compassion, respect, and communication can really create and establish harmony. These are ways to bring out the best in human beings. The power of forgiveness provides us with the path of healing.

Now for the feminine to be empowered, the masculine has to be re-educated. Man must re-evaluate women in his eyes, even the way he sees women. Women are so precious, so important for both peace and spiritual advancement. Both the masculine and feminine aspects must become enlightened and balanced so we can all understand each other. It is possible to achieve this balance since we are all part of the cosmos. The Creator does not discriminate between the two. A mindful person, man or woman, honors and empowers the other. It's all about education, education with awareness, education with heart, education with wisdom, education with love, education with kindness. An inner peace that reveres life is innate in women, because women carry life within their wombs. We women in harmony with men can bring global spiritual wisdom in this world with our love. Peace will prevail when our compassionate transformation of consciousness occurs, as our heart *chakras* open more and more, and our consciousness expands. Such is the potential glory of Divine Feminine right here now.

CHAPTER 16

Coalition of Religious Women at the United Nations

Jean M. O'Meara

Many of us remember clearly where we were and what we were doing on the morning of September 11, 2001. I was on a bus headed into Manhattan. Now, along with others, I try to make sense of religious beliefs, attempting to find meaning in a world so very changed.

Since that dreadful September date, I continue to reflect on my religious beliefs. As a Christian, I believe God revealed himself in Jesus. And we as human beings are an integral part of an ongoing redemption. Christianity sees the person of Jesus as the creative presence of the Transcendent One—in time, in space, and in history. The tension between transcendence and immanence finds resolution in the belief that the redemptive action of God continues through human activity—not only in Jesus, but also in every human being.

Certainly, these thoughts were not on my mind the morning of September 11, 2001, as I rode the Riverdale bus and headed for a luncheon meeting with Sister Catherine Ferguson at the United Nations. We had met the day before to finalize our strategy for establishing an NGO (a nongovernment organization) for a consortium of women's congregations.

There was a labyrinth of organizational matters that still needed attention before addressing some of the social issues, which were of concern. Suddenly, the bus driver announced that a plane had crashed into the World Trade Center. I turned to the woman next to me and said, "Strange—it is such a beautiful morning." Within the next few seconds, cell phones were ringing throughout the bus—a second plane had crashed into the other tower. I could see thick smoke rise over lower Manhattan, but like most commuters, I had things to do. When I reached the UN, it was being evacuated, and I joined thousands of people surging north as police and firefighters rushed south.

During the years since 9/11, which have been marked by violence, terror, and chaos, I have been challenged by the task of making known the reality of the Incarnation—to say nothing of rejoicing in it! Nevertheless, I continue to believe that joining with others to help improve the human condition is the great redemptive challenge. It is, to my mind, the human vocation. And I do rejoice in the infinite diversity of gifts and talents that are brought into play by this creative drama.

So in 2002, in the midst of all the chaos and disruption on the international scene, representatives from seven religious congregations of women met and discussed forming an NGO at the United Nations. We wanted to work together with a common belief that through a united effort, we could make a difference in a world where an increasing number of women and children had little or no voice.

Our mission statement says that we desire to work

- where the rights of women and children will receive the same respect as those of men
- where justice and respect for international law will protect immigrants and refugees
- where all people will care for and protect our planet

We chose UNANIMA-International as the name for our NGO. UNANIMA is a composite word is made up of two parts: ANIMA—a feminine life principle, that which animates—and UN, which together with ANIMA evokes the word unanimous and associated us with the UN organization. "International" describes our congregations, whose members and associates work in sixty-three countries on all the continents.

WHAT DO WE DO?

We bring the expertise of our members and associates to the United Nations. We act with other NGOs to create programs and help write policies seeking the economic and social advancement of all people, especially women and children. We educate our members about the programs and activities of the United Nations in New York and Geneva.

SPECIFIC PROGRAM: BRINGING TOGETHER THE EXPERTISE OF MEMBERS/ASSOCIATES

Two years ago, we decided to focus our efforts on human trafficking. We realized that we needed to have a realistic basis for advocacy against trafficking at the international level. With that in mind, we invited women from eight countries who are working directly with the issue of trafficking to join us for our bi-annual board meeting in New York. The guests were all women living and working in Brazil, Canada, Gabon, India, Ireland, Italy, Nigeria, and the United States. Our guests shared stories and circumstances about young women from Nepal and Bangladesh being trafficked to India, we learned about child slaves being transported between Gabon and Togo, and we heard about "safe houses" in Dublin for Eastern European women, whom we promised a better life. I want to share one of these stories.

Aecha came to Gabon when she was twelve years old. Her mother gave her to a woman from the same village in Togo, believing that her daughter would go to school, learn a trade, and earn money. Aecha never attended school, was forced to work as a domestic and as a street vender, but received no money. She was often beaten; she finally fled and found her way to a safe place.

Stories differ from country to country, but it is accurate to say that in every country, human trafficking is increasing and is the most violent crime against the human rights and dignity of children, women, and men.

We work actively with other concerned NGOs at the UN in New York and have taken some preliminary steps to work with the UN Council on Human Rights in Geneva. Drawing on the professional expertise of our membership, we have taken modest steps toward pushing back ignorance with compassion. In addition UNANIMA-International brings individuals to the UN to give them access to those in power so they can speak their truths, empowering them to say what is important in their lives and shape what they have to say in the ways that allow for their full development as human persons.

Recently, we invited a woman from the Philippines to make a statement at a UN hearing in order to bring the voices of the people into UN deliberations. She said: "I am Alma, and I am a survivor. I worked in the bars for almost four years when the U.S. bases were in the Philippines. If I didn't work, I had to pay a fine in the bars and clubs. . . . in the end I contracted venereal disease. I also gave birth to an Amerasian child."

Alma ended her statement by saying, "We call on the UN to address trafficking on the global and national levels, to address racism, economic inequality, and male domination existing in societies and the world that breed this form of violence against women."

There are many more poignant stories and accounts that I could share, but I just want to add that a year ago, UNANIMA-International became an accredited NGO with consultative status with the Economic and Social Council at the United Nations. With ECOSOC accreditation, we will be able to do more credible work for human rights.

Our collaborative work was undertaken not in the belief that this effort would actually achieve human dignity, especially for women and children, but in the belief that the work itself would be intrinsically redemptive (i.e., incarnational). It would be ongoing, and the step-by-step effort would reflect the presence of God among us.

What we are doing is very modest. Our human efforts are limited, but as an NGO, UNANIMA-International has formed a network of experts, educators, health care providers, social workers, and development workers to help those without voice. As written in St. Paul's second letter to the Corinthians, we are only the earthenware jars that hold this treasure, to make it clear that such an overwhelming power comes from God and not from us.

Part V

Religion, Spirituality, Science, and the Environment

CHAPTER 17

How and Why Science and Religion Share a Nexus and Are Both Indispensable for the Attainment of Ultimate Reality

Emmanuel J. Karavousanos

Consciousness has remained an enigma since the beginning of time. Science and religion have been in conflict for hundreds of years. Perhaps all this has been because we have failed to consider the larger aspect of seeing and analyzing the obvious. Most of us seem to simply ignore the obvious.

To question is a fundamental requirement central in any scientific endeavor, for solutions require proof. Faith is intrinsic in religion, and there is no questioning. No proof is required. Once we recognize that these two seemingly opposing forces actually complement one another, and once we understand that they share a nexus, and what that nexus is, we will recognize that religion can be a force for good, and we will have the impetus to put forth the effort needed to understand and attain ultimate reality. We will also discover that the consciousness question must be answered and realized independently by each soul. And for that to happen, science and religion are both necessary tools.

Science and religion each acknowledge the existence of what is called insight. An insight is born the instant a new meaning is apprehended. Insight is the sudden arrival of an idea. An unexpected realization is an insight. Insight is our *inside sight.* In our world, intellect and education are stressed, while development of insight is generally ignored. Insight is viewed as something that occurs—like a sudden, welcome summer shower rather than as a gift to be yearned for and sought. All this is not to say that negative insights are nonexistent: a terrorist gains an insight when he suddenly realizes a new target he can destroy or kill.

Hinduism teaches that one must look within to reach the gift that is Brahman. Brahman is ultimate reality in the Hindu religion. In Buddhism, too, one must look inward for that higher sense, and it is called Enlightenment. Jesus suggested we should look inward, offering that the kingdom of heaven is within. When we attain ultimate reality, only then do we realize that Jesus's kingdom, Brahman, and

Enlightenment are one and the same; there are many names for this higher state of consciousness.

We have often been encouraged to think about our thoughts, another idea that lends itself to looking inward. The German poet and novelist Johann Wolfgang von Goethe wrote, "My boy, I'll say that I've been clever. I think, but think of thinking never."[1] And historian James Harvey Robinson admonishes, "We do not think enough about thinking."[2] How similar to Goethe this is. Looking at our thoughts clarifies the idea of looking within.

A person might ask, "Fine, I'll look inward, and I'll look at my thoughts, but specifically what should I look for?" Perhaps if something could be found so that we know where and at what to look, and why, we would have the impetus to continue our search for ultimate reality. Until now, all calls we've heard to look inward and to think about thoughts have not succeeded adequately. Looking inward and thinking about thoughts are two elements that were established long ago as a basis for us to search for the ultimate reality, but few bother to search for that higher sense since the basis and the reasons for that search have not been sufficiently compelling.

Before we go to the third element needed to complete the foundation of the logic of why ultimate reality occurs, let us keep in mind the following: it is vital to stress, understand, and realize that many of our early observations and experiences as young children have to do with things that quickly become familiar and obvious to us, yet remain known only superficially and not intuitively. These are things we have taken for granted, continue to take for granted, and often completely ignore. These must be revisited, including the natural world, the light of day and the darkness of the night, the passing of time, the sound of birds singing, an apple falling from a tree. We know of, yet we ignore, the quiet of the silence that can give us an appreciation of solitude. Taken for granted are the trees, plants and flowers, the animals, the fish of the sea, and the moon and stars in the sky. We also take our senses and indeed, our health, for granted. And although it may not seem so, we take our thinking—and the thinking process—for granted as well. It is because we take these things for granted that we have been counseled to look inward and to consider our thoughts. At times we seem to overlook the fact that we, too, are part of nature.

We have already said that we must look inward and consider our thoughts while reaching for ultimate reality. In his book *Science in the Modern World,* Alfred North Whitehead wrote, "Familiar things happen, and mankind does not bother about them. It requires a very unusual mind to undertake the analysis of the obvious."[3] Newton looked at a familiar thing and analyzed it. It was an apple falling from a tree. He realized a force tugs at the apple. As a result, that force became known as gravity. Benjamin Franklin wondered about another familiar thing, lightning, and was right in believing that force could be harnessed. Many centuries before Newton and Franklin, Hippocrates wondered about disease and realized that disease arrives through natural causes. Insights brought these and countless other discoveries to light.

In the realm of consciousness, we can understand from Matthew 4:1 that Jesus analyzed his thoughts. He saw them as temptations. Some 500 years before, Buddha, too, had wondered about thoughts. He saw thoughts as attachments. Hindu mystics see thoughts as cravings. Socrates had an unusual mind that led him to wonder about a familiar thing. He wondered about knowledge, and when it was that he knew anything for certain. This led him to say that he knew only one thing, and that was that there was nothing he knew for certain.

As youngsters, at some point, each of us wonders about our individual thinking. We quickly accept the fact that thinking is a part of our nature, and for the rest of our lives, most of us do not again bother with that question. We live, work, play, act out, and entertain the *content* of our thoughts. What thoughts are, or when they are there, is ignored. Since so many of us do not have the curiosity of a Newton, a Franklin, a Jesus, a Buddha, a Hippocrates, or a Socrates to look at and analyze superficially known things, things obvious to us, we must have a substitute for curiosity. What could possibly replace curiosity? The substitute for curiosity is faith. If we do not have the curiosity of scientists and mystics, but we are able to apply faith in asking questions about familiar things, things that are taken for granted and are known to us only on the surface, insight will eventually be triggered.

The gift of ultimate reality does not happen overnight. It will happen when we begin to ask ourselves a question or questions with obvious answers. When is thinking taking place? The answer to this question is obvious, but do we ever dwell on it? No. Why? Because we already know the mind works all the time, and that thinking is a continuous process. We begin to think that only a fool would wonder about something already known. Yet, that is where enlightenment will be discovered. Another question could be this: what is this thing we call the present, and when are we living in the present? The present itself can be analyzed, and a sudden flash of insight can emerge. The factor of time is also a path to ultimate reality. Lacking curiosity, the conscious mind, by applying faith, will subconsciously, in time, turn toward curiosity. Just as Franklin wondered about lightning, we can wonder about the spark of light that we know occurs as an insight in the mind. And just as gravity tugs at an apple, causing it to fall from a tree, so, too, a force tugs at an insight until it arrives. That force can be curiosity, or it can be faith. Lacking curiosity, faith in the analysis of familiar things must be applied.

Richard Maurice Bucke, MD, also wrote that in order to enter into cosmic consciousness—his term for ultimate reality—"one must place himself (perhaps not intentionally or consciously) in the right mental attitude."[4] To reach enlightenment, we hear the Buddha say that those who seek the gift must be "a lamp unto themselves," and stress that seekers must be "anxious to learn."[5] Placing one's self in the right mental attitude, as Bucke suggests, is not unlike the Buddha's words that tell us we must be anxious to learn. We may begin to see that for one without a "very unusual mind," faith must replace curiosity. The playwright George Bernard Shaw said, "No question is so difficult to answer as that to which the answer is obvious."[6] In the Bhagavadgītā we can read virtually the same thing about the union of ātman—the individual self—with Brahman: "Subtle beyond the mind's grasp, so near to us, so utterly distant."[7] The Gītā goes on to say that nirvana is the light of all lights, and that it abides beyond our ignorant darkness. Not surprisingly it also says: "Those without faith in this, my knowledge, shall fail to find me."[8] The Gītā is talking about ultimate reality. We eventually discover that God and ultimate reality are one and the same. Yes, looking inward is one element in reaching for that higher state. Considering our thoughts is the second element. The third element is the analysis of familiar things. By analyzing familiar things, one is looking inward and is looking at thoughts. It is the analysis of familiar, obvious things that explains how ultimate reality is attained.

Although we have now come to know that analysis of familiar things explains ultimate reality, it still must be reached by each human soul independently of everyone else. This can only happen through faith. With this as a basis, we humans may have arrived at the point where we will be able to shift at least some faith from the skies above to the necessary task of directing faith at obvious things. Eventually we will realize that ultimate reality is our consciousness that has been enriched and is working full time. When we ask a question that is in the realm of science, and we have faith, which is the realm of religion, an insight will arrive with an answer. It is this insight that constitutes the nexus between science and religion.

In *Rocks of Ages,* Stephen Jay Gould asks for "non-overlapping magesteria," where Gould's two magesteria—science and religion—coexist.[9] Daniel Dennett, in his book titled *Breaking the Spell,* suggests religion should submit to scientific examination.[10] And in *The End of Faith,* Sam Harris calls for an end to faith itself. Science and religion can each examine and test the analysis of familiar, obvious things. Gould says that he cannot see how science and religion can be unified. Yet, they are unified by the fact that their nexus is insight. When we ask a question and have faith, insight may very well give us the answer. Each of us must ask, Where is thinking taking place? We will discover that thinking takes place within the ever-moving present.

The precious state of mind attained by mystics—ultimate reality—need not be esoteric. But the playing field must change from one where we look for, and pray to, a God in the skies above, to a field where we can include looking more seriously for the same God, who is also within. How often have we heard that God is everywhere? How often have we been told that God is in us? How often have we heard that we all have the same God? The many-splintered Christian denominations and all the religions of the world will come to see that looking at familiar things is compatible with all religions; syncretism will no longer be an impossible dream. Looking at familiar things, things that are obvious to us, can certainly be endorsed by all. The Buddha, Confucius, Jesus, Moses, Muhammad, and Socrates would approve.

Insight is by far the most underestimated, yet at the same time the most subconsciously sought-after gift from suffering that we have yearned for throughout human history. Awakening to the need to analyze familiar, obvious things that have not been fully realized, coupled with the knowledge that faith is the nexus between science and religion, can be the inchoate state of humanity's leap toward ultimate reality—and a saner world.

In *The End of Faith,* Sam Harris writes: "We must find our way to a time when faith, without evidence, disgraces anyone who would claim it."[11] We may not need to abandon faith, but rather shift it in another direction. We now have the evidence to claim a new, viable, grounded faith in the analysis of familiar, obvious things. We know that insight is something that occurs. It was Kahlil Gibran who said that the obvious is not seen until someone expresses it.[12] Let us once again express it: insight is the nexus between science and religion.

The mystical gift we seek requires work. It must arrive as an insight from within. This requires science by asking a question about something familiar, obvious, or superficially known, and it requires religion by having faith that an answer will arise from this mix. Insight is what allows one to segue from science to religion. We ask a question about something familiar—our thoughts—and with faith, insight arrives with an answer. The answer is ultimate reality.

Some scholars have tried to explain the creation, the existence, and the nature of angels. Through George Divry's *Modern English-Greek, Greek-English Desk Dictionary,* we learn that in the Greek language, *angelos* means angel, but it also has a second meaning: *angelos* is also a messenger. What should become obvious is that these angels, these heavenly messengers from God, are the message. Just as surely as a devil is a temptation (as in Matthew 4), an angel is an insight. We can believe that each time we realize something, anything at all, it is an insight—an angel. If we believe in the traditional idea of angels and devils, why not believe in fairies and goblins and ogres and ghosts! Gibran's words echo: "The obvious is that which is never seen until someone expresses it simply."[13] If the idea of angels and insights being one and the same "strikes a chord," we have just experienced an insight.

The Metanexus Institute's William Grassie writes that the constructive engagement of the seemingly "clashing opposites of science and religion may hold the secret to our well-being and our future."[14] Dr. Grassie may be right. We have known that we must look within. We have also known that we must look at our thoughts. But a piece of the puzzle has been missing. Now we can see that faith in the analysis of familiar and obvious things may be, or is, the missing piece of the consciousness puzzle. Knowing this, and knowing that insight is the nexus between science and religion, can give us confidence to overcome the inertia that has prevented us from realizing ultimate reality. It is possible that we may destroy ourselves, but it is also possible for us to know that there is salvation here on earth. Ultimate reality is not a product of the intellect. It is a product of insight.

Insight and ultimate reality can result from analysis of familiar and obvious things. The paradox of the mind keeps us from examining the question deeply. Why? Because we are, out of necessity, required to live in a world where we have not found it necessary to analyze things already "known." Although this concept has not as yet undergone scientific study—and it certainly should—our intuition speaks for itself, and it speaks to us loudly.

NOTES

1. Charles Pelham Curtis and Ferris Greenslet, eds., *The Practical Cogitator* (Boston: Houghton Mifflin, 1962), p. 100.

2. James Harvey Robinson, "On Various Kinds of Thinking," in *Readings in the Modern Essay*, ed. Edward Simpson Noyes (New York: Ayer Publishing, 1971), p. 3.

3. Alfred North Whitehead, *Science in the Modern World* (New York: Macmillan, 1925), p. 4.

4. Richard Maurice Bucke, *Cosmic Consciousness* (New York: Cosimo, Inc., 2006), p. 378.

5. *Maha-parinibbana Suttanta*, in *Buddhist Suttas*, trans. T. W. Rhys Davids (London: Routledge, 2001), p. 39.

6. George Bernard Shaw, *The Quintessence of G. B. S.* (London: Hutchinson, 1949), p. 168.

7. Ramesh Menon, *Mahabharata: A Modern Rendering* (New York: iUniverse, 2006), p. 137.

8. Swami Prabhavananda and Christopher Isherwood, trans., *Bhagavadgītā* (Los Angeles: Vedanta Press, 1951), p. 79.

9. Stephen Jay Gould, *Rocks of Ages* (New York: Ballantine Books, 2002). Also see Stephen Jay Gould, "Nonoverlapping Magisteria," *Natural History* 106 (March 1997): 16–22.

10. Daniel Dennett, *Breaking the Spell* (New York: Viking, 2006).

11. Sam Harris, *The End of Faith* (New York: W.W. Norton, 2004), p. 48.

12. Kahlil Gibran, *Sand and Foam: A Book of Aphorisms* (New York: Knopf, 1998), p. 54.

13. Gibran, p. 54.

14. http://www.metanexus.net/conference2006/.

CHAPTER 18

Taking Back Our Bodies: A Response to the Post-Human Ideal

Laura Gallo

It might be said that the events of September 11, 2001, were a display of how technology, when combined with ideology and negative emotion, can create catastrophe. Technology is, after all, created by humans for the use of humans, and as such, we are the ones who determine its use and effects. Biotechnology, a form of technology based in biology, is particularly acute technology applied to the human body. Biotechnology has had a profound influence on how we see our bodies as well as how we use them. Over the past two centuries, our bodies have been resolved into two different systems: the fragmented and the augmented. On the one hand, the body is perceived as a lack, while on the other hand, it is subject to technological compensation and the promise of perfection through technical means.[1] In effect, our bodies have become biotechnology's plaything, the site where Western medicine and technology meet in an effort to conquer our flawed natures. This chapter will discuss how the supremacy of science and biotechnology in our culture has affected the way we perceive and use our bodies. Using the transhumanist movement as a case study, I suggest that although biotechnology has offered utopian possibilities, it has also presented a wounding and fragmentation of the self.

THE WORLD TRANSHUMANIST ASSOCIATION

The word *transhuman* is shorthand for transitional human and is understood to be a stage along the path to becoming post-human.[2] The etymology of the word goes back to F. M. Estfandiary, who first used it in his book *Are You Transhuman?* where he defined transhuman as the "earliest manifestation of new evolutionary beings."[3] He maintained that transhumanity could be seen in everything from plastic surgery to mediated reproduction to artificial limbs. Transhumanists believe that the present state of human nature is a phase that will soon be overcome through technological advancements. They embrace any technology that can potentially "redesign" the human condition, since the current state of affairs is seen as nothing but a barrier to human progress.[4]

The World Transhumanist Association was formed in 1998 by Nick Bostrom and David Pearce.[5] It is an international, nonprofit membership organization that advocates the use of technology to expand human capacities. The transhumanist declaration begins as such:

> Humanity will be radically changed by technology in the future. We foresee the feasibility of redesigning the human condition, including such parameters as the inevitability of aging, limitations on human and artificial intellects, unchosen psychology, suffering, and our confinement to the planet earth.[6]

As the declaration illustrates, transhumanism is a rather loosely defined movement with quite lofty goals that has developed gradually over the past two decades into a subculture, social movement, and even academic discipline. The World Transhumanist Association runs similarly to a religious affiliation: members have a set of beliefs, a leader (Nick Bostrom), conferences that present and preach their belief system, "sacred" texts, as well as grand hopes for the future.[7] The quasi-sacred text that defines their mission is *The Engines of Creation* by Eric Drexler. In this book, Drexler discusses the possible advantages to nanotechnology, or the manipulation of matter on the smallest level possible.[8] This technology promises nothing short of a biomedical utopia, from the repair of damaged cells to bringing the dead back to life. For most transhumanists, Drexler's book holds the key to our impending post-human future since nanotechnology could allow us to upload our minds to computers and design new and better bodies. Transhumanists also believe in a type of afterlife. This belief is called The Singularity, an apocalyptic end point in the near future when technological developments will progress so rapidly that humanity will be transformed beyond recognition.[9] The World Transhumanist Association states that the most likely cause of The Singularity will be the creation of genetically enhanced, superintelligent beings. In other words, we will become post-human. But just what does post-human mean?

POST-HUMAN BODIES

Essentially, post-humans will be vastly superior to humans in both physical and intellectual ability. Many transhumanists insist that post-humanity does not mean the eradication of humans—but it does mean the eradication of everything we know as humans. For example, they envision resistance to disease and aging; unlimited youth and vigor; control over one's own desires, moods, and mental states; the ability to avoid feeling tired, hateful, or irritated about petty things; increased capacity for pleasure, love, artistic appreciation, and serenity; and novel states of consciousness that current human brains cannot access.[10] These ideas point to an entire restructuring of human beings. What would such a person look like? Natasha Vita-More, head of the Extropy Institute in California, is leading the way in designing the post-human body. Extropians are basically an extension or branch of transhumanists who work exclusively on the quest for perpetual beauty, longevity, and the avoidance of death.[11] Vita-More, who unabashedly extols a hedonistic view, asserts that our bodies will be the next fashion statement.[12] So far, Vita-More has designed "Primo," a prototype post-human body. Primo's body design is said to be more powerful, more flexible, and better suspended. Its body offers enhanced senses, a nano-engineered spinal communication system, parabolic hearing, and solar-protected skin.[13]

In the face of such a representation, the body we currently inhabit is sad. It is subject to change, illness, aging, and death. In light of this reality, embodied existence is our foe, and this supposition makes it easy to be casual about devising strategies to reject imperfect bodies and, in effect, replace them with perfect, designer bodies.[14]

The technocratic view of life is entrenched in a quest for control and a desire for power. The current state of affairs tells us that there is nothing more desirable than to conquer human nature, and nothing more powerful than the ability to control the natural world. However, there is something imperfect and damaging about this logic. What is at stake here is not only a quest to control the body, but indeed, it is part and parcel of the quest for immortality.

Transhumanism offers both a critique of human limitations as well as a promise of future power. Modern science can be said to be doing much the same since research is aimed toward curing disease, treating illness, and preventing decay.[15] The irony of the human condition is that we desire to escape death—or at least the anxiety surrounding death—yet it is life itself that gives rise to our fears.[16] In redesigning the human body, transhumanism is attempting to redesign life as well, so that it is a more comfortable place, free from the anxiety of impending death.

Historically, there have been three ways that death and the prospect of immortality have been discussed: philosophical treatise, various religious speculations on the afterlife, and most recently, the scientific ideal of overcoming aging and death.[17] The biotechnological vision of immortality is relatively new. There have always been some scientific imaginings of a medically transformed life, but few have gained as much momentum and built up as much hope as the current vision. Given the fact that progress is made in this area almost every other day, and is often featured as front-page news, the general public is more apt to find the scientific venture appealing and hopeful.

What is fascinating about biotechnology today is that it goes straight to the source of our mortal dilemma: the body. As we have seen, technologies are geared toward changing, fixing, and curing the body of every sickness, disease, and wrinkle—instead, replacing the human condition with a surreal version of bodily existence where nothing but perfect beauty and health prevail.

But in trying to destroy the fear of death, is biotechnology only increasing our anxieties and making death more difficult to accept? In the face of biomedical utopian visions of youthful bodies free from sickness and suffering, reality becomes a much harder pill to swallow. When in fact our bodies do fall ill, succumb to aches and pains, and grow old, we cannot help but feel frustrated. Somehow, this was not supposed to happen. Biotechnology's promises often turn up empty, with further hatred of our bodies as a result.

How did it come to this? According to Michel Foucault, it was early in the nineteenth century, when health and the prevention of disease made its debut, through a process involving both private and socialized medicine produced by the state, as the "priority for all." He attributes this phenomenon to the medicalization of childhood and to the emergence of hygiene as a form of social control.[18] Health and physical well-being became an essential objective of political power so that various power organizations took charge of bodies, making health the objective of all.[19] Medicine assumed an increasingly important place in the administrative world, making the doctor the ultimate governor and expert. The hospital also gained status as a "curing machine," set to purify the population and perhaps also serve as a reminder to the masses that health is the ultimate objective.[20]

By the twentieth century, many changes had taken place within the realm of biomedicine as new devices such as the stethoscope and the x-ray machine came into use. Medicine became a research-oriented, specialized, scientific endeavor, and the body came to be perceived as a complex biomechanical system.[21] At the same time, drugs, inoculation, and electricity were applied to this system in order to improve it. Modernity brought a desire to intervene in the body to make it part of what the modern age represented: a technological landscape. The body moved beyond being the site of control that Foucault perceived and became something that needed to be shaped and molded and tinkered with as well. Eugenics sought to govern reproductive potential; surgery became a daily practice; and eye therapy, dietary regimes, and hormone therapies were not just "cures," but the latest fads.

In the wake of modernity, we are now confronted with the body as object. Biotechnology also inherited a Cartesian dualism of embodiment so that the mind and body are understood as separate entities. The physical machine-like body is assumed to be separate from the self.[22] Conceptualizing the physical body in purely mechanistic terms has been "helpful" in furthering biotech's cause because as long as the body is a machine, it requires mechanical interventions.[23]

Courtney Campbell writes in her essay *Embodiment and Diminishment* how the Cartesian understanding of the body has allowed us to become machines, in need of technological repair where "the body becomes a *battleground* upon which the war against disease and the battle against the enemy of death is fought."[24] Part of the problem also results from the increasing extent to which medicine and technology are driven and controlled by the economy, so that the body is diminished to a commodity or understood in terms of private property. Other forms of diminishment such as illness, pain, suffering, and disability are the most revealing about the extent to which we have accentuated the otherness of the body and minimized bodily experience. For when we are ill or in pain, we are frustrated. Our lives are put on hold, and our intentions are let down by a body that presents itself as an obstacle rather than a means of self-expression.[25] Bodily limitation somehow necessitates a loss of control, so it is only natural to see it as the adversary. The body is the one thing left that presents itself as a challenge to biotechnology because it is subject to everything biotechnology is trying to overcome: aging, illness, disease, and even death.

TAKING BACK OUR BODIES

Essentially, the body can be understood in three ways: the individual body, or the body we experience; the social body, or the body as represented in social relations; and the political body or "body politic," which refers to the regulation of physical bodies by political and legal means.[26] These three bodies are interconnected: the social body overlaps with the political since they are both coercive, and in turn, both influence the experiences of the individual body. Typically, however, biomedicine and biotechnology have considered these entities as distinct, much in the same way that they consider the mind and body to be separate.

According to Margaret Lock and Nancy Scheper-Hughes, the problematic lies first and foremost in this mind/body dichotomy inherent in the biomedical model. In this paradigm, observable reality is equated with the purely material, thus equating persons with the purely material as well. But it is not just the mind and the body that are dichotomized; in fact, most of the concepts that make up our worldview are dualistic: nature/culture, passion/reason, individual/society, and so on. Lock notes that because of the complete overemphasis on the physical and the overuse of dichotomies, we are lacking a language with which to express interrelated interactions, such as mind-body-society relations.[27] As a result, we are lost in a sea of hyphenated concepts, such as the bio-social or the psychosomatic, which are all translatable as the ways in which the mind speaks through the body.[28]

Interestingly, these dichotomous relationships between concepts such as individual/society, which are central to Western epistemology, are also unique to it. Most cultures are sociocentric rather than individualistic in that they view the "individual" as comprised of several different selves so that these selves exist only in relation to other human beings. In Japan, for example, often described as the culture of social relativism, a person is always understood to be acting within the context of a social relationship and never as an autonomous self-entity.[29] Societies where the individual tends to be fused with the social body are better equipped to deal with illness and death because rather than trying to avoid or overcome these natural events, they are able to express them. Rather than pathologizing and medicalizing everything from a dry scalp to an episode of "mania," many non-Western cultures can experience these things without stigmatization. For example, in Haiti or Brazil, people can experience multiple selves or dissociative states through the practice of spirit possession.[30] This is not to say that non-Western cultures are "better" as such, but that the Western construction of an autonomous, individual self has aided the biomedical struggle to suppress bodily experience. The best we can do every time we try to express our somatic or psychosocial states is to fall back on the body-as-machine metaphor, saying that we are "worn out," "run down," "tuned in," "turned off," or that our "batteries need recharging."[31]

The body politic is another area where biomedicine and biotechnology have made their mark. Societies generally control the social order by reproducing and socializing the kinds of bodies they need. So in our society, which is largely governed by the likes of science and the biomedical assumptions discussed above, "the politically correct body is the lean, strong, androgynous, and physically fit form through which the core cultural values of autonomy, toughness, youth, and self control are readily manifest."[32] To this end, consumer culture leads the way by portraying the body as the most desirable asset one could have, and the closer one's body is to the idealized image of youth, health, and beauty, the higher its exchange value.[33] Within consumer culture, advertisements, television, and the popular press dictate the current trends in body image, all the while emphasizing the aesthetic benefits of living up to this image. Altering and molding one's body to the ideal image is not as much about improved health or spiritual salvation as it is about enhancing one's appearance to be a more-marketable self.[34] The illusion of *augmenting* the self and thereby transcending the lifespan is also entertained within consumer culture since it provides just enough fear of the decay involved in aging and the dirtiness of death to persuade people to consume body maintenance products.[35] All this is to say that biomedicine and biotechnology are not value-free entities, but rather they often work to regulate the body politic.

Margaret Lock lends some insight into how our bodily predicament can be overcome. She suggests that our current conception of the body needs a theory of emotions, for "emotions affect the way in which the body, illness, and pain are experienced and are projected in images of . . . the body politic."[36] Emotions are representative not only of feelings but also of cultural ideology and public morality. They are capable, therefore, of providing the "missing link," or filling the gap between the body and the mind.[37] Indeed, a "mindful body" is a person more capable of dealing with illness, injury, and death because rather than deconstructing the seeming unfairness and absurdity, a mindful body can identify with it. To be sure, a theory of emotions seems flaky to those immersed in the world of biotech, but it is even more absurd to deny the connection between mind and body. For all the advancements biotechnology has produced and for all the promises of improvements, these advancements have yet to improve the *quality* of life, they have yet to make illness and death more acceptable, and they have yet to realize the splendor of the human being. The mindful body that Lock proposes succeeds where biotech fails. It goes beyond the outdated Cartesian models for individuals and embraces the body as a form of communication, the medium where nature, culture, and society are given a language. The interactions between the individual, the social, and the body politic are given expression, especially when it comes to health and illness. Sickness is not a cumbersome, unfair occurrence in life; rather, it is a form of bodily communication that is better off expressed than suppressed by the ideals of biotechnology.

Technology's ideals can be wonderful, but there is a danger when they are applied to certain situations. When technology's principles are infiltrated into society, onto our individual bodies or into impressionable minds, its potential benefits are often distorted.

NOTES

1. Tim Armstrong, *Modernism, Technology and the Body: A Cultural Study* (Cambridge: Cambridge University Press, 1998), p. 1.
2. Carl Elliot, "Humanity 2.0," *Wilson Quarterly* (2003): 13–20.
3. Brian Alexander, *Rapture: How Biotech Became the New Religion* (New York: Basic Books, 2003), p. 54.
4. Alexander, p. 51.
5. World Transhumanist Association, "What Is the WTA?" http://transhumanism.org/index.php/WTA/about/.
6. World Transhumanist Association, "What Is a Posthuman?" http://transhumanism.org/index.php/WTA/faq21/56/.
7. Elliot, p. 16.
8. Elliot, p. 16.
9. Elliot, p. 17.

10. World Transhumanist Association, "What Is a Posthuman?" http://transhumanism.org/index.php/WTA/faq21/56/.

11. Langdon Winner, "Resistance is Futile: The Posthuman Condition and Its Advocates," in *Is Human Nature Obsolete? Genetics, Bioengineering and the Future of the Human Condition*, ed. Harold Baillie and Timothy Casey (Cambridge: MIT Press, 2005), pp. 385–411.

12. Winner, pp. 385–411.

13. Natasha Vita-More, "New Genre Body Design: Primo First Posthuman," http://www.natasha.cc/primointro.htm.

14. Jean Bethke Elshtain, "The Body and the Quest for Control," in Baillie and Casey, pp. 155–75.

15. Charles Rubin, "Artificial Intelligence and Human Nature," *The New Atlantis* (2003): 88–100.

16. Ernest Becker, *The Denial of Death* (New York: Free Press, 1973), p. 66.

17. Daniel Callahan, "Visions of Eternity," *First Things: Journal of Religion, Culture and Public Life*, 133 (2003): 28–35.

18. Michel Foucault, "The Politics of Health in the Eighteenth Century," in *Power/Knowledge: Selected Interviews and Other Writing*, ed. Colin Gordon (New York: Pantheon, 1980), pp. 166–82.

19. Foucault, pp. 169–82.

20. Foucault, pp. 169–82.

21. Armstrong, p. 2.

22. James Keenan, "Genetic Research and the Elusive Body," in *Embodiment, Morality, and Medicine*, ed. Lisa Sowle Cahill and Margaret A. Farley (Boston: Kluwer Academic Publishers, 1995), pp. 59–74.

23. Keenan, pp. 59–74.

24. Courtney Campbell, "Marks of the Body: Embodiment and Diminishment," in Cahill and Farley, pp. 169–84.

25. Campbell, in Cahill and Farley, pp. 169–184.

26. Margaret Lock and Nancy Scheper-Hughes, "The Mindful Body: A Prolegomenon to Future Work in Medical Anthropology," *Medical Anthropology Quarterly* 1 (1987): 6–41.

27. Lock and Scheper-Hughes, p. 8.

28. Lock and Scheper-Hughes, p. 10.

29. Lock and Scheper-Hughes, pp. 14–15.

30. Lock and Scheper-Hughes, p. 16.

31. Lock and Scheper-Hughes, p. 23.

32. Lock and Scheper-Hughes, p. 25.

33. Mike Featherstone, "The Body in Consumer Culture," in *The American Body in Context: An Anthology*, ed. Jessica R. Johnston (Wilmington, DE: Scholarly Resources, 2001), pp. 79–102.

34. Featherstone, pp. 79–102.

35. Featherstone, pp. 79–102.

36. Lock and Scheper-Hughes, p. 28.

37. Lock and Scheper-Hughes, p. 29.

CHAPTER 19

Humane Physics under Ekalavya Multiversity

Ravi Gangadhar

With the development of the larger human brain and cortex, another major evolutionary leap occurred, as significant as the emergence of life itself. This was the emergence of self-reflective consciousness. Humans are not only conscious, but they are conscious of being conscious.

Consciousness means different things to different people. One of the various definitions of the word "consciousness" is "knowing of external circumstances," which would imply that being asleep is a state of unconsciousness. Yet we certainly have experiences when we dream. We may use the word in the sense of intent or deliberation, as in making a choice with full consciousness of its consequences. We also talk of a person's social, political, or ecological consciousness, meaning that particular way he or she perceives the world.

The difficulty surrounding the meaning of the word *consciousness* arises in part from the fact that, in the English language, we have only one word to convey so many different meanings. In Sanskrit, the ancient Indian language, there are at least twenty different words that portray the various meanings ascribed to the word "consciousness" in the English language, each with its own specific meaning For example, *citta* is the "mind stuff" or an "experiencing medium" of the individual; *cit* is the eternal consciousness of which the individual mind stuff is a manifestation; *kriyā* is the experience of pure consciousness; and *puruṣa,* the essence of consciousness, is somewhat akin to the Holy Spirit.

For the purposes of this chapter, the word "consciousness" is used to mean the field within which all experiences take place. In this sense, consciousness is a prerequisite for all experiences, whether we are awake, in a trance, dreaming, in a coma, or in any other state. We might draw an analogy with a film projected onto a screen. We may watch many different films on the same screen, but without the screen, we cannot see any film.

Consciousness in this sense is not restricted to human beings; any being that experiences has consciousness. Anyone who has spent time with other beings, such as dogs, cats, or horses, has probably come to the conclusion that they are also conscious beings. They "know" the happenings in and around them. They are not automata. Birds, reptiles, and fish would also appear to have consciousness; maybe insects, snails, and worms do as well. According to some researchers, even plants appear to have some type of awareness. Sure of their very own karma, they live and perform their duty.[1]

An important characteristic attributed to conscious beings is the ability to form internal models of the world they experience: the greater the consciousness, the more complex the models. A worm probably has a relatively simple model of reality, whereas a dog's model would be considerably more complex. In human beings, the nervous system has evolved to a point where our internal models of reality are so complex that they include the self—the "modeler" himself or herself—in the model. This is the beginning of self-reflective consciousness. We not only experience the world around and within us, but also we are aware of ourselves in that world and are conscious that we are conscious.

The emergence of self-reflective consciousness is to some degree tied in with the development of language. Language allows humanity to communicate more vividly and more completely. It also allows us to focus attention on abstract and even hypothetical qualities of our experience, enabling us to separate the "experienced" from the "experiencer" (the self), a separation and objectification that the development of language led to in the exchange of information between individuals. Thus, a person could gain from the successes and failures of others, rather than having to learn everything from scratch. With drawing and writing came the ability to transfer information across time. This was as significant for the speeding of evolution as was the development of sexual reproduction, also a form of transferring information, through memes (building blocks of genes). The later invention of printing and the more recent developments of photocopying, computing, and telecommunications have likewise played chief roles in accelerating the evolution of civilization.

Accordingly, our brief review of evolution on this planet brings us to the present day. Suddenly, in a flash of evolutionary time, a new species has emerged—one that is aware of its own existence, and one that holds awesome potential for consciously affecting itself and its environment.

This product of 15 billion years of evolution is truly something to marvel at. Here we are, each of us, several septillion atoms arranged into an integrated system of some 100 trillion biological cells, experiencing the world around us as well as our thoughts, emotions, and desires. We can imagine alternative futures and make choices to bring them about. We can even fantasize the impossible. Furthermore, we can look back and wonder at the whole evolutionary process, which has resulted, step by step, in me and in you, in farms, automobiles, and computers, in men walking on the moon, in the Taj Mahal, the theory of relativity, and so much more.

If people had been around 4 billion years ago, could they ever have guessed that the volcanic landscape, the primeval oceans, and the strange mixtures of gases in the atmosphere would steadily evolve into such improbable and complex beings that constitute humanity? And if told, would they have believed it?

Could we now, if we were told what would happen in the next 4 billion years of evolution, believe it? Would the future seem as improbable to us as human beings were at the birth of the earth? What unimaginable developments lie ahead, not only in thousands of millions of years' time, but in just 1 million years?

And what of the next few thousand years? The next 100 even? Or the next 10 years? Where are we most likely headed? A look at the trends and patterns within the evolutionary process may give us some important clues to humanity's destination.

Creation can be understood only when it is viewed from a holistic perspective. Creation is not what we presume it is. Instead, we should understand it in its own way, for it is only then that we can imagine it. Everything in creation is nurturing humanity. Now it is humanity's turn to nurture itself and to nurture the creation. A day is made up of 86,400 seconds; 31,536,000 seconds make a year. During the years in the process of evolution, humanity has seen and experienced the growth of groups, communities, religions, nation-states, world governance structures, and so on, all of which convey the basic characteristic of humanity, which is to look for unification. In the present world, humanity is surviving in a world of "housing." Now we have to build one Home for humanity: Ekalavya Multiversity, an Ecumenopolis to accommodate generations to come. To irrigate humanity, to sustain nature, we have to establish Ekalavya Multiversity. Ekalavya Multiversity is a concept of one home for humanity, developed for the sustainable future of Humanity.

TOWARD ECUMENOPOLIS

Such cities, growing dynamically over the next two or three generations, will finally be interconnected, in one continuous network, into one universal city that we call the ecumenic city, the city of the whole inhabited earth, or Ecumenopolis. If we speak, therefore, of the cities of the future one century from now, we can state that they will have become one city, the unique city of mankind.

Because Ecumenopolis conceptually accounts for designing a humane habitat, addressing the users of ecumenopolis will be a concern for understanding humane living with limited recourses. This kind of study calls for understanding through overarching academic authority comprising political, economic, social, and administrative processes.

Ekalavya Multiversity is a supra academic authority to ordain political, economic, and bureaucratic authorities to function justly in this third millennium. Ekalavya is an ideal for volunteer learning, in the process of educating the self; we require volunteer involvement of citizens of earth, for the sustained brighter future of humanity. (An idol represents an ideal.)

Earth is our school; we citizens of mother earth are students of life. We all have to live to learn so that we will learn to live. Live and let live. Develop out our personalities and help our fellow beings to develop their humane personalities.

Which is the next step in evolution of Mankind.

HOME FOR HUMANITY: BUILT WITH MIND AND HEARTS WITH TRUST

Housing is built with material. Creation has provided us housing; we need to make a home for humanity.

The desire of humanity in the present context is to build a "home" that accommodates all of humanity, not just in a physical or materialistic sense, but in terms of uniting humanity in consciousness. We need to build a *home* in order for humankind to sustain itself meaningfully; to flourish; to exercise truth, faith, and goodness; and to develop along with the creation. This is our instant karma or present factual duty.

Creation makes up the gap of a billion years of evolutionary stages in nine months in the case of humans ("birth"). In creation every entity is unique and has identity of its own.

In the process of evolution, the first step is from nonliving to living entity, the second step is from living thing to human being, and the third step is from human being to Humane (Divine) Being.

Mother earth is our Karma Bhumi (Karma = Duty). Living a humane life is our Karma (i.e., Duty).

This is the need of our time, which results in the new discipline of Humane Physics. Humanity in its awakened thought has persistently returned to some of the basic questions of life and its meaning. Questions such as, What is human life for?—that is, the eternal search for the meaning and purpose of human life. How is man to plan his life to attain his ideals set for himself? If life is a part of reality, how is man to know this reality?[2] Answering these questions is the basic quest of every civilization.

Philosophy, along with the religion and spirituality, has been one of the proudest achievements of India. Periodically, people have explored and persistently expressed "Truth" to humanity, the aim of which was to revitalize and spiritualize the collective life of the people. Sri Aurobindo's understanding is the synthesis of Eastern and Western thoughts, but it also offered India's message to the new world civilization.

RESEARCH METHODOLOGY

Aurobindo is a teacher for building moral humanity, a moral civilization. We have just reached lower civilization. We have to move properly toward higher civilization.

1. Aims and Objectives

To initiate the diversified understanding of humankind under one system as Humane Physics. Some of the important areas of the proposed discipline may be as follows:

a. To build a home for humanity
b. To know that reason alone really unites humanity (study of reason and human minds)
c. To end the present mind suffering and to have a resolved mind for all forever
d. To exercise the new universal religion, Humanism
e. To establish the faith of humanity for its sake
f. To make one capital for planet earth
g. To grant the citizenship of mother earth for all along with their existing national citizenship

2. Scope and Limitations

The purpose of this chapter is to initiate the study of the articulation of the human mind toward a new discipline of the convergence of reasoning capacity and evolution, thereby breaking away from the traditional methods of studying humanity. It proposes the ideal set of principles that need to be followed for the achievement of the ultimate human consciousness.

The proposed study is based on human consciousness and the brilliance of the human mind. It does not cover within its ambit the currently established notions of civil society, nation-state, the impact of geographical situations on human behavioral patterns, and so on.

3. Research Purpose

a. To render altruism as religion for the present and present-future humanity
b. To grant citizenship of the earth for citizens of earth
c. To formulate the law of everything
d. To establish the faith of present humanity for future humanity
e. To exercise truth for present humanity to evolve
f. To educate and civilize the educated and civilized humanity

Indeed, with 6 billion different human forms, we do share a common mind. Because of the lack of proper understanding, humanity is facing a present crisis of faith. If this alienation is eliminated, perhaps we deserve to desire aliens to visit us. We get what we deserve, not what we desire, so we need to desire what we deserve, such that all of our deserved desires can be fulfilled.

> Humanity should desire what humanity deserves, not what humanity desires.
> The limits for humanity to observe for secure present-future humanity.
> By nurturing minds with, proper understanding,
> Lifetime understanding for every mind forever, to end this mind suffering.

Ekalavya Multiversity, an Ecumenopolis, is the term coined by Mr. Ravi Gangadharaiah Nayaka (www.ekalavyamultiversity.blogspot.com), Dr. A. K. Mukhopadhayay (http://www.akmukhopadhyayconsciousness.com/), and Prof. S. Sathish Rao (www.ergopolis.blogspot.com) for 222 nations under one roof. Multiversity is a learning place, Earth is our school, we citizens of mother earth are students of life, and humane physics is the lifelong education in their lifetime protocol. Ekalavya is an ideal for volunteer learning; in the process of educating the self we require volunteer involvement of citizens of earth. An idol represents an ideal in India. Ecumenopolis is the concept of world city, a city of the entire inhabited earth.

To establish this multiversity, this is what is needed:

a. A very large university with many component schools, colleges, or divisions and widely diverse functions, the purpose of which is to accommodate, educate, and civilize humanity

b. Academic authority to ordain economic, political, and bureaucratic authorities to function fully

4. Research Context

At the time of universal faith deceit, speaking truth becomes a revolutionary act. The truth is: "We have 6 billion different human forms; we share a common mind-conscience-morality-understanding-consciousness, which [is] the gift of creation for its human creation."[3]

> All human miseries are the result of our own acts and are within humankind.
> Every other entity is as it should be.
> So let humanity observe how it should be.

The present humanity has to plan for present-future humanity to prevail. At this time, this act to establish Ekalavya Multiversity is the Third Millennium plan of action for humanity. Twenty fifty-year plans make a Millennium plan. We are in the first phase of it, which has already begun: 2000 to 2050.[4]

5. Research Problem

1. To make room for the present-future humanity to accomplish its destined destiny.
2. To resolve the present mind suffering of humanity. Humane physics is the tool, under Ekalavya Multiversity, to put an end to mind suffering.
3. To establish and exercise the faith and truth of humanity for humanity.

This is to resolve the present crisis of faith for the brighter future of humanity.

Indians are the oldest civilized race of our planet earth. Epics and *Purāṇas* are the proof of this; India has never invaded any country. Being invaded by others, Indians are good at building civilizations. In is now our responsibility to build the democratic globe.

India was the richest country in the world until the seventeenth century, after which the British drained us.

The last fifty years has seen an exponential increase in human population, which is to stabilize by another fifty years. Presently, developed nations have reached saturation in population at 1.2 billion. Developing regions have 4.8 billion population, which is to increase to 7.8 billion by 2050–2100.

1. 50% of the present population is under 20 years of age. We will be as we are molded in childhood and adolescence for the rest of our life. We need to nurture the upcoming generations cautiously to evolve further.
2. 30% of the present population is in the age group 20–40.
3. 15% of the present population is in the age group 40–60.
4. 5% of the present population is in the age group 60–100.

6. Research Questions

1. Who, why, and what of humanity?
2. How to accomplish the destined destiny of humanity?
3. Answers for unanswered questions?
4. Answers for the meaning and purpose of humanity?

7. Research Hypothesis

To create protocols for the diversified understanding of humanity under one stream as Humane Physics, which is compulsory lifetime education for every mind within each person's lifetime.

1. To integrate the diversified understanding of humanity for a brighter future of humanity, which lasts for all forever
2. To know that although the future is safe, the present is in trouble

8. Methodology

The accounted history of humanity in the last 5,000 years gives us a view of the possibilities of conscious blunders mankind has committed, which can't be imagined. Now we are bearing the effects of the same.

It follows that misunderstanding is the first step toward understanding.

First we need to stop the conscious blunders being committed by the present humanity. Because we are repeating conscious blunders, we have to realize what we are doing to evolve further—which is the next step in evolution of humanity.

Humane Physics' moral laws of understanding: Live to learn, and we will learn to live. To learn to live, we need to live to learn.

- **Karma** as **duty**
- **Gravity** as **silence**
- **Levitation** as **understanding**
- **Thinking** as speedier than **light**
- **Silence** as cooler than **Zero Kelvin**.

Understanding is the only factor, which varies with time in a mind's lifetime. Until the mind procures a proper understanding, it fluctuates, after which it resonates, and finally it levitates.

NOTES

1. For example, Dr. Jagdish Chandra Bose proposed that plants do breathe and are living beings. Every entity has life on its own accord. We have to see life in every entity. Gaia Hypothesis: mother earth is a living organism. True friends are like crystal clear mirrors of real life; likewise nature has always nurtured humanity to evolve. We have to help humanity to evolve further by restoring biosphere.

2. See Indian Council of Philosophical Research, "Introduction," http://www.icpr.nic.in/intro.htm.

3. Where injustice rules, it is a crime to be a silent spectator. This was the question asked in English in a question paper of Indian Forest Service exam in 2001: "We have limits to growth. Maximum number of humans who can be present at a given instant of time will be 9 billion. Medium fertility rate to 12 billion with high fertility rate. With 2–3 billion families make 9–12 billion Human population." Quoted by Ravi Gangadhar. (www.ekalavyamultiversity.blogspot.com).

4. (a) 0-1000 CE: people flourished in their regions; (b) 1000–2000 CE: people mutually exploited each other; (c) 2000–3000 CE: it is time to harmonize and live together. Toward oneness (*vasudhaiva kuṭumbakam*).

SUGGESTED READINGS

Books

Barney, Gerald O. *Threshold 2000: Critical Issues and Spiritual Values for a Global Age.* Cape Town: Millennium Institute, 1999.

Kenny, Anthony. *The Metaphysics of Mind.* New York: Oxford University Press, 1989.

Leslie, John. *The End of the World.* London: Routledge, 1996.

Mukhopadhyay, A. K. *The Millennium Bridge: Towards the Mechanics of Consciousness and the Akhanda Paradigm.* New Delhi: Conscious Publication, 2000.

Nath, Ravindra. *History of Creation.* New Delhi: Akhil Bharathiya Ithihas Sankalam Yojana, 2000.

Russell, Bertrand. *The Problems of Philosophy.* Oxford: Oxford University Press, 1980.

Sanford, Anthony J. *The Nature and Limits of Human Understanding.* Edinburgh: T&T Clark, 2003.

Sprague, Elmer. *Metaphysical Thinking.* New York, Oxford University Press, 1978.

Stonier, Tom. *Information and the Internal Structure of the Universe.* London: Springer-Verlag, 1990.

The World Guide: An Alternative Reference to the Countries of Our Planet, millennium ed. Oxford, UK: New Internationalist Publications, 1999.

Websites

A. K. Mukhopadhayay (http://www.akmukhopadhyayconsciousness.com/).

Ravi Gangadharaiah Nayaka (www.ekalavyamultiversity.blogspot.com).

S. Sathish Rao (www.ergopolis.blogspot.com).

CHAPTER 20

Cultural Astronomy and Interfaith Dialogue: Finding Common Ground in the Skies

Andrea D. Lobel

Human beings have been fascinated by the night skies for millennia. Under clear, starry skies devoid of the light pollution we experience in today's modern cities, the view of the universe seen by ancient humans would have been nothing short of spectacular, imbuing viewers with a sense of awe. In those days, thousands, even tens of thousands of years ago, the sky and astronomical phenomena were inextricably bound up with religion. Indeed, it is easy to imagine the ways in which ancient civilizations—steeped as they were in their distinct mythologies—might have come to associate the sun, the moon, the stars, and the planets with deities such as the sun god Ra in ancient Egypt, or Shamash in Mesopotamia.

Moreover, in addition to this linkage of astronomical objects with sky gods, nearly every world culture eventually came to organize the stars into patterns, or constellations, based on their cultural perceptions. As the late astronomer and educator Carl Sagan described human perceptions of astronomy, "in the night sky, when the air is clear, there is a cosmic Rorschach test awaiting us. Thousands of stars, bright and faint, near and far, in a glittering variety of colors, are peppered across the canopy of night."[1]

The patterns handed down to us today include asterisms such as the Big Dipper, in the constellation Ursa Major.[2] However, approximately 6,000 years ago in Sumer, the Big Dipper was seen as a wagon, likely reflecting an everyday tool found in that civilization.[3] By way of contrast, in ancient Egypt, the asterism was seen as a large hook. Since this hook was seen to rotate around the North celestial pole, and never set, it became associated with immortality.[4] This is but one example among many of the ways in which the sky and religious conceptions were linked. Other examples include the evolution of calendar systems designed to keep track of state and religious holidays based on the sun or the moon—or both, in the case of lunisolar calendars.

This chapter is neither specifically focused on the current relationship between science and religion, nor upon the interactions that have existed between them throughout history. These are in themselves wide-ranging topics extending back through numerous historical points of importance, from the rise of astronomy in Mesopotamia and the later astronomical and religious speculations of the Greco-Roman era, to the discoveries of Copernicus and Galileo. Debates on these broad topics have spanned questions such as, Is the Big Bang compatible with the creation account in the Book of Genesis? Is evolution compatible with the Bible? and of course, one of the most challenging questions of all: How can we continue to believe in a God at all in an age of science, which serves to demystify and illuminate?

These questions are well beyond our scope in this brief examination. However, for our purposes, suffice it to say that throughout the history of the sciences, some amount of tension, or outright conflict, with religion has rarely been far away. Keeping this in mind as a background assumption, the main focus of this chapter is the state of astronomical education today, and on what I suggest is its great potential for contribution to interfaith dialogue despite these historical and contemporary tensions. Ultimately, my goal is to present several of the key arguments for including an astronomical education curriculum in the effort to build bridges between religious groups by using this curriculum as a value-neutral point of mediation.

To what do I refer when I use the term *value-neutral?*

By this, I certainly do not intend to suggest that neutrality should imply religious agreement on all points. As Catherine Cornille has argued, "a neutral meeting point upon which all religions may agree is *not* a necessary condition for dialogue. To the contrary, if a belief in a unified reality is presupposed, it cannot but be defined from *within* a particular religion."[5] Nevertheless, Cornille asserts that there is a need for common ground in interreligious dialogue, whether it is a shared perspective on the importance of truth in religion, or some other presupposition.[6] It is my contention that astronomy offers educators and facilitators this common ground, and more.

But first, it is important to keep in mind that there are many different approaches to interfaith dialogue. Some are more directly focused on issues such as world peace or conflict resolution, and others on more neutral topics to be examined by participants from differing religious perspectives. An interfaith group of this type might, for example, discuss ways of understanding life cycle events such as birth and death within their individual religious traditions. This, I would suggest, may well be less threatening than immediately delving into some of the more controversial and challenging issues that must ultimately be faced within interreligious dialogue. In essence, it is a way in—a way to begin the discussion. The topics are in themselves value neutral even though the discussions may find their way toward different religious interpretations. Of course, it is then up to a skilled facilitator to navigate and guide such discussions so as to maintain an atmosphere of discovery and respect.

Astronomy is a similar topic that can be approached as a way into more direct dialogue later on. However, I would also suggest that unlike other topics that can be examined from differing religious perspectives, astronomical education offers interfaith groups a number of added benefits that serve to enhance and underscore the process of religious dialogue.

The most important basic prequalification of astronomy is suggested by J. Edward Wright in his examination of religious perceptions of heaven. Referring to the popularity of astronomy in the public imagination, he asserts that although our scientific knowledge has advanced dramatically over the millennia, "when many people look to the skies, they see more than stars, planets, and galaxies: they see the Divine lurking just behind the mystic veil of the cosmos."[7]

According to the 2001 report of the United States National Research Council on the state of astronomy education, this particular science "resonates with some of the most basic questions of humanity: When did the universe begin? How has it evolved? What will be its ultimate fate? Is there life elsewhere?"[8] Indeed, the study of astronomy allows for a fuller comprehension of humanity's situation in the universe. As astronomer and director of the Arecibo Observatory, Daniel R. Altschuler, sees a place of astronomical education, as our universe is immeasurably vast, and we humans are relatively small.[9] As a result, "it is time to get off this great collective ego trip and look at ourselves from a different perspective."[10] Altschuler believes that it is astronomy that holds the greatest opportunity within it to remind people of their origins, and to come to view our planet with the reverence it deserves.[11]

However, to this, I might add the caveat that even when conveying to participants the sheer scope and size of the cosmos, the goal should not merely be to impart a sense of human engulfment, or smallness. I am in basic agreement with J. Edward Wright when he cautions that this can lead to "existential despair," and is best avoided.[12] Rather, he suggests that knowledge of the universe—and its expression in many religions as the location of heaven and the residence of God—"has an unfaltering permanence and regularity [that] has given meaning to human lives throughout history. The images we create of our cosmic neighborhood . . . give meaning and structure to life."[13]

Other benefits of incorporating astronomical education into interfaith dialogue include the fact, described by University of Toronto astronomer John R. Percy, that astronomy has traditions in nearly every world culture, and that astronomical discoveries have revolutionized our thinking about the universe. Astronomy is also practical in nature, being related to calendars, diurnal cycles, the seasons, weather, navigation, the tides, and even the search for comets and asteroids that might one day collide with the earth.[14] These are matters that affect all of us on a collective level, and it is this universal perspective that astronomy education can serve to strengthen.

Percy further asserts that teaching astronomy fosters a global sense of environmental awareness when participants come to realize that our ecosystem is ultimately a fragile unity, and that we may—or may not—be alone in the universe.[15] The very practice of astronomy calls for cooperation and international collaboration because of the need for observers at many different longitudes and latitudes around the globe. This cooperative effort extends not merely across vast geographical distances, but over lengthy periods of time as well—indeed, astronomical collaboration can span many decades, calling for long-term planning and relationship building.[16]

Astronomy also has aesthetic and inspirational value. As Percy explains:

> [It] reveals a universe that is vast, varied, and beautiful—the beauty of the night sky, the spectacle of an eclipse, the excitement of a black hole. Astronomy thus illustrates the fact that science has cultural as well as economic value. It has inspired artists and poets through the ages. . . . and harnesses curiosity, imagination, and a sense of shared exploration and discovery.[17]

Perhaps most importantly, however, astronomy might be considered "the ultimate interdisciplinary subject"—one that transcends the sciences to touch upon core human issues.[18] Other astronomy educators, including Leonarda Fucilli, agree with Percy. Fucilli considers the integration of interdisciplinary areas such as art, religion, literature, and music essential to the venture of imbuing students with a strong emotional attachment to the skies.[19] It is for this reason among others that I suggest that astronomy education properly belongs not only in the realm of the sciences, where it currently resides, but within the humanities as well. For in its exposition of the wonders of the universe and our place in the cosmos, a basic knowledge of astronomy helps to illumine the very experience of being human—that is, not simply *Homo religiosus*, but our shared, elemental existence as *Homo sapiens*.

Now that I have listed some of the key arguments for the inclusion of astronomy within interfaith dialogue, we are left with several practical questions. Most of the recommendations made by educators such as scholars at the United States National Research Council emphasize outreach programs and formal astronomical education, from kindergarten through university levels.[20] Yet, what kind of astronomical curriculum should be developed and taught to adults within an interfaith context? How might this be done, and who might be best qualified to teach this subject? How advanced should the material be, and how can facilitators accommodate participants with limited scientific background knowledge? Finally, what kinds of challenges might be faced when attempting to unite astronomy and interfaith dialogue?

This is, as I see it, where the integration of astronomy must be effected quite differently than it would be in a scientific context. To offer my own recent experience as one example of such integration, I recently designed and taught a course on astronomy and religion in the ancient Near East at McGill University. The class consisted mainly of arts undergraduates with no scientific backgrounds, and while my goals were not specifically related to interfaith dialogue, I often found myself responding to questions presented from various religious perspectives.

Within this pedagogical setting, theological questions were brought back to the texts themselves. This was done not for the sake of synthesizing one religious tradition with the others, but in order to properly understand the place of astronomy in the lives of individuals within specific ancient faith traditions. This approach avoids syncretism, and has been supported by scholars such as Catholic theologian Jacques Cuttat, who has written that although intolerance is indeed one major barrier to interreligious encounter, so is religious syncretism, for in combining religious traditions "in order to bring them to a common denominator . . . it claims to place itself over and above all religions as such," and in effect "dissolves itself into a metaphysical relativism."[21]

However, Cuttat asserts that it is also important to maintain the "consciousness of the sacred" as a common religious foundation, and this is, in my view, one of the great strengths of using an astronomical curriculum.[22]

An interfaith astronomy curriculum should ideally be presented as simply as possible, remain focused on one topic at a time, and should be relevant to the participants. This is not as difficult as it might seem. To this end, I would suggest that the astronomy best suited to interfaith dialogue is a survey of a list of astronomical topics, each enhanced with astronomical photos to better illustrate each concept. My own presentation of the material was organized beginning with the earth, the moon, and the tides, and it subsequently progressed outward through the solar system. We eventually covered such phenomena as solar and lunar eclipses, the cultural organization of stars into familiar patterns (or constellations), and galaxies and their formation, as well as significant astronomical events, including asteroid collisions and comets. Most importantly for the students without science training, this was presented without any use of mathematics or, indeed, any assumption of background knowledge.

Fortunately, this is also the type of curriculum that can be easily imparted to interfaith facilitators even if they themselves have no science background to speak of. Its emphasis on astronomical concepts rather than mathematics can also help circumvent concerns raised by a fear of science and/or math. Ideally, the training would take place in collaboration with cultural astronomers, but since this is not always practical or available, it might also be offered by astronomy or science educators who are familiar with the needs of participants from diverse backgrounds.

Finally, this brings us to some of the challenges that might emerge while discussing astronomical material within an interfaith group. For example, returning to some of the aforementioned tensions that have existed between science and religion, what should happen were participants to take issue with a topic such as the Big Bang theory or the dating of the earth?

Here, the aim of the group facilitator is not to foist the notion of a 15-billion-year-old expanding universe onto unwilling participants, but to guide them through many different religious and scientific interpretations of the same phenomena. This, too, is a way of building understanding and tolerance of individual truths, and of navigating some of the tensions that continue to exist between science and religion, and among religious interpretations of nature. Finally, this understanding serves as a way into a more accepting way of thinking—a way of processing religious and interpretive difference that might be used in later interfaith dialogue more directly focused on areas of conflict.

Several other recommendations that can help make an interfaith astronomical curriculum a success include maintaining the relative simplicity and relevance to which I referred earlier. That is, presenting an image of the Milky Way in order to demonstrate the size of our galaxy can be very useful; however, a discussion of orbital mechanics is neither relevant nor simple, and might well be intimidating to many participants. Next, according to David R. Smock, director of the Religion and Peacemaking Initiative at the United States Institute of Peace, there is evidence that multisession interfaith meetings in small groups are more successful than single sessions.[23] As I have also suggested, it is helpful to make use of many visuals. It is one thing to describe the high-impact collisions of fragments of comet Shoemaker-Levy 9 with the planet Jupiter, and quite another to present these images on streaming video. To this end, there are large collections of downloadable digital photos and videos on the Internet that may be used for educational purposes. These images can help ensure that the astronomical content remains both emotionally and intellectually compelling for participants.

Finally, it is important to continue to bring the subject matter back to the interfaith discussion itself. Ask participants to describe their experiences of the material, and attempt to address areas of conflict in ways that keep the field of inquiry open.

Incorporating an astronomical curriculum is one way of enhancing interfaith dialogue and education, but it is almost certainly one of the roads least traveled. However, as religious thinkers and group facilitators concern themselves with ever more creative and innovative approaches to dialogue, this type of methodology may well find its way into common use in due course. For not only does it offer a way into interfaith dialogue, but it brings the study of our natural world into the arena of the humanities in a meaningful way—one that serves to bolster our sense of cohesiveness, and above all, our sense of global unity. This is, after all, what the late Carl Sagan meant when he advocated the adoption of what can only be called a "cosmic perspective for mankind."[24]

NOTES

1. Carl Sagan, *Carl Sagan's Cosmic Connection* (Cambridge: Cambridge University Press, 1973 [reprint]), p. 9.
2. Philip S. Harrington, *Star Watch* (Hoboken, NJ: John Wiley & Sons, 2003), p. 102.
3. E. C. Krupp, "Sky Tales and Why We Tell Them," in *Astronomy Across Cultures: The History of Non-Western Astronomy*, ed. Helaine Selin (Dordrecht, Boston, and London: Kluwer Academic Publishers, 2000), p. 24.
4. Krupp, p. 25.
5. Catherine Cornille, "Conditions for the Possibility of Interreligious Dialogue on God" in *The Concept of God in Global Dialogue*, ed. Werner G. Jeanrond and Lande Aasulv (Maryknoll, NY: Orbis Books, 2005), pp. 13.
6. Cornille, p. 17.
7. J. Edward Wright, *The Early History of Heaven* (New York and Oxford: Oxford University Press, 2000), pp. vii–viii.
8. National Research Council, *Astronomy and Astrophysics in the New Millennium* (Washington, DC: National Academy Press, 2001), p. 47.
9. Daniel R. Altschuler, *Children of the Stars: Our Origin, Evolution and Destiny* (Cambridge: Cambridge University Press, 2002), p. 150.
10. Altschuler, p. 151.
11. Altschuler, p. 236.
12. Wright, p. 214.
13. Wright, p. 214.
14. John R. Percy, "Why Astronomy Is Useful and Should Be Included in the School Curriculum," in *Teaching and Learning Astronomy: Effective Strategies for Educators Worldwide*, ed. Jay M. Pasachoff and John R. Percy (Cambridge: Cambridge University Press, 2005), p. 11.
15. Percy, p. 12.
16. Percy, p. 12.
17. Percy, p. 12.
18. Percy, p. 12.
19. Leonarda Fucilli, "Implementing Astronomy Education Research," in *Teaching and Learning Astronomy: Effective Strategies for Educators Worldwide*, ed. Pasachoff and Percy, p. 74.
20. National Research Council, p. 48.
21. Jacques Cuttat, "The Meeting of Religions," in *Relations Among Religions Today*, ed. Moses Jung, Swami Nikhilananda, and Herbert W. Schneider (Leiden: E. J. Brill, 1963), p. 107.
22. Cuttat, p. 107.
23. David Smock, "Conclusion," in *Interfaith Dialogue and Peacebuilding*, ed. David R. Smock (Washington, DC: United States Institute of Peace Press, 2002), p. 131.
24. Sagan, p. 59.

CHAPTER 21

Vedic Science and Quantum Physics

Shantilal G. Goradia

Modern physics addresses all topics regarding the early universe except consciousness. Religions have addressed consciousness and its beginning. In order for religions to be consistent with physics, there must be a connecting link. Meditation is recognized as science and practiced by medical institutions very successfully. Religion may be considered a result of meditation. Science cannot deny the importance of such meditation. The body-mind connection is not a speculation anymore. Religions offer a valuable contribution in this area. The fundamentals of molecular biology and computer science are common knowledge.

OBSERVATIONS

We know our bodies are made of trillions of cells. The cells have the information to clone a baby human being. Where does this information come from? How is it stored? How is it communicated? What is there in nucleotides of genetic tape that enables them to store and express information? They are made of elementary particles. How do the elementary particles work in groups to generate such capability? Particle physicists do not seem to have an answer. These are profound questions raised by biological observations. Physics is supposed to explain observations. For example, Newton compared the propagation of gravitation with that of light and postulated the inverse square law of gravitation. There are many such examples of the fruitful value of comparison.

VEDIC SYMBOL OM

There is a technical justification for a postulation that every particle has a quantum (Planck size) "mouth" that links an elementary particle to space-time.[1] The expression "by the mouth" in the form of binary bits of Open and Closed states is analogous to the expression of OM in the Vedas. Both these expressions relate to the elementary particles. The particles were created before the rest of the universe. The word *OM* was given a special symbol and is pronounced as if giving out resonant vibrations or waves. Its pronunciation has variations of varying pitch and wavelength. Ancient thinkers must have realized the importance of their conclusion to take the trouble to document the findings of their meditation. The Vedic contribution of the body-mind connection is well recognized. A political but practical paraphrase says that if it walks like a duck, and if it talks like a duck, it is a duck, raising the possibility that there is some validity in the creation of the special word OM, given its credibility. Our mouths radiate sound waves when we speak. Nobel laureate Richard Feynman says the fine-structure constant, an interaction between particles, is like the hand of God.[2] Do the probabilistic bits of Open and Closed states of particles radiate some messages somehow and communicate with each other? A hidden physical motive may provide the answer.[3]

The symbol OM looks like the Sanskrit number 3. Bhagavadgītā, Chapter 13, compares the material body with the field (*kṣetra*), and links it to the mind and the knower of the field (*kṣetra-jñam*), unifying the three basic elements of life forms. There are exactly three repeats of the word *śānti* after the initial word of creation, OM, as supported by John 1:1–1:4, linking (1) the word of God with (2) light and (3) life, as if the all-unifying formula (*śānti*-Sūtra, if I may) of nature is OM: *śānti, śānti, śānti*. How does the tiny quantum mouth of particles generate field and biological life? The blinking characteristics postulated in my paper, "What Is the Fine-Structure Constant?" can create a statistical law of quantum states, such as the simple binary bits of computation capable of carrying out complex calculations.[4] The statistical law (the second law of thermodynamics) is the most certain and intriguing physical law as repeatedly recorded by Einstein.[5] Newton and Einstein believed God is fundamentally simple. An intriguing statistical implication of more interest to the physicist is that the fine-structure constant (what physics recognizes as the word of God) equals the reciprocal of the natural logarithm of the square root of the inverse of the cosmological constant (numerical value: 10^{-120} Planck lengths) introduced by Einstein. This is my simple, verbal, statistical equivalent of the unifying formula of nature, consistently linking nature's encryptions of blinking quantum states with biology and cosmology.

THE OMNIPRESENT SOUL

There are Sanskrit songs that describe the soul. Their idea of soul stretches to the scale of elementary particle size. They describe the soul as ten thousandths of the size of the tip of a hair. If we consider the tip of a hair as an atom, the size of the soul they envisioned is that of the nucleus of an atom. The songs state that all souls are eternal. This statement is somewhat like the law of conservation of baryon numbers. The songs state that all souls are connected to the supreme soul. This is analogous to a 1935 paper linking particles to space-time, co-authored by Einstein, titled "Problem of Particles in General Relativity."[6]

Expressions by the mouths of the particles could be by radiations of particles of light, called photons, and their characteristics. The continuities and discontinuities for varying amounts of time could have a coded meaning for particles to communicate with each other. There is no viable theory that can mathematically explain such communications. The following paragraph is technically simple. However, nontechnical readers may skip its statistical approach.

THE WORD OF GOD IN PHYSICS

The fine-structure constant is an important number in physics. It is considered as the word of God. It is the magic number of 1/137. "Since it is a God-given number (independent of mortal choice of units) one tries to relate it to fundamental numbers such as π, e, e^{π}, π^{e}, the number of space-time dimension, etc."[7] The number challenges conventional mathematics. What is hidden behind it, I say, is Boltzmann statistics. At the beginning of the last century, Ludwig Boltzmann suggested a formula of entropy, $S = k \log_e W$. Here k is Boltzmann's constant; one in natural units, W is the number of microstates of a system. Age of the universe in microstates of Planck times is 1,000,000,000,000,000,000,000,000,000,000,000,000,000,000, 000,000,000,000,000 Planck times. This huge number with sixty zeros is approximate since it increases very rapidly and continuously. Physicists make it easy to handle large numbers by describing them in order of magnitude. In this case, the order of magnitude is sixty. Even with continuous inflation, it will take 90 billion years to increase the age of the universe to 10^{61} Planck times. The substitution of W in the equation gives $S \approx \log_e 10^{60} \approx 138$. As the universe inflates, the fundamental units of nature, such as Planck length or Plank time, shrink to make up for the inflation, as indicated in my proposal in "What Is the Fine-Structure Constant?" For example, if the economy inflates, wages seem to be going up although the value of the currency drops with no real increase in real (inflation-adjusted) income. If we use a negative number for each microstate of deflation, we will get its effect on the entropy as approximately -138, making the sum of the entropy increase of the universe approximately zero. The entropy of the universe does not decrease for a closed system according to the second law of thermodynamics. A technical interpretation in terms of the rate of increase of order would give the number 1/138. This number is close to 1/137. The difference is too small to challenge my proposal. There could be many subtle causes for this difference.

One of the causes is consciousness. Consciousness cannot be quantified mathematically. Mathematics describes a lifeless universe. Our real universe contains life, full of consciousness. The Vedic view of particle soul implies that a particle knows itself and is conscious of its surroundings. It does not reject the position of the uncertainty principle that we cannot simultaneously determine the position and velocity of a particle. Physics is based on observations. The evolution of life mandates variations of the magic number 1/137. This proposal accomplishes variability as a function of the age of the universe consistent with the uncertainty principle. It links the oldest science of meditation with the latest views of great minds. George Gamow, the proponent of the Big Bang theory and credited with the insight about the sequences of the four nucleotides of genetic tape, had a deeper insight into a link between the magic number 1/137 and cosmology. Sometimes scientific insights are too simple mathematically. Simplicity is the beauty of nature. Sir Arthur Stanley Eddington, one of the first minds to understand Einstein's theory of gravitation, spent a good portion of his life deriving the magic number 1/137 and other such constants of nature based on multiplicity.

Boltzmann had a profound impact on Einstein, and Einstein on Eddington. Einstein is reported to have believed that "a particle should know where and what it is . . . even if we do not, and it should certainly not receive signals more quickly than the speed of light."[8]

VEDIC SOUL

Size Arithmetic

A version of Śvetāśvatara Upaniṣad 5.9 states the size of the soul as the size of the tip of hair divided by the fourth order of magnitude in physics language (*keśāgra-śata-bhāgasya śataṁśaḥ sadṛṣātmakaḥ*), giving a reduction factor *r*, where

$$r = 10^{-4}$$

The tip of the hair can be considered an atom. The diameter of an atom is

$$d = 10^{-10} \text{ meter}$$

Multiplying these two equations, we get

$$\text{size of the soul} = 10^{-14} \text{ meter}$$

This is almost the size of the nucleus. There seems no possibility that anyone could guess this so precisely. If there were millions of numerical guesses with one correct, one would think that the correctness was a mere chance. That is not the case. Does meditation sometimes work better than mathematics? If not, what is the counter proposition for such rare findings? Spooky action at a distance does not seem to need a mathematically valid pathway.

Characteristics of Vedic Soul

Muṇḍaka Upaniṣad 3.1.9 states that the soul can be perceived by perfect intelligence (*eṣo' ṇurātmā cetasā veditavyo, yasmin prāṇāḥ pañcadhā saṁviveśa* . . .). Physicists cannot determine the sizes of particles without mathematical and experimental interpretations (intelligence). Both Upaniṣads lead us to establish a link between soul and particle, potentially indicating that soul resides in every particle we see. The Bhagavadgītā descriptions of the soul in chapter 2, verses 16–20, are eternal (*sat*), imperishable (*avināśī*), immeasurable (*aprameya*), impossible to kill (*na hanyate*), and one that is never born or dies (*na jāyate mṛyate vā*), respectively. These descriptions are consistent with modern physics, knowing that baryon number is conserved, a proton does not decay, and so on. The particle and soul link may explain the paradox of Schrödinger's cat.

Vedic Cosmology

Kaṭha Upaniṣad 1.2.20 states that the Supreme Absolute Truth can be found throughout the whole range of existence (*aṇor aṇīyān mahato mahīyān*). This statement connects the souls to the universe and vice versa. I am connecting nucleons to the normal space-time. I see that the Vedic picture is the same as my picture. If combined, they both imply that souls are part of the Supreme Absolute Truth, making the universe isotropic. There is no fixed and distinct line or point of separation between the particle and its surrounding space-time. The inflationary universe is consistent with Swami Vivekanand's interpretation that everything came from nothing (*puṛṇamidam*), speculating nothing as a quantum entity, something smaller than what we can see.

Particle Communications

A stone thrown in the air follows a path described by the theory of gravitation. A bird thrown in the air does not follow such a path. The bird makes its own decision about the path to follow. The individual path followed by each bird can be described in terms of probabilities. If we throw the bird in a northerly direction, 50 percent of the birds would go eastward, and the remaining 50 percent of the birds would go westward. The uncertainty that applies to the birds applies to particles in general at a quantum level. The Vedic description of the size of the soul matching the nucleus injects consciousness in particles. Kaṭha Upaniṣad 1.2.18 states that the soul has knowledge (*vipaścit*), potentially implying it makes its own decisions, as does a bird. Cloning is a process that confirms that the cells of our body know how to make a carbon copy of us in the right environment. Cells of bone marrow, when placed in the liver, make liver protein in mice. The subject decision-making process cannot be explained mathematically (in terms of Lagrangian formalism).

UNIFICATION OF RELIGIONS

The Sanskrit songs referred to here are really Vedic science, consistent with many religions at a fundamental level of creation. Long after their creation, Jainism has accepted the concepts of its souls. The radiations of photons come close to the biblical quotation, "There shall be Light."[9] Even remote civilizations, including those of Native Americans, prayed to the sun to create light. Vedic literature incorporates consciousness by stating that soul radiates light (*jyoti*). A word search for the phrase "relativity in Islam" shows a dynamic view of a photon's movement. We do not know the coded information in the sequences of photon radiations. Vedic science states that particles have souls (*aṇu-ātmā*), and souls have knowledge (*vipaścit*). The Bible also states that "Initially there was the word, and the word was with God and the word was God."[10] This is OM, containing the vibrations at the time of creation. Biblical and Vedic statements point to the existence of preexistent energy prior to the immergence of light. The Dalai Lama envisions a link between neurology and thought processes, a case of body-mind connection and mind over matter. His recent book addresses unity between religion and science.[11] The title of his book is similar to Kaṭha Upaniṣad 1.2.20, merging *short range* with *long range* in one *whole* range. This paper points to one unknown dancing behind the scene, somewhat like the dance of Hindu lord Śiva, controlling faraway particles simultaneously. The unknown is beyond the reach of mathematics to challenge its existence. We cannot probe the primordial soup. Its preexistent energy far exceeds the capability of our particle colliders. The word *Ba* (soul) is inscribed in ancient sculptures in Egypt. Mahatma Gandhi insisted on the intermingling of cultures, the lack of which, and not religions as such, is making mobocracies overtake the good intentions of democracies in fundamentalist states (creating an increase in macroscopic social entropy).

Consistent with (not based on) the above biblical quote, I predict that lightning appearing before thunderstorms causes chemical and nuclear reactions that fuels their energy. Biochemical reactions would be too rare to test.

CONCLUSION

When we see motion picture on a TV screen, we are looking at particles of light in the form of waves, particular to the message to be conveyed. If we go inside the TV set to break open the human speaker, there is something, but no live speaker—just the hardware. Breaking open the nucleon gives no sight of quarks. Likewise, the quantum foam or primordial soup is as far as we can probe. The rest is unknown and beyond us. My explanation of the word of God in physics has a special significance to physics, evolution, and consciousness.

NOTES

1. Shantilal G. Goradia, "Why Is Gravity So Weak?" *Journal of Nuclear Radiations and Physics*, 1 (2006): 107–17.
2. Richard Feynman, *Six Easy Pieces* (Cambridge, MA: Perseus Books, 1995).
3. Peter Martin, "Probability as a Physical Motive," *Entropy* 9 (2007): 42–57.
4. Goradia, "What Is the Fine-Structure Constant?" http://www.arXiv.org/pdf/physics/0210040v3.
5. Albert Einstein, "Considerations Concerning the Fundaments of Theoretical Physics," *Science* 91.2369 (1940): 487–92.
6. Albert Einstein, Boris Podolsky, and Nathan Rosen, "Can Quantum-mechanical Description of Physical Reality Be Considered Complete," *Physical Review* 48.73 (1935): 777.
7. Ramamurti Shankar, *Principles of Quantum Mechanics* (New York and London: Plenum Press, 1994).
8. J. R. Minkel, "The Gedanken Experimenter," *Scientific American* 297 (2007): 94–96.
9. King James Bible, Genesis 1:3.
10. King James Bible, John 1:1.
11. Dalai Lama, *The Universe in a Single Atom* (New York: Random House, 2005).

CHAPTER 22

Incarnation and the Environment

Mary Ann Buckley

When I say "we" are facing a crisis, I mean all of earth's creatures—humankind, plant and animal life, water, air, and land—the whole of our living planet. Many say that this crisis is the major sign and call of our time, because if we don't respond to this one, it won't matter what response we make in other situations. Furthermore, the violence that has been unleashed in the post-9/11 world exacerbates the crisis and accentuates the truth that nothing happens in isolation from anything else. We're an interdependent, earth community—for good and for ill—whether we're from a part of the world that marks time by the September 11 event or not.

So, within the time frame of the years since September 11, I'd like first to tell you a story of one small, yet bold, agricultural project that is, in its own modest way, beginning to make a positive difference to the earth community. Then I'll explore briefly how this project is nourished and sustained by an incarnational vision.

The story begins in 2003. That's when a few of my Nigerian sisters and their colleagues opened what is now called the Holy Child Integrated Agricultural Center. It's in the village of Owowo Lala in southwestern Nigeria—West Africa—in the homeland of one of Africa's largest ethnic groups, the Yoruba people.

This agricultural center is one sign of hope in the much larger context of the vast, marvelously diverse continent of Africa—a continent with an enormous wealth of peoples and natural resources, and a heavy weight of human suffering and the degradation of life-supporting habitats. Owowo Lala village is situated in a rural area in the region around the big urban center of Abeokuta, a city important, among other things, for its University of Agriculture. Our sisters went to this locale to be at the service of a new and burgeoning diocese of the Roman Catholic Church. They wanted to meet the people at the point of their most pressing needs. And they found that what the people needed first of all was food and better-balanced diets, and then they needed to be taught how to produce affordable, nutritious food for themselves in an ongoing, sustainable way. As they responded to these immediate needs, our sisters and their co-workers also dreamed of creating jobs and training future farmers in innovative methods that would enable them to be independent and self-reliant. This was the vision that fired the launching of the project.

And the story has continued its hopeful trajectory through the past three years. Five Holy Child sisters have worked hard with a staff of local people to translate that vision into practical reality. They have purchased, cleared, and cultivated 48 acres of land (the size of about forty-eight soccer fields); they've installed an infrastructure for water and electrical power, and constructed housing; they've begun to raise pigs, chickens, turkeys, and rabbits; they built and stocked ten fish ponds; and they've started biogas energy production. In effect, they've incarnated their vision. The farm is up and running now. But that's just the first chapter of the story. The plan for the next six years is to raise funds to expand all of this over 197 acres, and eventually construct classrooms for workshops and courses on organic farming. And it's really happening, day by day.

This dedicated team of Holy Child sisters and local people has created an organic farm. That means they're committed to not using any chemical fertilizers, but what they do use very creatively is an "integrated" method of agriculture. Therefore, every process on the farm is designed to be incorporated into every other process: waste from latrines is filtered to irrigate crops; when a chicken is slaughtered, its waste is fed to the catfish, then water from the catfish pond is used for the crops, and so on. Everything is recycled, nothing is lost, and thus the whole becomes greater than the sum of all the parts. This is the underlying philosophy—the soul, really—of integrated agriculture. It's a very ecologically friendly approach. I see it as a mirror that reflects back to us the basic principles of the universe: that life in all its myriad forms is essentially one, and that all living things are interconnected, interdependent. This approach is like a model, not just for organic farming, but for every dimension of living. Our sisters say, in their mission statement for this center, that "we [Holy Child sisters] are passionate that our dream of organic agriculture will bring food, hope and a better life to the people of Nigeria."

How then, do they sustain that passion? What belief system and spirituality ground and nourish a project like this, day in and day out? I'd like to answer those questions in two ways—by saying what I think sustains the people involved, and by sharing with you what they say gives them energy and will from day to day.

I believe that if you were to put those questions to any member of my international community, sooner or later she would start talking about the mystery of the Incarnation. And that's where I would start.

In Chapter 9 of this volume, Tobie Tondi writes that incarnation is "the creative and nurturing activity of the Transcendent One." Those who designed and now run the agricultural center continue this creative, nurturing activity through the very earthy ordinariness of raising animals, planting crops, grinding grain, and teaching others to do likewise, so that everyone may share the table of earth's bounty and live more fully human lives, and so that earth itself will flourish and not be depleted. Their farming activities give expression to the love of the Transcendent One. Their lives repeat the pattern of the Incarnation and continue it in a new time, place, and situation. That idea of continuing the Incarnation happens to be expressed in the very first line of my community's constitution—that God needs men and women in every age to make known the reality of the Incarnation. This belief is the deep source of our life and energy.

And that fundamental belief has even further theological depths. The lives of those who run the center repeat the pattern of the Incarnation, and in so doing, they also express the pattern of the inner life of God, the Transcendent One. The Incarnation is the outward manifestation of this inward life of God. And in my Catholic Christian tradition, we say that the inner life of God is communitarian; it's Trinitarian—Father, Son and Holy Spirit—is how we say it in classical language. The Trinity is simply a way of talking about the inner life of God, and incarnation is simply the outward expression of that rich interior life of love—love made accessible as something we can touch, taste, and see with our own eyes in our distinctive human way.

The philosopher/theologian Beatrice Bruteau says this in more contemporary language, in an article titled "Eucharistic Ecology and Ecological Spirituality." For her, the symbol of the Trinity means that the inner life of God is a "mutually feeding, mutually indwelling, community, in which all the persons give themselves to one another as food, for the sake of life, abundant life."[1] So, quite literally, the agricultural center staff is committed to becoming that mutually feeding, interdependent community of love that is a sure sign of God's sustaining presence among us. And their integrated approach to organic farming, in which everything gives itself to be redirected to some further need, is an expression of this communitarian life. This dynamic of interdependent love is at the very heart of the cosmos, too—for creation bears the stamp of the Creator.

But these are lofty ideas, and I doubt that the staff of the Holy Child Integrated Agricultural Center has time to think such thoughts when the chickens are cackling to be fed in the cool of the early morning—or when the bore hole fails, and they have to haul water in drums from the village to keep the crops from withering in the heat of the midday sun.

Maybe, in the press of daily life, those at the farm are more in touch with the simple fact that the Incarnation is essentially a movement toward earth and its needs, rather than away from it in retreat—a movement toward the world out of love, because they've fallen so deeply in love with it that they're part of it, inseparable from it. They and the pigs and the cassava plants are all one, so to roll up their sleeves and do what needs to be done is the way they love.

When there is some leisure to ponder the meaning of all that's entailed in running a small organic farm, I think the staff would be encouraged by a revelation of an eleventh-century German woman. She's Hildegard of Bingen, a mystic who saw deeply into the mystery of the Incarnation in relation to earth. This is what she had to say:

> The earth . . . is the mother of all,
> for contained in her are the seeds of all.
> The earth . . . is in so many ways fruitful.
> All creation comes from it.
> Yet it forms not only the basic raw material for humankind,
> but also the substance of the incarnation of God's Son.[2]

Earth itself is the substance of the Incarnation of God's Son. If you take time to think about this, you can see that it must be very nourishing indeed to touch into the truth that the soil that collects under one's fingernails in the course of a day's work is the same substance from which the body of Christ was formed. It all erupted from the same, original flaring forth of creation 15 billion years ago.

Whether these truths are at the level of consciousness or not, I think they are the deep truths that must nourish and sustain the passionate commitment of my sisters on their wonderful farm in Yorubaland.

When I asked them to speak for themselves about what sustains their passion, my sisters spoke excitedly about the nourishment they receive from the enthusiasm and joy of the villagers. The people of the area are very poor, and the farm has become for them a place where they really can buy good food at an affordable price, find employment, and learn methods for producing their own food. In the process, they grow personally in a sense of their own power and dignity. One of the added side effects of this growth has been an increased respect for the capabilities of women. Farming is men's work in this part of Nigeria, and little by little, the men are growing in admiration for what our sisters have achieved on the land with the help of other women.

So the realization of the dream that launched the farm just a few years ago is like daily bread, on many levels, for staff and villagers. And my sisters continue to be fed by even more dreams. As I listened to their reflections on what sustains their passion, I heard them say that new dreams keep on exploding in their minds and hearts. In fact, they dream that one day the farm will even become a village—Holy Child Village is what they'll call it! They dream there will be a school, a conference center, and a library there; a restaurant, too, and a pastoral center, and perhaps even a clinic. Women and men will farm side by side in this village. University students will continue to come to study methods of integrated agriculture. It will be a place of refreshment and renewal—tourists from far and wide will travel there to enjoy an eco-holiday. Others will come in search of spiritual nourishment and a time of prayer and retreat.

In other words, the Holy Child Integrated Agricultural Center, and the village it could someday become, is essentially a place of unbounded hope for life, a metaphor for a worldview, a very real sign of the Reign of God. That's the "fire in the belly" that burns in my sisters and their friends from day to day.

NOTES

1. Beatrice Bruteau, "Eucharistic Ecology and Ecological Spirituality," http://www.crosscurrents.org/eucharist.htm.

2. Gabriele Uhlein, *Meditations with Hildegard of Bingen* (Santa Fe, NM: Bear & Co., 1983), p. 58.

Part VI

Toward a Holistic Future

CHAPTER 23

Religion, Fundamental Questions, and Human Society

Vinesh Saxena

Our universe began 13.7 billion years ago, and the earth was formed 4.5 billion years ago. Invertebrate life started to appear 600 million years ago. Fish evolved 150 million years ago. Dinosaurs started roaming the earth about 80 million years ago. Evolution continued—humans as we know them appeared 70,000 years ago. They started to use words about 30,000 years ago, to farm about 11,000 years ago, and to write about 5,000 years ago.

The first organized religion was Judaism, which started in 2085 BCE. Then came Hinduism in approximately 1500 BCE, then Buddhism about 560 BCE. Jainism and Taoism originated at about the same time as Buddhism. Christianity goes back to 30 CE, and Islam originated about 610 CE. Sikhism originated about 1500 CE. Thereafter, only subreligions seem to spring up: Protestantism in 1515 CE, Mormonism in 1830 CE, Bahá'í Faith in 1844, Jehovah's Witness in 1870, and so on. More recently, Scientology originated in 1955, and the Hare Krishna movement began in 1968. There are many more that I have not mentioned here.

We have briefly reviewed the evolution of human society on the one hand and of religions on the other. It seems that religions originated at different places, and at different times, in response to human needs in a specific part of the society at a specific time. When we gaze at the universe and ponder over its mystery, many questions come to mind, including these: Where do we come from? Why are we here on the earth? Where do we go after death? Are we just this mortal body or something more?

To me, the principal fundamental unanswered questions are

1. Does the soul exist?
2. Is there life after death?
3. Does God exist?

The first two questions are interconnected. If we are more than this mortal body, that is, if there is a kind of life force in our body, then it is likely that this life force, which we can call soul, does not die with the mortal body. Hence, it is quite likely that this soul can continue, and the notion of life after death becomes a likelihood.

The third question is very basic. When we look at a house, there is an owner and creator of that house. Similarly, for this immense universe, there must be a creator or owner. Thus we can arrive at the existence of the God. This is simple deductive logic; however, to provide a universally acceptable rational answer is another matter.

I find this very strange and kind of sad that we as humans have existed for 40,000–70,000 years, but there are no universally acceptable and proven answers to these basic questions. Maybe it is not easy to answer them, but society owes itself answers to these questions. Let us look at the religions and see what they say.

DOES SOUL EXIST?

- Judaism: Yes. It is only through the granting of a soul that man becomes animate flesh.
- Hinduism: Yes. Believes ātman is eternal, invisible, imperishable, and unchanging.
- Buddhism: Denies the existence of an eternal soul but believes in the notion of constant change.
- Christianity: Yes. Each soul is judged upon death.
- Islam: Yes. Believes the soul has distinct parts: nonrational and rational.

IS THERE LIFE AFTER DEATH?

- Judaism: Jewish ideas are relatively fluid. A Jew might believe that the souls of Jewish people go to heaven, reincarnate into new beings, or get resurrected at the coming of the Messiah.
- Hinduism: Yes. After death, the soul goes to heaven or hell to be rewarded or punished, and then is placed in a new body depending upon deeds performed in this life. This cycle continues till one attains the state of Nirvana.
- Buddhism: Yes. People are reborn until they are free from the cycle of birth and decay.
- Christianity: Believes that all who have died are immediately judged, and their souls are sent to heaven, hell, or in some belief systems, purgatory. At the time of second coming of Jesus, the bodies of the righteous will be resurrected and united with their souls.
- Islam: Believes that on the day of resurrection, all people will be held accountable for their actions.

DOES GOD EXIST?

- Judaism: Yes. There are two words for it: Yahweh, or Lord, and Elohim, or God
- Hinduism: Yes. God is eternal. Millions of deities are but manifestations to help us visualize the unknowable Godhead.
- Buddhism: Does not believe in God but believes that there are beings that inhabit the various celestial realms.

- Christianity: Yes. God is both one and triune as the Father, the Son, and the Holy Spirit.
- Islam: Yes. Allah is absolute, eternal, incorporeal, and unknowable.

While examining different religions regarding the three fundamental questions, I see contradictions and marked differences in the answers. For example, Hindus say that there is reincarnation; according to Islam, there is no reincarnation; and Christians believe in resurrection. What does this mean? Then there are atheists, communists, the followers of Jedi, and so on. If religions are true as their followers strongly feel, then there would have to be pigeonholes in God's administrative kingdom that pertain to adherents of different established religions and diverse nonreligious people; in other words, each faction will go to a different distinctive quarter after death. Does this make sense? To me it does not. I believe that all religions are man-made and do not provide logical, rational, or universal answers to the fundamental unanswered questions mentioned earlier. Furthermore, humans have been on the earth for 70,000 years, while organized religions have been here for fewer than 3,000 years, so what was happening when humans were dying earlier than 3,000 years ago?

Furthermore, we have been witnessing horrific events. Certainly, 9/11 was one of them. Fundamentalists are even killing people of other religions in the name of religion. Hindus and Muslims fight each other, Catholics and Protestants do the same, and Jews and Muslims are killing each other in the Middle East. The situation is so horrific and baseless. Communists were and are even today suppressing all religions. Christians and Muslims (as well as followers of other religions) convert people of other religions to their religion to "save the souls." I am sad. To me, religions may be acceptable so long as they teach some morality and as long as they respect each other. That is it, but no more.

I am baffled and concerned that society has existed for so long without making any concerted effort to answer the unanswered questions listed earlier. Society has spent more than $10 million to develop an artificial heart, trillions of dollars on space programs, and so on. Then why has society not even established an institute to examine and research the answers to the above questions?

One may explain why it is important to have answers to the fundamental questions listed earlier.

- If soul exists, and if there is life after death in the form of reincarnation based on deeds performed in this life, then the implications would be very different. There will be fewer criminals and less criminal activity; monsters such as Hitler, Idi Amin, and so on would not evolve. People will not be killing each other. Episodes such as 9/11 and the bombings in England, Madrid, and Bombay will not occur. People will be concerned about the moral implications of their deeds. They will become busy preparing for the next life.
- On the other hand, if the answers to the above questions are negative, then we, as well as all events, are random and statistical. Under this scenario, people will want to own and enjoy all material goods and comforts in this one lifetime—imagine how ultramaterialistic such a society would be. Further, what would prevent human beings from carrying out immoral acts and turning into

monsters if they can do so with impunity? We would need more laws and more expenditure on law enforcement, otherwise society would in all likelihood just disintegrate.

To conclude, we should encourage society to establish an institute and spend funds to carry out impartial research into answering the questions mentioned above. For my small part, I have established a registered charitable foundation.[1] This foundation has two objectives: the first is to help the needy, and the other is to fund research to provide logical and universally acceptable answers to the three fundamental questions mentioned above.

NOTE

1. "Welcome to the Vinesh Saxena Family Foundation," Vinesh Saxena Family Foundation, www.vsffoundation.ca.

CHAPTER 24

Religions as the Gateway to Peace

Jagessar Das

On September 11, 2001, the world suddenly changed. In an instant, our values, our spirituality, our way of life, and the essence of our very being were all shaken to the core. In an instant, it became very apparent that the nature of violence in the world had changed. In an instant, it became clear that the perception of religions, too, was about to change. Although 9/11 and other acts of violence have been perpetrated in the name of religion, it is my fervent belief that in the wake of this tragedy, religion can serve as the guiding light toward peace.

First of all, we need to admit that the world needs new solutions to an age-old problem that has grown more intense, more destructive, more complex, more expensive, and more ubiquitous with the increase in technology and speed—and that is violence in the world. It is obvious from general observation that violence becomes a part of human nature when the positive attributes of love, compassion, acceptance, co-existence, and mutual respect are lacking in people. Band-Aid solutions will not be of much benefit, especially when dictated or proposed by a few in authority, without the capacity to execute the remedy on a worldwide scale.

Religions, as practiced in the world over the millennia, have failed to reduce or eliminate violence at the individual, family, national, and international levels. As such, a new paradigm is needed. In this chapter, I shall propose some ways and means that if seriously considered and implemented, should enable the people of the world to benefit from greater peace.

A HISTORY OF RECENT VIOLENCE

a. 1938 to the present: World War II, Vietnam, Korea, the Cold War, racism, Indian independence, Pol Pot of Cambodia (1.5–2 million killed), Idi Amin of Uganda (300,000 killed; Indians driven out), Joseph Stalin of the USSR (20 million killed or starved; 1 million executed; many sent to the Gulag), Rwanda and Kosovo genocides, South African Apartheid, massacres in Sudan, the current wars in the Middle East involving Israel, Palestine and the Hezbollah, the wars in Afghanistan and Iraq, and Al Qaeda terrorists

b. 1900 to 1938: World War I, fall of czarist Russia, brutal rise of communism, Fascism, and Nazism
c. 1800s: slavery, feudal China, European slave trade, American Civil War (1861–65)
d. 1400s to 1800s: brutal colonization of the New World, decimation of indigenous populations, American Revolution, Napoleonic wars

Once we take into account historical figures and forces such as Genghis Khan, Alexander the Great, the Crusades, the brutal treatment of Christ by the Romans, and the Roman wars of conquest, we begin to see that violence forms a backdrop against which we live.

When assessing the impact of violence on our world, we must take into account the fact that all of these examples entail physical, emotional, and spiritual violence.

In order to make inroads against this backdrop of violence we need

a. A shift in paradigm, as the present "system" is not working
b. A look at peace in terms of the butterfly effect: every person adopting peace would make more people peaceful over time

THE NEED FOR PEACE

Ever since the dawn of human history, there has been need for peace, unity, and understanding among all people. However, these goals have been ever elusive. In earlier times, people waged war among themselves, using primitive weapons and hand-to-hand combat. As society became more complex, and science developed, people waged wars with ever-increasing sophistication and destructiveness. Will Durant has remarked in his *Story of Philosophy* how science both heals and kills. It reduces the death rate in retail, but then also kills us wholesale in war.[1] There has hardly been any time in the history of the modern world when some war was not occurring. It is paradoxical that there have been two sociological constants throughout history: man's desire for peace and society's penchant for indulging in warfare.

Sometime ago the United Nations stated that stress is the number one health problem in the world at an individual level. This stress is brought about by many factors, and among them is the lack of peace, unity, and understanding among people, whether in families, nations, or the world in general. Perhaps the greatest stress producer is violence leading to loss of life, property, family, and means of survival.

A few years ago, the Council for the Parliament of the World's Religions proclaimed a Global Ethic: "We affirm that there is an irrevocable and unconditional norm for all areas of life: for families and communities; for races, nations and religions; there already exist ancient guidelines for human behavior which are found in the teachings of the religions of the world and which are the condition for a sustainable world order."[2]

Specific topics of the Global Ethic: Embracing Difference, Transforming the World indicate that every human being must be treated humanely:

1. Commitment to a culture of nonviolence and respect for life
2. Commitment to a culture of solidarity and a just economic order

3. Commitment to a culture of tolerance and a life of truthfulness
4. Commitment to a culture of equal rights and partnership between men and women

This Global Ethic was meant to reemphasize that there are common denominators in the lives of all people that can make life more meaningful, peaceful, and enjoyable. Why are peace, unity, and understanding so elusive? The answer lies within people themselves. People create problems, and people also come up with solutions to problems. Peace is embedded, and is latent, in the heart and soul of human beings. All that is required is an awareness of its presence, which has been overshadowed by the passions of hate, egoism, selfishness, anger, and intolerance, among others. Once a person becomes aware of these, and makes a sincere effort to control them for the greater good of self and others, then we can say that there is "heaven on earth."

THE ROLE OF ORGANIZED RELIGION

Throughout the ages, people have thought that religion will bring peace, unity, and understanding in life, but it has failed to do so. One religion is not able to get along with another, and religious people fight among themselves to preserve their own religious values and traditions. Great thinkers of various eras and traditions have often pondered the oneness of God and its connection with peace. Religion, in its purest form, can be a powerful force in the lives of people, and ought to bring peace, love, unity, and understanding among all peoples of the world. Approximately 80 percent of the world's population belongs to one religion or another. If they truly practiced the precepts of their religions, then certainly there would be peace in the world, but because of the realities of power, politics, and ego, and the belief in the superiority of one religious tradition over another, people generally (and often times unwittingly) make their religions hollow and superficial.

THE ROLE OF PEACE

Merriam-Webster's Collegiate Dictionary defines peace in terms of "freedom from public disturbance or disorder," "freedom from disagreement," "an undisturbed state of mind," "an absence of mental conflict," and "peace of mind."[3] From these definitions, it becomes obvious that practicing these attributes will be of benefit to every person, and to the world in general. Perhaps we may question, what is the reason for the absence of these attributes? From analysis, it will be found that the root cause for the absence of these attributes lies in the ignorance of spiritual values, aided by egoism, greed, and selfishness, among others.

THE LOGICAL REASON FOR PEACE

All religions teach humanity to live a noble and righteous life of love, harmony, tolerance, service, humility, forgiveness, and other values. We need to remember that the source of our being is God, and that God dwells in the hearts of all. The Vedas state, "Human beings, all, are as head, arms, trunks and legs one on to another." The Bible states, "No man liveth on to himself . . . we are all parts of one another . . . God hath made of one blood all nations that dwelleth upon the face of the earth."[4] There is a great unity in the cosmos, including among all beings on earth. All things in the universe are made up of atoms. All atoms, whether they are in humans, animals, plants, or stars, are made up of protons, neutrons, and electrons. These subatomic particles are the same in all things, all beings. Carl Sagan, a renowned astronomer, in his television series *Cosmos* (1980), said: "We are all made of star stuff." Shouldn't this knowledge foster peace, love, unity, and understanding?

THE IMPORTANCE OF THE INDIVIDUAL

World peace is possible only when there is peace in the hearts of people. Peace in the hearts of people is possible only when there is peace in the heart of every person. Peace in the heart of each person is possible only when each person sees the unity of humanity. The unity of humanity is realized when there is universal love for all. Universal love for all is possible only when everyone gets rid of ego-based motivations and behavior spurred on by anger, greed, hate, intolerance, condescension, and possessiveness. These are not easy goals for people to attain, but they are not impossible. They are made possible by understanding the relationship between all of us, all of nature, and God. Peace is possible by removing the obstacles created by religious doctrines, dogmas, creeds, castes, social status, power, control, passions, and lack of empathy for others.

People are generally occupied with the material, worldly life, neglecting their spiritual part. If they considered themselves to be the spiritual beings they are, then they would be motivated by love and understanding, which will result in world peace. All of us say that we are children of God, and that God is our Father, but we quickly forget this when we are engaged in the pursuit of our material pursuits. God is the abode of love, and we must seek to realize God in our own life, and see that God manifests in the life of all beings. He is immanent in his own creation, hence his omnipresence. But as practiced, religions suffer from a great weakness, namely, their inability to make God real to their devotees.

VIOLENCE AT THE LOCAL LEVEL

When dealing with the topic of "World's Religions after 9/11," we should not confine our deliberations to civil or international wars. We need to look also at violence in young people since they are the future of society. Violent behavior occurs even among children, as is obvious all over the world. Violence is common among youth in most "developed countries" and is often related to illegal drugs. It includes suicides and homicides. It is sad to see that youth are engaged in activities that will make for an uncertain future for them, their families, and society.

Perhaps we can try to understand some of the underlying causes of such violence among youth by considering the following points:

1. There is a lack of proper training and supervision by parents, teachers, and other significant adults that prevents young people from developing good ethical, moral, and spiritual values in life.

2. Educational systems often do not stress moral, ethical, cultural, ethnic, and spiritual values in children. These are underlying human values that cross all religious boundaries, and are equally applicable to people of all religions.
3. Racial and religious intolerance exists. This is unfortunate since the world is made up of people of different cultures, races, and religions. The law of variety is the law of nature. Everywhere you look you see differences. There are different breeds of horses, cattle, dogs, and other animals. One breed of animals does not fight with those of another breed. Why does it happen in human beings? God, in his infinite wisdom, has made varieties, and we need to accept them.
4. Much of youth violence is related to the acquisition of street or illegal drugs. The news media frequently relate stories of killing, robbing, breaking and entering, and other criminal activities by drug addicts in order to "feed" their drug habit.
5. There exists too much freedom for youth and the assertion of individual rights, especially in Western countries. Youth often do not have enough maturity and responsibility, and they use their idle time hanging out with others who can influence them toward negative activities. They often develop a group mentality and take part in activities that may result in violence. Society has become too permissive, to the extent that "anything goes," and no one has the right to correct another's behavior. At fault are parents, the educational institutions, the religious leaders, and law enforcement at all levels.
6. Children and youth are bombarded with violence on television and in electronic games. The entertainment industry is interested in making money, not in cultivating good character. At a subconscious level, these are often the triggers that result in outward violence. We may say that these are cases of "copy cat" violence. Religious leaders need to show strong leadership in ending these violent types of "entertainment."

These are only a few examples of the underlying causes of youth violence. There are many others, depending on ethnicity; religious, moral, and cultural values, or lack of them; and society's condoning of such behaviors. It is important to realize, however, that when one chooses a pattern of behavior, then one also chooses its consequences. Committing a crime and then trying to escape the consequences is the mark of a coward. The courts are full of cases dealing with violence, with perpetrators putting up legal defenses to escape punishment. Youth violence will decrease only when society—including the family, school, church, and the law—creates a milieu in which violence will not be tolerated. Individual rights and freedoms must be subservient to what is good for all people.

THE PARADIGM SHIFT

After having given a great deal of thought to the violence and suffering occurring in many parts of the world, I believe that steps need to be taken to develop people from childhood onward into loving and caring individuals who will not resort to violence. Let us remind ourselves of the violence perpetrated on September 11 in the United States that was morally and economically devastating, and brought untold sorrow to those injured and to the families of the thousands killed. People all over the world were deeply saddened. This resulted in the war in Afghanistan to oust the Taliban regime and to eliminate the Al Qaeda terrorist network. It has led to incalculable suffering among the civilian population. The Middle East wars are another example. Similarly, there have also been other significant wars, ethnic cleansings, and other atrocities in recent memory. As we think about them, a feeling of helplessness and sorrow assails us. We empathize with all the suffering people, especially when they are innocent. This applies more so to the children, who do not understand why violence is thrust on them, and the uncertain future they face. I believe there must be a way to decrease, or even mostly eliminate, the atrocities happening in the world.

Although both the 9/11 attacks and the war in the Middle East involve many political and military factors, both, in the end, are the results of the collective violent actions and thoughts of individuals. It was the actions of individuals that led to the hijacking of the jetliners, and it is ultimately the actions of individuals that lead to each escalation of violence in the Middle East.

How then do we inculcate a culture of peace throughout the world?

In the shadow of the madness of 9/11, the late Pope John Paul, speaking for the Roman Catholic Church and its 1 billion members around the world, told the gathering of religious leaders of various faiths in Assisi on January 24, 2002,

> Never again violence!
> Never again war!
> Never again terrorism!
> In the name of God
> may every religion bring upon the earth
> justice and peace,
> forgiveness and life, love![5]

Other religions equally teach love, peace, tolerance, and brotherhood. Mahatma Gandhi taught peace. Hinduism's main tenet is nonviolence, and the unity of all in God. Islam teaches mercy and compassion, as does Buddhism. Jesus taught us to love one another. Jainism's main tenet is universal nonviolence. I reemphasize: 80 percent of the world's people adhere to a religion. If 80 percent of the world's people are taught truly to adhere to the teachings of their religions, we will indeed have a peaceful and happier world.

Thus, if violent actions are ultimately carried out by individuals and we need to develop a worldwide culture of peace, then we must focus our efforts on the individual through the framework that follows.

PROPOSED ROLE OF THE UNITED NATIONS

The United Nations is in a unique position to offer a solution to the problems noted above. The United Nations is the world government, and it should have a great deal of influence on its member countries. It needs to develop a protocol, in consultation with significant leaders of all its 192 member countries and, through invitation, with leaders of the nonmember countries as well. Since violence occurs in the whole world, it will make sense to have participation of all countries for the welfare of their own citizens. Unless world violence is tackled universally by a world government, any solution developed by, or imposed on, any country, or instituted by organizations within any country, will not solve the problem. It is for this reason that I believe the United Nations is the only proper authority to deal with this problem.

The military-industrial complex of every nation is so pervasive that it devours a huge portion of each country's GNP. There would be healthier, happier, and more prosperous people in the world if even a portion of that expense were diverted toward the welfare of the civilian population. It is estimated that since 9/11, the United States has spent about $400 billion on wars. The hundreds of billions of dollars spent by the United States in wars could provide better housing, dairy cows, clean water, and health care for millions of poor people around the world.

The premises on which I base my suggestions are as follows:

1. Life is sacred, and we must have reverence for life.
2. Everyone wants peace, health, prosperity, and happiness.
3. Everyone wants to avoid pain and suffering.
4. Everyone has an innate desire for family, community, and brotherhood.
5. All the world's religions teach peace and love for one another.

There are certain identifiable causes for war and violence:

1. Hate and anger in those having power to cause violence
2. Greed and possessiveness for territory and resources
3. Religious intolerance/bigotry, fanaticism, religious sectism, and fundamentalism
4. Egoism and need for power
5. Economic inequalities/poverty and lack of opportunities
6. Political ideologies such as democracy vs. dictatorships, theocracy, oligarchy
7. Racism, casteism, classism, and other divisions

The above causes of conflict may appear simplistic, but they are definitely the root causes of violence. Any or all of these causes start in the heart of an individual, and then spread to others by indoctrination, imposition, opportunism, and recruitment. If these causes are removed from each individual, then there is an excellent chance of having peace in the world.

This is a strategy for achieving peace at the world level:

1. Teach all children the noble qualities of love, compassion, respect, understanding, nonviolence, and brotherhood.
2. Teach all children to reflect upon their own thinking, and what may be the consequences. Actions in thoughts, words and deeds will produce appropriate consequences.
3. Teach all children reverence for life: hurting anyone causes suffering that one would not like inflicted on oneself.
4. Teach all children what egoism is, and its power to do harm.
5. Teach all children acceptance of one another based on understanding, empathy, sharing, love, and respect.

In order to achieve the above, I would suggest that the United Nations convene a summit of the departments or ministries of education of all the countries. Prominent, liberal-minded religious leaders and educators should also be invited. The purpose of this meeting would be to formulate a core curriculum, and to develop ways and means of implementing it. The curriculum will place emphasis on the items listed above, and on their implementation at the first-grade level or its equivalent. The content will need to be upgraded in terms of vocabulary and complexity of ideas as students advance to higher grades. It will need to be a core subject no less than language, science, or mathematics. It will need to be taught until children grasp the fundamental importance of these values and apply them in life.

If the above values are taught in the formative years of children, then just as they learn the other subjects, they will also learn the values that bring peace, happiness, and shared co-existence into everyday life, and make them manifest in the world. This need not be a religious course, but a course in shared human values. We must recognize that some people may not subscribe to these principles, but that does not mean that we need to abandon the whole idea. It would be necessary to point out the logic and necessity for this approach to them in order to achieve world peace.

ROLE OF RELIGIONS AFTER 9/11

1. All religions have an equal right to exist in freedom and dignity, without pressure or censure in any form from other religions.
2. No religion should consider itself superior, or that it has the monopoly on God or spirituality, and should not seek to convert others to its fold. A sense of superiority is egotistic and leads away from God.
3. God is spirit and dwells in the hearts of all through his omnipresence. Let all "religious" people see this unity and practice universal brotherhood.
4. Truth is God and God is Truth, and is Absolute. Truth is God that is immanent in his creation. Religious people need to live with this understanding.
5. All religions need to tackle violence from the ground up, that is, from childhood, by teaching love, respect, charity, compassion, reverence for life, and coexistence with religious and nonreligious people everywhere. A tree cannot be nourished by watering the leaves but by watering the root. Children are the root of society. This is outlined above under strategy.
6. Nonviolence must be stressed at the individual level, so that the world would in time have a population of nonviolent people.
7. Leaders of all religions need to commit themselves to peace and gather annually at a summit meeting to formulate ways and means to propagate peace from childhood onwards, whether through the places of worship, homes, or schools.
8. Every religion should monitor its adherents for violence. If a violent group develops, then the majority of the adherents of that religion should make every effort to stop it.

I believe that my vision as outlined above is a comprehensive and universal one and, once implemented, will reap rich dividends in love, peace, health, harmony, happiness, and economic well-being throughout the world.

Here is a short poem I composed on peace:

Please allow peace to be with you,
Each and everyday of your life;
Allow it to work its magic,
Comforting you and humanity,
Enshrining peace in your loving heart.

NOTES

1. *The Story of Philosophy: The Lives and Opinions of the Great Philosophers* (New York: Simon and Schuster, 1953), p. 2.

2. Hans Küng and Karl-Josef Kuschel, eds. *A Global Ethic: The Declaration of the Parliament of the World's Religion* (London: SCM Press, 1993), p. 14.

3. *Merriam Webster's Collegiate Dictionary*, 10th ed. (Springfield, MA: Merriam Webster, 2002), p. 852.

4. *The Essential Unity of All Religions,* compiled by Bhagwan Das (Wheaton, IL: The Theosophical Press, 1932 [Reprinted 1966]), p. lvi.

5. See http://www.vatican.va/news_services/liturgy/documents/ns_lit_doc_20020124_assisi-giornata_en.html.

CHAPTER 25

Religious Tolerance and Peace Building in a World of Diversity

Issa Kirarira

Throughout history, religious differences have divided men and women from their neighbors and have served as justification for some of humankind's bloodiest conflicts. In the modern world, it has become clear that people of all religions must bridge these differences and work together to ensure our survival and realize the vision of peace that all faiths share.

Presently the "clash of religions" is resonating so powerfully and worryingly around the world that finding answers to the old questions of how best to manage and mitigate conflicts over religions has taken on renewed importance.

The earliest recorded evidence of religious activity dates from only about 60,000 BCE. However, anthropologists and historians of religion believe that some form of religion has been practiced since people first appeared on earth about 2.5 million years ago.

Religion (Latin *religare,* "to bind," perhaps human beings to God) is a code of belief or philosophy that often involves worship of a God or gods. Belief in a supernatural power is not essential (absent in, for example, Buddhism and Confucianism), but faithful adherence is usually considered to be rewarded, for example by escape from human existence (Buddhism), by future existence (Christianity, Islam), or by worldly benefit (Soka Gakkai, Buddhism).

Among the chief religions are

- Ancient and Pantheist religions: Babylonia, Assyria, Egypt, Greece, and Rome
- Oriental: Hinduism, Buddhism, Jainism, Parseeism, Confucianism, Taoism, and Shinto
- Religions of a Book: Judaism, Christianity (the principal divisions are Roman Catholic, Eastern Orthodox, and Protestant), and Islam (the principle divisions are Sunni and Shi'ite)
- Combined derivation such as Bahá'í Faith, the Unification Church, and Mormonism

On the other hand, theology is the study of religion. The word itself refers to the interpretation of the doctrines of God. But modern theology includes the study of various religions and such topics as church history, sacred writings, and the relationship between religion and human needs.

Theology teaches the importance of rejecting violence and adapting to peaceful and civilized means of resolving conflicts and disagreements. It is a vital instrument in enhancing societal transition without recourse to volatile methods. This is through revelation as in the scriptures of Christianity, Islam, or other religions that religious communities are formed by people coming and staying together. Each religion therefore serves as an example for the other.

If we are to live peacefully in our diversity, we must first successfully confront the challenge of how to build all-inclusive, tolerant societies, and look at religion as a better way of fostering peace than of fueling war. People of different religions must be allowed to express and practice their beliefs, and at the same time, they should respect the beliefs of others. There can be no coherent social life unless there are social relationships that bind people together to at least some degree of order. As the dictum goes, when Christ enters sectarianism has to leave. To maintain an orderly system, every individual should be left to exercise the religion of his or her choice.

The Holy Qur'an says, "I worship not which you worship nor will you worship that which I worship. And I shall not worship that which you are worshipping nor will you worship that which I worship. To you be your religion and to me my religion."[1] People of one religion must be allowed to not only to criticize the practices and beliefs of other religions but to respect them.

RELIGIOUS TOLERANCE IN PEACE BUILDING

We both commemorate the sad events of September 11 and celebrate the heroes whose spirit of oneness soared above the grief and pain of that time. I wish to categorically state that we are in every way opposed to the acts of September 11. The perpetrators of those acts were evil and have absolutely no connection with the truth of Islam or any other religion.

The true spirit of heroism that ensued in the wake of the events of September 11 should be emulated by future generations without the need for more tragedies to convince them of the fact that we are really one people of different tongues, races, educational backgrounds, cultures, and religious orientation, and yet of very like needs. We may pray differently, but our destiny is the same.

What brings us together is the universal cry for peace, peace that leaves us the freedom to bring up our families in an atmosphere of love and conviviality with our neighbors. Our cry is for a future of prosperity that can spread around our nations that there may be no more frustration in our communities, and that there may be less disagreement and more of a spirit of working together in the very ultimate of tolerance to differences in beliefs and in choices of non–antagonistic behaviors.

Religious communities are, without question, the largest and best-organized civil institutions in the world today. They claim the allegiance of billions of believers and bridge the divides of race, class, and nationality. They are uniquely equipped to meet the challenges of our time: resolving conflicts, caring for the sick and needy, promoting peaceful co-existence among all people, and allowing some degree of tolerance.

Islamic civilization has in the past proved capable of, for the times, extraordinary feats of toleration. Under the Muslims, medieval Spain became a haven for diverse religions and sects. Following the Christian re-conquest, the Inquisition eliminated all dissent. The notion that Islamic civilization is inherently less capable of tolerance and compassion then any other religion is hard to square with facts.

When Meccan pagans severely persecuted the early Muslims, Prophet Muhammad himself instructed a group of his followers to migrate to neighboring Abyssinia, now Ethiopia, which was ruled by a Christian king. He was known as a just ruler, and so the prophet trusted that his followers would be safe under this king's rule. The king not only provided them safe refuge but also refused to deport them back to Mecca when a Meccan delegation requested him to do so. It should be noted that the Muslims sought protection under a Christian king, which goes against the generalization that a Muslim cannot take a Christian as his protector. There are numerous examples of good relations, tolerance, and neighborliness shown by non-Muslims in authority or otherwise to Muslims the world over.

It is a relief that the mainstream theologians have came out so unanimously against the terrorists. What we must now ask them is to campaign more strongly against the aberrant doctrines that underpin them. It is the responsibility of the Islamic world to defeat the terrorist aberration theologically. In what sense were the World Trade Center bombers members of Islam? This question has been sidelined by many Western analysts impatient with the niceties of theology, but it may be the key to understanding the attack, and to assessing the long-term prospects for peace in the Muslim world.

Without a theological position justifying the rejection of the mainstream position, the frustration would have led to a frustration with religion and then to a search for secular responses. It should be noted that religious studies involves instruction in the beliefs of a particular religion. This type of education is the work of organized religions, through their school and religious organizations. Religious education therefore may be defined as general education that follows religious instructions and ideals. It is the clergy and various religious orders that offer the best opportunities for religious study and education.

At the heart of the global crisis currently afflicting humanity exists a pervasive lack of moral leadership in all sectors of human society. The lack of moral leadership is demonstrated in the continuous uncovering of unethical behavior at all levels of society in all parts of the world. Religions traditionally offer guiding wisdom, yet the disparity of belief systems results in fragmentation and often works against the common good. Are religions responsible for caring for the soul of humanity? If so, how can we encourage religious leaders to move beyond concern for their specific faith communities to caring for the whole of humanity?

It is true that because of the politicization of religions and cultures, political elites and religious leaders fail to consolidate unity in their countries or communities. In turn, the international community (the UN, Amnesty International, Human Rights Watch, etc.) comes in with solutions that it deems reasonable for cushioning or ending a crisis. However, these solutions ignore the real and fundamental issues at the back and front of the crisis. In turn, they produce short-lived solutions and answers to complex and complicated problems.

Rarely is religion the principal cause of international conflict, even though some adversaries may argue differently. Religious adherence continues to play a significant role in legitimizing the social order as well as reducing conflicts. This becomes an effective mechanism for power sharing between diverse religious groups. Power-sharing arrangements between different groups prevent conflicts and violence. This conception of democracy emerges when the "study of politics" is linked to the "study of religion" by the concept of power.

For instance, high government officials are sworn into office while holding Bibles and Qur'ans, and they make public demonstrations of church attendance and prayers in mosques. Legislative sessions are opened with public prayers, and court proceedings involve taking oaths involving the name of God. Such arrangements are important in legitimizing social order while at the same time reducing conflicts in countries without social order. There is no serious attempt to achieve world peace that can ignore religion.

Many religions suffer from various forms of exclusion, sometimes resulting from explicit suppression of religious freedom or discrimination against that group—a problem particularly common in nonsecular countries where the state upholds an established religion.

But in other cases, the exclusion may be less direct and often unintended, as when the public calendar does not recognize a minority's religious holidays. India officially celebrates five Hindu holidays but also four Muslim, two Christian, one Buddhist, one Jain, and one Sikh holiday in recognition of the diverse population. France celebrates eleven national holidays: five are nondenominational, but the six religious holidays all celebrate events in the Christian calendar even though 7 percent of the population is Muslim and 1 percent is Jewish. Similarly, the dress codes in public institutions may conflict with a minority's religious dress, or state rules about marriage and inheritance may differ from those of religious codes.

These sorts of conflicts can arise even in secular states with strong democratic institutions that protect civil and political rights. Given the profound importance of religion to people's identities, it is not surprising that religious minorities often mobilize to contest these exclusions. Some religious practices are not difficult to accommodate, but often they present difficult choices and trade-offs.

France is grappling with whether the wearing of headscarves in state schools violates state principles of secularism and democratic values of gender equality that state education aims to impart. Although a law was passed in 2004 banning headscarves in state schools, the debate continues today. Nigeria is struggling with whether to uphold the ruling of Sharia courts in the case of adultery. A high-profile case involved a woman, Safiya Husaini, being convicted of adultery in 2001 for having a child out of wedlock and sentenced to death by stoning. She has since mounted a successful appeal of the conviction.

What is important is to expand human freedoms and human rights and to recognize equality. Secular and democratic states are most likely to achieve these goals when the state provides reasonable accommodations for religious practices, where all religions have the same relation to the state, and where the state protects human rights.

In order to live peacefully in the world, one must first successfully meet the challenge of building religiously tolerant societies that allow people religious freedom. Such a world would be more stable, more peaceful, and free from much disturbance and confusion.

Religion can have a strong role of guiding wisdom and enabling individuals to weigh their cultures and decide on those aspects that might be of benefit or of detriment to themselves and to society. The Holy Qur'an says, "Piety doesn't lie in turning your face to the East or West. Piety lies in believing in God."[2] This through the influence of faith has encouraged the followers to move beyond concern for their specific faith communities into caring for the whole of humanity.

Having noted these relationships, we should become particularly interested in how best to enable students and academics to become agents of social change imbued with spiritual, technical, moral, and spiritual capacities. The maintenance of a liberal society depends largely on respecting the rule of law, listening to political claims, protecting fundamental human rights, and securing the rights of diverse cultural groups and minorities. The need to find ways of forging unity amid this diversity is the responsibility of the states; it is also their responsibility to protect rights and secure freedoms for all their members, and not discriminate on the grounds of race, religion, or culture. Religious adherence plays a significant role in legitimizing the social order as well as reducing conflict.

Islam as a religion is an organized system of beliefs, ceremonies, practices, and worship that center on one supreme God (Allah). Islam developed a form of religious life during the eighth century CE through the Sufi movement. The members met regularly to recite the Qur'an and worship together. The Islamic system has preserved and even maintained prior cultural expressions, including the Egyptian sphinx and the Persian persepolis, all signs of religious tolerance.

The Qur'anic command of tolerance explains why Greece, in spite of 500 years of Ottoman rule, emerged as a Greek Orthodox nation; why en route to the Cairo airport, one sees more Coptic churches than mosques; why the Bible is available in Moroccan bookshops; and why church steeples in Damascus bear neon-lit crosses at night. All these are examples of the willingness to live together in tolerance.

The principal aim and object of every religion is service to humanity, and both prayers and fasting have been the basic teachings of every religion the world over. To Muslims, fasting during the month of Ramadan inculcates within them tolerance, sacrifice, purity, and total submission, and helps strengthen them to live by their faith within the realities of life. The impact of fasting is immense. It teaches us in a practical way to live up to the human standards that Allah has ordained for mankind.

Islam places great emphasis on the unity, both of thought and action, of the Muslim Ummah (community). The objective is to establish peace on earth and eradicate oppression and mischief from society; failing that, crisis, turmoil, and catastrophes will prevail in the world.

Muslims have uniformity in their religious practices. Allah created different groups of people, and they were expected to get to know one another. Allah says, "O mankind, we created you from a single male and female, and made you into nations and tribes that you may know one another (not that you may despise each other)."[3]

Dividing people into sects, denominations, and group is a sinful act. In this regard, Allah says, "As for those who divide their religion and break up into sects, you have no part in them in the least their affair is with Allah; He will in the end tell them the truth of all they did."[4] Allah commands believers to "hold fast together to Allah's code (the way prescribed by Allah) and let nothing divide you."[5]

Muslims must strive to create this unity not only among themselves but also with other religious faiths. If we unite, then Allah will send his mercy and grace upon us. He will also guide each of us on the straight path, and grant us peace and honor.

We do agree that some Muslims, as men themselves, have not been followers of the truth of their religion. There are cases of discrimination, and even humiliation, of Jews, Christians, and even of their own Muslim brethren living under some Muslim rulers. That is why it comes out as particularly painful to the entire Muslim world whenever, in sharp contrast to the Qur'anic teachings, a few extremists attack and hurt non-Muslims as happened in Pakistan when some innocent Christian worshipers were killed. The Afghanistan war, Osama Bin Laden, Saddam Hussein's attacks of Kuwait, and the July 7, 2005, bombing in Britain are some additional examples.

On behalf of the peace-loving peoples of the Islamic world, we do advocate that perpetrators of these heinous crimes be exposed to real Islam. We ask both Muslims and the non-Muslims in the rest of the world to do their utmost to protect the security and welfare of the minority communities living under their protection.

Although it is understandable that the expression of anger and loss of tolerance is not too infrequent a phenomenon during times of warfare or political crisis, it is just as important to balance out this understanding with a deep contemplation of the possibility of what could happen if threats and other proclamations are acted upon. The bottom line is that the resulting effect on our planet earth on the next years and next centuries has to be thoroughly analyzed before conflict should be permitted.

There are misled Muslims who may cherish disrespect or even hatred for Westerners or non-Muslims. That can, however, be found among people of other faiths as well. Numbers of such people are not many. I believe, we, the majority, Muslim, Christian, Hindu, Buddhist, Bahá'í, and all other world religions can overcome the power they have amassed. History has replayed this scenario over and over. Let us emulate the example of our more balanced forbearers and stamp out these social evils by developing a culture of forgiveness, mercy, peace, love, and tolerance.

WAY FORWARD

Dr. Hassan Hathout, a scholar of Islam, says, "In my late sixties, and after lifelong study, reflection and insight into my Islamic faith, I feel my heart bursting with love. It is non-specific love that has no address attached to it. I feel love towards my fellow humans, animals, birds, trees, things, and the earth and universe in which we live and deep in my heart I wish it were contagious."[6]

Such is the result of his true understanding of his faith and its reflection in him. Hopefully many of us and our own children will be able to walk in his footsteps. It is our heartfelt belief that our planet earth can adapt his culture of thinking and action. The question should be, Why not? What has gone wrong, and can the situation be salvaged and how? The answer to these questions is quite simple.

It is important to realize that our fellowship is with God alone and not with the belief system that we have. In many cases, even though we proclaim our loyalty to

God, in our actions, we really adhere to the teachings of the school of thought with which we associate ourselves. Loyalty to God, in contrast, means evaluating our actions with this question: is this want God wants?

Related to the above is that the shape and substance of the value of teaching religious studies need to provide a better understanding of the common values of all religions and assist in the formulation of nonsectarian curricula. The curricula considered should meet the needs of quality, access, and lifestyle; they should be all inclusive and flexible, and should be undertaken after a comparative analysis of different values. Also, a program in moral leadership should be considered for school teachers to understand relationships of domination and contribute to their transformation into relationships based on interconnectedness, reciprocity, and service.

We have seen the effect of media, both positive and negative, on the masses. We can harness this same power and bestow this one good above all upon our own future.

The religious opinion concerning the acts of terrorism provides for deterrent punishment against persons who carry out bombing attacks against installations and housing complexes, or hijack airplanes, trains, and other means of transportation with the intent to intimidate or terrify innocent people—the so-called refugees. Islam urges the protection of human life and honors, property, religion, and intellect—Allah says: "If any do transgress the limits ordained by God, such persons wrong themselves as well as others."[7] Peace-loving nations, people, and organizations should endeavor to protect humankind from all forms of evil and contribute to any effort that aims at realizing security and peace for humankind.

By studying Islam rationally rather than emotionally, one would be able to see the equity of Islam and its compatibility with humankind's natural disposition on one hand and the scientific realities on the other. Islam is not only a religion of peace and nonaggression, but it also contains solutions to humankind's problems as well as its favorable view of justice, tolerance, dialogue, and human interaction.

Identifying the facts, both causative and resultant, nurtures a culture of tolerance that creates an atmosphere for peace to thrive and enables people of diverse religious and cultural backgrounds to live together in harmony. Hence, due rights are returned to their rightful owners, and wrongdoing is stopped.

The media, the government systems, the donor community, and all sympathetic to the cry for peace need to agree on an immediate plan of action and work with communities the world over to bring about realization of this dream.

CONCLUSION

Overall, the world must address the challenge of how to build inclusive, religiously diverse societies in order to achieve the goals of reducing tensions in the world and solving the problems facing humanity. When we talk about tolerance, we don't necessarily mean that we should agree with or love one another, but we mean that we should respect the rights of others, especially the right to be different. At times intolerance should be promoted, by this I mean let's not tolerate acts such as those of September 11, Bali, Nairobi, July 7 in Britain, and Pakistan, to name just a few, because they only make us insecure and cause untold suffering to us all. Freedom of self-expression is not without restrictions, however. Transgressing the sanctity of others' honor and spreading rumors lead to confusion and disorder, and upset the atmosphere of stability and the feeling of security among citizens. None of these can be condoned in the name of religious freedom.

NOTES

1. Qur'an 109:2–6.
2. Qur'an 2:17.
3. Qur'an 49:13.
4. Qur'an 6:159.
5. Qur'an 111:103.
6. Hassan Hathout, *Reading the Muslim Mind* (Plainfield, IN: American Trust Publications, 1995), p. 141.
7. Qur'an 2:229.

SUGGESTED READINGS

Al-Hageel, Sulaiman bin Abdul Rahman, *Human Rights in Islam and Their Applications in the Kingdom of Saudi Arabia* (Riyadh: King Fahd National Library, 2001).

Human Development Report 2004: Cultural Liberty in Today's Diverse World, United Nations Development Programme (New York: Oxford University Press, 2004).

Huntington, Samuel and Mahmood Mamdani, *Clash of Civilizations* (Kampala: Fountain Publishers, 2004).

Mbiti, John S. *African Religions and Philosophy*, 2d ed. (Oxford: Heinemann, 1989).

CHAPTER 26

Toward a Culture of Peace

Fabrice Blée

In today's world, we are desperately in need of a culture of peace. Interreligious dialogue is seen as a key element in such a development. Although many initiatives have been taken in this area since the first Parliament of Religions was held in Chicago in 1893, we are reaching a point when we must consider what to do to foster more realistic and less idealistic relations. This concern was raised by the World Council of Churches in a congress titled Critical Moment in Interreligious Dialogue, held in Geneva in June 2005.[1] Being sensitive to this need, I am skeptical regarding the tendency to focus only on common points, an attitude that consists in avoiding all situations that might lead to conflict. Is it fair to ask religious leaders to support peace at all costs? Does this serve peace? If yes, what kind of peace? Or does it serve a specific world order? How then can a culture of peace be developed?

A culture of peace cannot be reduced to simply the effort of reaching a peace accord. Rather, it must be based on a pluralistic attitude that holds together an awareness of the interdependency of people, cultures, nations, and religions, and the respect for what makes us truly different and unique. Unity, peace, and harmony cannot gloss over or ignore the difficulties in dealing with the differences, in particular hopes and concerns, either doctrinal or political. Such a confrontation is a necessary step on the path of interreligious dialogue. That is why I find the role of a spirituality of dialogue so important.

The central idea of my presentation is this: there is no culture of peace possible without the emergence of a spirituality of dialogue. Only such a spirituality can promote respect for religious otherness while accepting that there is no real separation between religion, politics, and spirituality. Here are three elements that must be considered as interactive if our intention is to promote mutual respect and understanding.

I propose to develop this idea briefly in four points. First, I would like to say something about what I mean by spirituality of dialogue. Second, I want to point out the relevance in not separating religion and political concern too quickly. Third, it is vital to reconnect religion and spirituality. Fourth, examining the last two points will allow me to show the importance of considering the link between spirituality and political concern. Finally, all these points will be followed by some concluding thoughts.

WHAT DO I MEAN BY SPIRITUALITY OF DIALOGUE?

My intention is neither to describe the historical development of a spirituality of dialogue nor to point out its theological implications. Instead, I refer you to my book *Le désert de l'altérité,* published in 2004. Here, let us just ask this question: What is at stake in a spirituality of dialogue? As soon as a dialogue is more than a mere conversation, as soon as our partner is received in our heart, as soon as we accept that we are received in our partner's milieu (that is, in another religious context), as soon as we are touched by another universal truth and worldview, dialogue becomes existential and begins to transform us deeply.

The relationship that comes out of such an encounter is certainly enriching and promising, but it also becomes a question for oneself, a source of tension, a challenging space wherein we face ourselves with our strengths as well as our weaknesses, a space wherein God talks to us in unknown ways. The inner dialogue resulting from this relationship is not easy. Our faith and beliefs are put at risk. Then the meeting, which is going on within oneself between two religious universes, two ways of feeling and praying, requires spiritual qualities and virtues. That is the reason why dialogue is seen as a spiritual act in itself.

A spirituality of dialogue comes out of a hospitality process through which we can accept being deeply touched by another religious experience while witnessing our own faith. It refers to a new religious consciousness stemming from a dialogue of religious experience, one of the four types of dialogue identified by the Pontifical Council for Interreligious Dialogue, that is, a sharing focused on each other's connection to the living God, the divine mystery.

In a spirituality of dialogue, religious otherness, that is, other believers as received in their religious differences and uniqueness, is not seen as a threat to our own religious identity, but as the space where our identity is fully expressed, where I apply concretely what it means to be a Christian. Therefore, a spirituality of dialogue is not universal; it is always specific and has to be developed by each religious assembly in accordance with its own worldviews and doctrinal characteristics. However, in every case, a spirituality of dialogue will promote deep respect for religious otherness, true listening to those who are different from us, and sincere mutual understanding. But this cannot be done unless we accept the impossibility of separating religion, political concern, and spirituality.

RELIGION AND POLITICAL CONCERN

The events of 9/11 have changed the perception of religion and its role regarding society and world development. Since then, it has become common to talk about religion on TV, in the news, and in political debates, a situation which would have appeared odd and unusual ten or fifteen years ago. Religions have become an issue. More and more people want to explore religions in order to understand more deeply the world they live in as well as many local and international tensions and conflicts. Peace has no future on this planet unless we pay attention to the various religious claims and hopes, unless we promote dialogue and mutual understanding among them.

One thing, however, must be remembered: for the majority of believers, religion is not a private activity; rather, it plays a great part in determining their behavior and decisions on social and political levels. In other words, religious identity "has direct repercussions for ethnic, political, and national identity."[2] Religions are not something added to cultures that would otherwise be naturally secular in themselves. On the contrary, culture and religion are often so intertwined that it would be impossible to extract what is properly cultural or religious. Each culture promotes a specific order and social organization, and the religious dimension is never neutral in such representations.

The ideal that promotes the separation between religion and politics certainly serves valuable and pragmatic goals, but it does not neutralize the will of many believers to act for a better world and society in accordance with their own religious values. In our global context, however, such an ideal cannot be imposed, even by force, as the only one to be applied in all contexts and cultures.

We are, therefore, led to ask this question: within religion, how can we determine the correct course of action? In most religions, at least in the way they have been applied for centuries, a right action is determined not primarily by the welfare of the individual, but in accordance with a specific cosmotheandric order that has to be preserved and promoted. From a religious point of view, peace cannot be reduced to individual security and the absence of conflicts, two elements that are overestimated in our Western world.[3] Considering this point, is it realistic and fair to invite all religious leaders, especially Muslim leaders, to promote a specific vision of peace at all costs?

If a culture of peace is vital, it should not be based on such a request. The shock between religious worldviews will be dramatic in today's world unless we facilitate dialogue. However, dialogue cannot succeed unless we pay serious attention to the interconnection between religion and political concern—between one's relationship to the sacred and the momentum to be involved in the structure of the city (*polis*). This momentum is inherent in all relationships involving the sacred.

If religions are not political institutions, they are at least circles wherein political actions are made. It is possible to ignore the social and political concerns of Hindus, Muslims, Jews, or Christians in various contexts, but this will not serve dialogue and peace; we will only play the game of a dominating political worldview, nourishing by the same token fundamentalism and violence. Here Raimundo Panikkar's question is relevant: "Is pluralism the stratagem to induce people to give up their own identities in order to create a new world order in which all cats are gray, all differences abolished under the pretext of tolerance and peace?"[4] It is precisely because the link between religion and political concern must not be neglected that it is necessary to recognize the interconnection between religion and spirituality.

RELIGION AND SPIRITUALITY

A spirituality of dialogue can be seen as part of today's spiritual renewal, especially in the West. However, it does not yield to the current tendency to see spirituality as exclusive of religion. Such an opposition is inappropriate and damaging in many respects. Three remarks will help in understanding the present situation: First, religions have not become irrelevant, as was predicted decades ago; they have not been replaced by a disincarnated and multiform spirituality. Second, religions have no future except in the revitalization of their spiritual dimension. Third, in our pluralistic context, such a revitalization will be accomplished by taking an interreligious approach. Keeping these points in mind, it is clear why a spirituality of dialogue is so relevant: it actually prevents two dangers threatening interreligious dialogue and peace.

First of all, there is the danger that interreligious dialogue will be reduced to a mere diplomatic activity. This risk is all the more real because current political conflicts often have a religious dimension, and because the word "dialogue" itself, so often mentioned in the news regarding the geopolitical scene, refers to negotiation and aims at compromises.

The danger here is to see this approach becoming the main one: the opportunity to talk about peace and at the same time the pretext to stop the development of a spirituality of dialogue that would engage the church in new and challenging ways. Are we actually ready as Christians to make this step? Are we ready to lose in some ways to gain in others? The question is important, because if we refuse to make the step, dialogue could become simply a new strategy to meet particular and provincial interests; then it would become a tool at the service of political powers, and if so, peace has no chance.

Generally speaking, we see religions only as sociopolitical structures that have a strong influence on people. However, when we come to talk about faith and the spiritual dimension, we often focus on pathological, irrational, or other extreme behaviors. In my opinion, this means that, even though religions have a space in our society, they are not yet taken seriously. This will be the case as long as their deepest hopes, linked to salvation or liberation, of the spiritual encounter with the divine, or inner awakening, are not heard and respected. Only a spirituality of dialogue can preserve the "prophetic" voice of an interreligious encounter, in the sense that such a spirituality is rooted in a more profound dialogue with the divine presence, in the silence of love and humility.

What is at stake, then, in interreligious dialogue is not peace at all costs, for the simple reason that peace cannot be forced, just as the rules of dialogue cannot be imposed. We cannot control the other in dialogue; the little control we have, however, is over ourselves. What is at stake in dialogue is our openness to religious otherness, our effort to understand and respect the religious system and experience of the Hindu or Muslim partner, in the full affirmation of our own faith and identity. Here, compromises do not exist.

A second danger related to the opposition between spirituality and religion is to believe in a universal spirituality beyond all religious belonging to which everybody would join sooner or later. This would be the pretext to call every religious leader to promote peace without paying attention to local and contextual problems and concerns. A spirituality of dialogue rejects such an opposition between spirituality and religion. It does not yield to the temptation that consists of believing that religion is an obstacle to dialogue, and spirituality its solution. On the contrary, religious structure can offer an important support in helping dialogue last and progress, whereas circles known as the most spiritual sometimes sustain rivalries and unhealthy tensions.

A spirituality of dialogue does not aim at the fusion of interacting religious systems or at the creation of a universal spirituality beyond all religious structure. It does not promote a unique and abstract truth that every believer should adopt, whatever his or her religion. If a dialogue lived at the spiritual level is considered promising, it is neither because it requires ignoring religious doctrines and structures of one's partner, nor because one minimizes the fact that they are different from ours. It is because these religious doctrines and structures are considered seriously and rooted in the effort to reconnect with the divine mystery in which they find their raison d'être.

A spirituality of dialogue takes seriously religious systems while opening them to the unlimited and uncontrolled presence of God. This prevents all risk of absolutism. Hence, religious systems are kept incomplete, therefore always open to dialogue, and to mutual understanding and enrichment.

SPIRITUALITY AND POLITICAL CONCERN

It is perilous to think that spirituality has nothing to do with political concern, or that it leads necessarily to peace and harmony. True, spirituality is the driving force allowing religion to accomplish its goal of peace—peace understood, however, not as an absence of war, but as liberation or salvation, a fullness transcending both the visible and invisible worlds.

Now, this liberation has an individual aspect as well as a collective aspect, and implies, to some extent, a fight. There is the fight within, the battle of Jacob against the angel, and there is also the fight without, a fight for social justice and liberation. Both of these battles go together. Even though the call for liberation is universal, it is always rooted in a specific community facing specific problems requiring specific battles for justice and freedom.

Liberation, justice, and freedom are based on the search for respect, dignity, and integrity. No one can contribute to peace without first receiving respect and dignity. When there is no respect, there is humiliation, and humiliation nourishes hatred and violence. Respect is the key condition to peace, and respect is sustained by love and humility. In many ways, respect is beyond our own capability; that is why it can be seen as a divine gift, sustained by the Holy Spirit. The divine power helps us to pay respect as well as to receive respect and dignity. This is true at the individual and collective levels.

It is not surprising, therefore, to see spiritual people, or mystics, involved in political debates, in battles and conflicts in order to fight for what they think is right, for justice and dignity. History teaches that interiority has a great impact on the organization of the city. Saint Benedict, Saint Bernard, Saint Joan of Arc, and Martin Luther are among those who have initiated great changes in social consciousness and behaviors. The more the fight for change is rooted in faith and transcending reality, the deeper the changes.

Each religion has its own understanding and vision about liberation and its process. Certainly there are similar ethics among religions, but I doubt these ethics are applied with the same logic and priorities. The idea of global peace including and involving all particular religious communities and cultural contexts is a new idea. I do not say that such an idea is impossible to concretize; I say only it is not an automatic process.

It is a demanding process that requires the participation of everyone, every partner of dialogue. In this process, one cannot avoid the step that consists of understanding with respect the doctrinal and political coherence of our partner's religious experience. We need to elaborate a new approach of religious otherness, an approach in which religious otherness is not an obstacle to the process of liberation but part of it.

CONCLUSION

I like Panikkar's idea: there is no "pluralistic religion" but only a "pluralistic attitude" toward religion.[5] This means that Christians, Muslims, and Hindus have their own conceptions of the ultimate reality, the absolute, the universal, and from their conception comes their approach to other religions. A Christian will never be fully at home among Muslims or Hindus; the Muslim never fully at home among Christians and Hindus, and so on. However, each of them can choose to practice hospitality, to welcome the religious otherness, and to develop this approach within their own tradition and from their own categories.

As far as Christians are concerned, they are called to apply Jesus's commandment in a new way: to love their enemies. In Christian history, enemies par excellence have been members of other religious traditions and heretics, those who prayed and believed in a different way. Christians are called to receive others in their hearts with what is important to them: their faith, beliefs, hopes, and deepest aspirations. This can be done only if we accept the connection between religion, politics, and spirituality.

It is much easier to deal with political concerns in interreligious dialogue when this dialogue is rooted in a spiritual perspective, supported with a spirituality of dialogue, and based on values such as faith, love, humility, and detachment. Peace does not depend on security, on building a fortress around us. Rather, it depends on faith and confidence: confidence that friendship can grow out of tensions and conflicts; confidence in the divine presence who, in her glory, transforms us and the world toward harmony; confidence that this divine presence expresses herself through unknown ways; and confidence that love awakens love, respect awakens respect, whereas too much security kills it.

However, a "pluralistic attitude" toward religions cannot be improvised. A spirituality of dialogue must be elaborated, developed, and taught. Spirituality does not lead necessarily to this attitude, and it can promote sectarian views. That is why interreligious education is so important in our societies. It is urgent that a new spiritual and religious consciousness prevail, a new consciousness based on respect and dignity. But the question still remains: are we ready to go in this direction, and to face the difficulties attached to it?

NOTES

1. See the World Council of Churches website, www.oikoumene.org.

2. Raimundo Panikkar, "Religious Identity and Pluralism," in *A Dome of Many Colors: Studies in Religious Pluralism, Identity, and Unity*, ed. Arvind Sharma and Kathleen M. Dugan (Harrisburg, PA: Trinity Press International, 1999), p. 27.

3. See Douglas Hall, *Bound and Free: A Theologian's Journey* (Minneapolis: Fortress Press, 2005), p. 112.

4. Panikkar, pp. 28–29.

5. Panikkar, p. 26.

CHAPTER 27

The Call to Unite

Debra Behrle

It is for me to speak of what I have discovered for and about myself, and, in turn, about all of life. I share this information with you and encourage you to look within your own heart to discover the interconnectedness of all life.

As individuals of humanity, we are aspects of and create the whole of humanity, a tapestry of life on planet earth. I believe it is up to us as individuals to create the qualities that benefit all life.

How, you ask? Well, I believe we can agree that there is a Universal Power greater than we are.

It is known by many names: Yahweh, Allah, God, Spirit, Krishna, Buddha, and Christ. Scientists refer to it as a high frequency unified field of energy consisting of formless waves and particles. This description is like that of the mystics and sages of the ages, who refer to it as a vast sea of tranquility and love.

Regardless of the name we choose to assign this Power, I know we are all referring to the same Power.

Perhaps we can agree that this Power to which we have assigned these names has created out of itself the form of this world and all upon it? If so, can we then agree that in order to create, there must be a conscious choice to do so?

I know that we are each aspects of this One Creative Energy that is life itself, and because we are created in its image and likeness, we, too, must have these creative characteristics. Consider then, that we are each an individual expression of this one life. Wow!

And in order to express this Creative Energy, we are each given free will, the power of choice in our lives, and in turn the appearance of diversity within the One.

Individuality must be spontaneous, it can never be automatic. This Creative Energy has planted the seed of freedom in the innermost being of each individual, yet like the Prodigal Son, we must make this discovery for ourselves.

There are many distractions in our lives, yet it is up to us, as individuals, to choose to take the time to contemplate the meaning of life and our part in it, by ourselves.

We turn to our respective religions for guidance, yet they have fallen short in their efforts to explain our deepest connections to this Creative Energy.

I believe that now is the time for all religions to focus their teachings on the spiritual truths that are common to and at the back of all religions, and to teach practical ways of applying these truths in our everyday lives. We thereby empower every individual in the realization that who they are makes a difference.

So what are these truths, and what are some of the ways in which we can apply them?

The most common spiritual truths are that this Creative Energy, or God, is

Omnipotent—has unlimited Power and Potentiality
Omniscient—knows all things
Omnipresent—is present in all places at the same time
Love—gives unconditional love, love without condition

I now remind you that we are all created in its image and likeness.

We are to this Creative Energy, known as God, as a wave is to the ocean—a part of the whole appearing separate. We are continuously connected to this source of all life.

It is our very nature.

Just as this One Creative Energy created out of itself all life through its word, we create in this same way.

We express our thoughts as words and actions; these thoughts and actions are based on our perceptions and beliefs. Our perceptions and beliefs are based on what we have been taught, our past experiences, and even the past experiences of other people who have influenced our lives.

Some of these beliefs have been with us since childhood and may no longer serve us.

We may go through life never questioning our beliefs or even realizing what they are, yet they are still operating in our lives, subconsciously affecting our thoughts, words, and actions, and creating our experiences of life now.

This affects how we view our world, our neighbors, our family, and, most importantly, ourselves.

There are many tools out there to assist us on our journey to truth, yet they all require preparing an inner inventory, as well as a willingness to look honestly at ourselves and ask the tough questions.

It is time to give ourselves permission to consciously create the life we choose to live. It is all a matter of choice. What is stopping us? Only ourselves.

We are responsible for every aspect of our lives. We determine whether the words or actions of another hurt or anger us, bring us joy or peace.

The most profound moment of my journey thus far, was when I realized that I, Debra Behrle, was an expression of this Creative Energy known as God. I had to be sure, so I opened my heart and mind and set my intention to know the truth. I researched many of the world's religions and found spiritual truths that are common to all religions jumping off the pages. I know that all paths lead to the One Source of all life.

I then asked myself, what are the qualities of this Creative Energy, or God? And how can I embody these qualities that are described by these religions in my life?

The qualities are Love, Light, Peace, Wisdom, Beauty, Joy, and Power. I decided that the best way for me to embody these qualities was to define them for myself. And so I did. I will share with you a few examples.

Love—self-givingness. It is free of condemnation, fear, and judgment. It is compassion, kindness, forgiveness, and caring. It is a feeling. It is invisible in its essence, yet apparent in its action. Love overcomes both hate and fear by the subtle power of transformation. Anything that is unlike love is a call for love.

Light—a form of energy, the first words used to call creation into form, to illuminate, to shed light, to see more clearly. "In light of" invokes awareness, to be light hearted. I am the light; how brightly do I shine?

Peace—the serenity of knowing my connection to all of life. For me, it has come by releasing others from judgment and, in turn, releasing myself from judgment. It has also come through refusing to take things personally. Instead of looking at things as right or wrong, good or bad, I choose to look at them from a viewpoint of what works for me, and what does not.

Wisdom—using knowledge wisely. We have within us all the knowledge and wisdom we could ever need; the answer to every question is within. We receive as much as we are ready to understand. As we continually seek and ask for truth, we increase our wisdom and understanding. Wisdom is to be applied and shared.

Beauty—something we see. There is beauty all around us. It is in nature, in one another, in ourselves, in every situation and circumstance. Beauty is an opportunity to be discovered in all things if we simply choose to see it.

Joy—a feeling I have when I'm inspired, when my heart is uplifted, delighted, and happy. It's the sound of a child's laughter, the chirping of the birds, a sunrise, a sunset, a windy day, the rain. We can find joy in anything and everything if we choose to see it. I choose to find joy everywhere and keep joyful thoughts in my mind.

Power—represents strength, the ability to act, and energy. It can be constructive or destructive. Power arises from meaning and has to do with motive. My power comes from the knowledge and understanding of how I create my world through my thoughts, words, and actions. Power comes also from the realization of the principles of cause and effect, the law of attraction, and the statement "it is done unto me as I believe." This inspires me to be the best that I can be. When I align myself with the Power that is God, with the motive of benefiting all involved in any given situation, all of humanity benefits.

I know that we all want peace in the world.

I invite you to now take a couple of deep cleansing breaths. Imagine peace in the world. What does it look like for you?

Is it an end to all war and conflict?
Is it to end starvation and hunger in the world?
Is it to live in harmony with nature and one another?
Is it a just and fair society? And who decides what is just and fair?
Is it to live our lives knowing we are safe?
Is it to trust and respect one another?
What does peace look like for you?
What is your part?

I know peace begins with each of us. Let us first be at peace with ourselves and with the people in our lives.

Allow yourself to stop the inner war and conflict within yourself.
Allow yourself to be fed and nourished with the truth of who and what you are, a powerful, creative, spiritual being.
Allow yourself to choose to live in harmony with nature and one another.
Allow yourself to be just and fair in all you say and do.
Allow yourself to live your life, knowing you are safe because you are one with all life.

Trust and respect yourself and all life.

When we are at peace individually, everyone with whom we come into contact benefits. Its effects ripple outward from one to the other, touching lives that we may not be aware of.

I invite you in this moment to focus on the Light, Wisdom, Power, Joy, Beauty, Peace, and Love that already exist in your life and the world, for I know what we focus on grows. This, too, is a Universal Principle.

I call you to unite in the knowing that we are all aspects and beautiful expressions of the One Creative Energy that is all life.

You already know the truth.

Allow yourself to remember!

I invite you to be the peace you choose to see in the world.

Namaste.

The divine in me honors the divine in you.

Gratitude, and rich blessings.

CHAPTER 28

Beyond Religion: A Holistic Spirituality (Alternatives to Realizing Oneself through Loving-kindness)

Mabel Aranha

What does "holistic" mean in reference to "spirituality"?

- A desire for integration and wholeness, an awareness of equality and reciprocity
- An understanding of the connections between various aspects of our reality as we know it
- A harmonious relationship for the ultimate welfare and productivity of a person and those that inhabit our universe
- A dynamic process that includes every dimension of one's life—including every object and every person that constitutes our world, and connecting us with every aspect of human development
- A religious maturity accepting human life and our earth as a gift

A holistic spirituality means an outlook that will integrate our lives sufficiently to give us a sense of increasing wholeness in order to heal the dichotomy between the human and the holy, the secular and the sacred.

A holistic spirituality starts from the premise that there are many ways to achieve peace: through prayer, social action, singing, chanting, writing good literature, painting beautiful pictures, and creating beautiful artifacts and sculptures. The greatest way is the training of the mind in love, kindness, contentment, compassion, and wisdom.

In *By Way of the Heart*, Wilkie Au, a Jesuit, says, "By way of the heart is to take a path to holiness or spirituality that is both graceful and human. It is a spirituality wherein our cold hearts of stone are replaced with warm hearts of flesh capable of loving—a transformation that calls for personal responsibility and effort. It is human because it requires the whole self—body, mind and feeling, as spiritual growth is a multifaceted process."[1] So is human growth.

Many factors contribute to violence in society. We are born with the legacy of greed, hatred, and ignorance passed down through generations, and the social and cultural consciousness of a nation or groups of people. Kids imitate adults around them because kids are still in the process of forming their identities and their sense of right and wrong. Often, they are confused by the behavior of adults—exploitation and competition at the expense of the other. If we want our children to be happy, we have to present alternatives for a happy and peaceful life.

Our understanding of the world comes to us through our senses. Our perceptions and reactions are colored or sieved through individual, family, and social legacies of the past. Conditioned patterns of living and beliefs must be constantly replaced with patterns of understanding, tolerance, and friendliness by leading the people to a place of peace within themselves, when the stress of life and their emotions overwhelm them. We use the feeling of love they are familiar with, and widen the circle of that love in boundless ripples touching most aspects of their life with the meditation of loving-kindness.

Loving-kindness is like radiating the rays of the sun in all directions; it is like the rain falling on every person and creature irrespective of who or what they are. A loving-kindness meditation helps us put loving-kindness into practice. When we are constantly sending love, a transformation of the consciousness is initiated. We will not fight or say harsh words. We will not harm or plan to harm others. Loving-kindness understands one's own suffering and through that experience understands the suffering of others. It is a mental attitude that does not want us or others to suffer. Loving-kindness is the beginning stage of compassion. A person of compassion wants all beings to have everything they wish for. The main idea is that all beings must have happiness and the causes for happiness.

Based on a scheme from Donald Goergen, used by Wilkie Au to explain "A Holistic Christian Spirituality," I have attempted to create a framework for the practice of loving-kindness within a holistic spirituality. According to it, the practice of loving-kindness, known as *metta* in Pali and *maitrī* in Sanskrit, can be divided into

1. Self sphere
2. Family sphere
3. Friend/Foe sphere
4. Community and the Mediator sphere

Within this holistic framework, self-love must be looked at first. Self-esteem is primary because all other healthy love springs from it. This love is different from the egoistic or narcissistic love of oneself; it is a love that accepts the humanity within us, whenever or wherever we come across it. Embracing the totality of who we are gradually helps us accept the totality of others and the worth of us all. By understanding our pain, our success, our joys, and our need to be happy, we understand the pain and needs of all beings.

Self-denial and self-hatred block us from loving others, and such self-rejection often leads to rejection of the sacred in us and other people. Self-denial is not a negation, but an understanding that we are more than what we think we are, and recognition of the inherent goodness, which is our true Self. Wishing for our own well-being is the root of the wish for the well-being of all beings.

The family, which is the cornerstone of society, is the cradle of love, for here it is that we see the pure love, the unconditional love of a mother and a father for a child, for whom they are willing to give up everything to nurture and keep safe from harm. Love that makes us whole usually begins with our family.

Leisure for all, including parents, must be a component of family life to avoid conflicts, resentments, and the feeling of helplessness. It is necessary to give each member a certain amount of space, time, and opportunity for responsibility, interests, and creativity to flourish and be fulfilled.

Healthy family life must strike a balance between fostering intimacy within the home and developing life-enhancing ties outside domestic walls. We all have known the value of friends and the attachment we have for them. Good friends are like the summer roses, whose fragrance makes the garden smell sweeter. We love our friends but have to use a certain amount of discernment in our friendships. Discernment and discretion distinguish between right and wrong associations and lead to wisdom.

Our reaction to those who are not our friends—a picky boss or spiteful colleagues—is a story we are familiar with. They are also part of our lives, and we need to use the same discernment not to bring on suffering for ourselves and others. If there is a problem, send loving-kindness to a hostile person. Try to persist or leave it aside for the moment and come back to it later. When there is no distinction, we truly radiate kindness.

Our community today is far beyond the little village or town in which we were born. It includes all those who inhabit the planet. Mindless actions in one part of the country or the world have tremendous consequences thousands of miles away. Too much in one place means too little in another. Misuse of mother earth and her exploitation bring about tremendous loss of life in the remotest parts of the globe. We have to understand our needs are the same as the needs of those living in other parts of the world.

All of us deserve to live with sufficient means and achieve happiness. Yet it takes just a few thoughts to convey our empathy and feel the unity in our innermost being. We are able to make this connection through loving-kindness meditation. Sending vibrations of love and friendliness can heal the world and ourselves. Practicing it often will work at the innermost cellular structure of the body, making us truly happy.

LOVING-KINDNESS MEDITATION

We will do a simple loving-kindness meditation. Because of lack of space, we will not follow the pattern in the book, which gives readers a greater understanding of the practice.

The meditation is divided into four parts. When we first introduce the meditation, we do some reflection on the part we are going to meditate.

1. Myself, my parents, my children, relatives, and teachers
2. Friendly persons, indifferent persons, and unfriendly persons
3. Beings in our country, the world, and the universe
4. All living creatures

Sit quietly with your spine straight, eyes closed gently, and hands in your lap. Try to be as relaxed as possible. Send all your tensions through the windows at least for the next twenty minutes. Concentrate on good thoughts. Take three deep inhalations and exhalations.

THE FIRST GROUP

Ia: Reflections on Myself

> I suffer from discomfort, pain, and sickness. I am hard on myself because I want everything to be perfect according to my wishes. I suffer when I cannot get the things I want. I also suffer when I get what I do not want or have to give up what I have. I have faults, but only if I love myself, I can accept myself as I am, and that will make me happy. That will help me to accept others and to come to love others. So, I send loving-kindness to myself.

Now I send loving-kindness to myself, accepting fully all that I am. Let the feeling of warmth and radiance start from my heart and flow through my whole body.

Ib: Meditation of Loving-kindness for Myself

May I be well, happy, and peaceful
May I be free from every harm
May I be free from difficulties
May I have patience and courage
To overcome anger and suffering
And have success in all that I do

IIa: Reflections on My Family

> My parents worked hard to make a home, give me the things I needed, and good values. I think they did the best they could for me, but sometimes I do not agree with them. My parents suffer, too. My brothers and sisters have the same needs, desires, and ambition that I have. This brings conflict in the family. If I try to understand that in some ways they are different and unique, like myself, and send love and kindness to them, I can find a way of making myself peaceful and making them happy, too. If I understand that we all suffer, it will make it easier for me to make allowances for the members of my family and my relatives.

Now send loving-kindness to family members, accepting all that they are. Let the feeling of warmth and radiance start from the heart and flow toward each of them.

IIb: Meditation of Loving-kindness for My Family

May my family be happy and peaceful
May they be free from every harm
May they be free from difficulties

May they have patience and courage
To overcome anger and suffering
And have success in all that they do

At this point, we can extend our love to our children, relatives, and teachers, with the appropriate reflection on their lives and their suffering, and be grateful to them for what we have received.

THE SECOND GROUP

IIIa: Reflections on Friendly Persons at School or Work

We know we suffer, and sometimes we know why we suffer. Our friends suffer, too. Start with good thoughts about a friend and send him/her loving-kindness, then include all those with whom you have had good times or who have helped you when you were sad or were in difficulties. However, we should not do things that are not right just because we love them. If anyone is sick, send extra love.

Being thankful, we send loving-kindness to them. True love is wishing for their ultimate happiness.

IIIb: Meditation of Loving-kindness for Friendly Persons

May friendly persons be happy and peaceful
May they be free from every harm
May they be free from difficulties
May they have patience and courage
To overcome anger and suffering
And have success in all that they do

IVa: Reflections on Indifferent Persons

There are many people who pass us by on the streets, in trains and buses, in buildings, and on the highways. Although we do not know them, they suffer because they have the same legacy we have. They also have the same potential for goodness. Until our craving and ill will toward others is eliminated, we will be ignorant of our true self and we will suffer.

With increasing compassion in our hearts, let us send loving-kindness to indifferent people we meet. You can send loving-kindness to people who are neutral but help you in your life, such as the letter carrier, store attendant, newspaper carrier, grocery attendants, garbage collectors, bank officials, and others.

IVb: Meditation of Loving-kindness for Indifferent Persons

May indifferent persons be happy and peaceful
May they be free from every harm

May they be free from difficulties
May they have patience and courage
To overcome anger and suffering
And have success in all that they do

Va: Reflections on Unfriendly Persons at School or Work

We would like everyone in our life to love us. If we do not do that, how can we expect everyone to be friendly to us? People have different ways of behaving with people. Sometimes our friends turn against us, or people who do not seem to like us are not friendly to us. Perhaps we have given them cause at some time without knowing it, or they are doing it out of ignorance without paying attention to the hurt they cause. We should calm ourselves, and think of the harm and suffering they bring on themselves. If we change this bad result into a good cause by sending kind feelings, we get more credit and ensure our greater happiness in the future.

With the constant practice of sending loving-kindness to those who hurt us, we will not have any enemies. Even if they try to harm us, it will not offend us so much the next time we feel hurt.

Vb: Meditation of Loving-kindness for Unfriendly Persons

May unfriendly persons be happy and peaceful
May they be free from every harm
May they be free from difficulties
May they have patience and courage
To overcome anger and suffering
And have success in all that they do

THE THIRD GROUP

VIa: Reflections on Beings in My Country

We have people of different states and nationalities living in our country. They follow different religions and come from various cultures. We all want enough food, drink, clothing, and shelter, and good air to breathe. Some are hungry and unemployed; others have no shelter or clothing. Some are addicted to drugs and alcohol and cannot think of the consequences of their actions. Some suffer because of floods, earthquakes, natural disasters, or terrorist actions. Every human being wants caring and loving.

Let us send loving-kindness to all the infants and all the people in our country that they may be loved, that their wishes may be met, and that they may be able to live without hurting each other.

VIb: Meditation of Loving-kindness for All Beings in My Country

May all beings in my country be happy and peaceful
May they be free from every harm

May they be free from difficulties
May they have patience and courage
To overcome anger and suffering
And have success in all that they do

VIIa: Reflections on Beings in Our World

In our world, there are people of many cultures we know nothing about. Some people live on hills and mountains and in dense forests. Whatever they are—rich or poor; white, brown, yellow or black; advanced, underdeveloped, or primitive; with resources or trying hard to make a living—all go through wanting, sickness, ageing, and death. The desire to want more and more than we need is a sickness. We suffer because we cannot get the things we want. If we do get them, we are satisfied for brief intervals, but our lack of satisfaction is a permanent state in our life.

Let us think of the suffering of the people in the world, make a wish that everyone will have what they need, including ourselves, and send loving-kindness.

VIIb: Meditation of Loving-kindness for All Beings in the World

May all beings in the world be happy and peaceful
May they be free from every harm
May they be free from difficulties
May they have patience and courage
To overcome anger and suffering
And have success in all that they do

THE FOURTH GROUP

Let us visualize the creatures of the universe, and then follow it with a loving-kindness meditation.

VIIIa: Reflection on Creatures

Imagine you are transformed into a snow-white dove with beautiful, silver-tipped wings and a heart of gold. Golden rays of loving-kindness are streaming from your heart. You gently lift yourself and are now flying through the air. As you fly over the lakes, seas, and oceans, you see the most beautiful creatures in the waters. Their life appears peaceful, but it is full of danger. Now we fly over the meadows, woods, and forests. There are all kinds of creatures, small as the ant and big as the elephant. Some have to hide from other animals, which may eat them; others are hungry and thirsty and have to travel long distances to get food and water; many are cold, sick, ageing, and dying. We see that creatures of the air have the same difficulties. We return back to the city. Dogs and cats are homeless and are scrounging for food. We see some animals ill treated by their masters, and horses and oxen that are overworked.

Send loving-kindness to all creatures of the world, including our pets, that they may have good lives.

VIIIb: Meditation of Loving-kindness for All Creatures in the World

May all creatures in the world be happy and peaceful
In the sea and in the air
On the land and everywhere
May they have patience and courage
To overcome danger and suffering
And live in harmony all the time.

The benefits of a wishing prayer cannot be seen. The results of purely mental activities are not visible immediately, yet the extent of their power is very great. The conditioned walls of our own prison gradually break down, and we experience a freedom of mind and spirit.

A **loving-kindness meditation** can be done during the day in parts or when we face a particular situation before we react to it. We will become calm and do our work with more energy. Our perceptions of others will gradually change. It does not have to be in a structured order. It can be done while standing, walking, playing, or driving, and it is recommended to be done when we start our day or before going to sleep. By teaching children a loving-kindness meditation, teachers, parents, and significant others can replace disintegration with integration, hatred with love, brokenness with wholeness, and division with unity in their lives.

NOTE

1. Wilkie Au, *By Way of the Heart: Toward a Holistic Christian Spirituality* (Mahwah, NJ: Paulist Press, 1991), p. 3.

CHAPTER 29

Healing Consciousness

Laj Utreja

Just as there is more to religion than just faith, there is more to healing than just medicine. The well-being of the human being involves the health of body, mind, and soul in recognition of the fact that the human being is a spirituo-psycho-physical organism, and all three of these components of a human being need to be given full recognition. It may not be a question of mind over matter, or vice versa, so much as one of taking care of both mind and body simultaneously. More importantly, intentional pursuit of spiritual practices has an additional benefit of providing clarity of purpose, and therefore, it helps orient the person toward suitable goals while providing concentration and focus for mundane activities. Medicine may or may not address these important parameters simultaneously, but healing must.

The use of prayer and visits to places of worship to improve health were a common practice in Āyurveda dating back thousands of years. While many diagnostic and therapeutic tools of modern medicine were not available during those times, the use of spiritual practices in addition to Āyurvedic medicine provided a way for Āyurveda practitioners to approach care for patients.[1] The use of spirituality in treating patients, lacking in the modern practice of medicine, recognized the need for holistic healing to restore health to normalcy. The human body comprises three bodies: a physical body, a subtle (thinking and feeling) body, and a causal (spiritual) body in the context of Āyurveda.[2] The entire body is considered in need of healing if any one of these bodies deviates from its normal state.

THE HUMAN BODY AND ITS MALADIES

Physical Body

We can perceive only the physical body, including the outer cover called skin, which encloses the physical senses of perception, organs of action, and a complex physiology comprising the central nervous system, respiratory system, cardiovascular system, digestive system, and reproductive system. The main function of the physical body is to perform actions toward some intended goals that are in the physical consciousness, and undertake some free-will goals of unknown origin. We become aware of the physical body in the waking state.

Subtle Body

The subtle body includes the mind, intellect, and the subtle senses of perception. The presence of subtle body is felt when we may be seemingly looking at an object, but our mind is somewhere else so that we are not able to perceive that object. We become aware of the subtle body as we wake up from a dreaming state. No life is possible without a subtle body, or the mind. The main function of the subtle body is to provide a storage area for all intentions, thoughts, feelings, and emotions. All that is intended, or is thought of, may be manifested. Whereas the mind is endowed with a capacity to reflect on events and experiences, analyze experiences, and feel emotions of pleasure and pain, the intellect guides one to discriminate between right and wrong. There are various levels of subtle consciousness that are associated with the physical consciousness on one end and the causal consciousness on the other.

Causal Body

The causal body is comprised of the soul, which carries the primal intention to know the supporting consciousness. Its presence is felt when a person begins to dream from the state of dreamless sleep. It is the cause of the subtle body and the physical body. The results of actions performed by the human beings are felt by the causal consciousness. The causal body, along with the subtle body with the intention of the last thought, called *consciotron*, separate from the physical body at death.[3] Under appropriate space and time conditions, the *consciotron* manifests into a physical expression. The grosser elements possess the knowledge of their preservation, as well as the knowledge of the group order.

There are three maladies inside the body that control and regulate physiological, psychological, and emotional activities of the body. According to Āyurveda, these maladies are called *vāta, kapha, and pitta* (*vkp*). The constituent nature of a particular body is sustained when these maladies are in harmony, and the body is in good physical, mental, and emotional health. But when the maladies are not in harmony, the constituent nature is thrown out of balance, and the body experiences physical sickness, mental sickness, or emotional sickness.

Spiritual ignorance, clouded intellect, disturbed mind, and fatigued or unhealthy body, or any combination thereof, compromises the soul's innate quality to stay connected to the source (sheer joy or bliss). There are techniques that prepare the human body to achieve a state of awareness to realize the state of well-being within the confines of its condition and its environment. Ultimately, the awareness begins to break the bonds of ignorance that lead to the state of happiness.

ĀYURVEDA

Āyurveda deals with the functional and structural elements of a human being, the state of health and diseases that alter that state, and methods to balance the functional elements for health. According to Āyurveda, *svasthaya* (health) comprises *Sva*, or self-normalcy (it covers the psychosomatic well-being of a person), and *Sthaya*, or state of staying. Sushruta (one of the earliest Āyurveda practitioners) maintained that self-normalcy not only comprises psychosomatics but also includes spiritual awareness. Correspondingly, health implies a state of spirituo-psycho-physical well-being of a person. In other words, health is called the natural state of all three aspects of the human body (normal function of the physical organs, calmness of mind, and spiritual awareness).

The ancient Seers saw the universe as the macrocosm and human beings as the microcosm. Human beings are made from food, and the body grows by the constant intake of food. Both are evolved from their subtle (unstable-element) states expressed in gross (stable-element) states. Human beings are made up of five gross elements that express themselves with their qualities. Space is the field where matter acts with its quality of containing matter. Air is the gaseous state, with the quality of motion. Fire is the combustible state of both solids and liquids, with the quality of purifying any substance. Water is the liquid state, with the quality of flexing when subjected to external force. Earth is the solid state, with the qualities of rigidity and stability.

The five gross elements are represented as three functional elements, called *dośas* (defects) in the human body. As stated before, they are *vkp* and govern the physiological functions of the body. *Vāta* constitutes space and air, is dry, anabolic, light, and cool. *Kapha* is made up of water and earth, is oily, catabolic, heavy, and cool. *Pitta* is made from fire, is sharp, oily, light, and hot. Each *dośa* dominates in a specific region of the body. The functions of *vāta* are respiration, movement, and evacuation, and it dominates below the navel. The functions of *kapha* are lubrication, joint integrity, and virility, and it dominates in the chest and head. The functions of *pitta* are digestion, metabolism, and appetite, and it dominates in the middle region of the body. Any disturbance of the proportion of *vkp* in a human body causes disease.

Each human being comes with a certain *Prakṛti* (nature) at the time of birth. Nature is the psychosomatic constitution of a person determined by the combination and proportion of the three functional elements, *vkp*. At the moment of conception, genetics, lifestyle, and emotions of the parents determine each person's psychosomatic constitution. This does not change during one's lifetime, except in very rare cases. The equilibrium of the psychosomatic elements is called health.

As a person interacts with the environment through diet, habits, and attitudes, there is a change in the *vkp* proportion of psychosomatic elements leading to the current state of health, or *vikṛti*. In a person of excellent health, the proportions of psychosomatic elements in *vikṛti* are the same as in *Prakṛti*. But more likely, there will be a difference, for *vikṛti* reflects all aspects of diet, lifestyle, age, environment, and emotions that are not in harmony with *Prakṛti*. *Roga* (illness or disease) is disequilibrium of the psychosomatic elements. Disease is the lack of balance among the three somatic elements of *vkp*. The difference between *vikṛti* and *Prakṛti* can be restored or established by the principles of Āyurveda by an Āyurvedic practitioner through a variety of procedures such as taking life history, analyzing the face and tongue, and taking a pulse. That is called healing. *Vikṛti* emanates from *Prakṛti* and in the end dissolves in it. Similarly, disease springs from health and again moves to attain the state of *Prakṛti*.

The food consumed gets converted to seven structural elements, called *dhātus* (substances) of the body, which act as hosts to the three functional elements mentioned above. These are as follows in the order of formation: *Rasa* (plasma), *Rakta* (blood), *Māṁsa* (muscle), *Medas* (fat), *Asthi* (bone and cartilage), *Majjā* (bone marrow,) and *Śukra* (reproductive fluid). *Śukra* produces *ojas* (the fluid that also generates aura), which provides immunity. The bones are host to *vāta*, the blood is host to *pitta*, and the rest of the *dhātus* (plasma, muscle, fat, bone marrow, and seminal fluid) are host to *kapha*. The increase or decrease of *dhātus* affects the body with a physical condition that is treated by bringing *dośa* in control. The excess of *dośas* in the *dhātus* is discarded as three *malas* (wastes) from the body. The excess of *vāta* from the bones is represented by the growth of nails and hair, the excess of *vāta* and *pitta* by feces, the excess of *pitta* from the blood and *kapha* from the fat by sweat, and the excess of *kapha* from the plasma by urine.

Pitta is the manifestation of *Agni* (fire element in the body) that transforms food into energy. All metabolic diseases are produced as a result of impairment of *Agni*. *Agni* is present in all the *dhātus*, especially in the stomach. A normal-functioning *Agni* keeps *dośas* normal. It is the chief protector of the body. An impaired *Agni* puts *dośas* in imbalance, resulting in *vikṛti*. Food, activity, or stress disturbs *Agni*. Improperly digested food results in *Amā* (toxin), the cause of disease. All *dośas* depend upon *dhātus*. Any symptom of disease is expressed in *dhātus* that brings imbalance in the *dośas*. The treatment is done to bring *dośas* in balance.

If you visit an Āyurvedic practitioner, he will first determine your *Prakṛti*. On the basis of the symptoms from the *dhātus*, he would look for off-balance *dośas*. He would make a prognosis based on vitiated *dośas* and any accompanying complications. His knowledge would help him decide whether the condition is curable, controllable, and/or maintainable. Then he will suggest a treatment based on food and medicine. Medicines are either oils or decoctions made from herbs. They can be in tablet form, powder form, or made with alcohol as a preservative. The Āyurvedic treatment is holistic in the sense that it heals the body, mind, and soul. Therefore, a knowledgeable practitioner may prescribe chanting of specific mantras, meditation, and visits to holy places for the well-being of the patient.

HEALING CONSCIOUSNESS

Healing Consciousness (HC) is an approach to bringing to awareness our inherent characteristic of being happy and complete. Whereas happiness is tied to fulfillment of an objective or achievement of a goal, completeness is a synonym for a state of accomplishment devoid of mistakes and failures in the process or path of a pursuit. When thinking is clear and no universal values are compromised, there is no basis for mistakes or sickness, and no impediments to pursuits. Good health is one of the key elements necessary for our well-being leading to the state of happiness. HC allows one to develop a sense of well-being by following a lifestyle that finds a basis in many cultures but is mostly ignored. The term *well-being* is here used to imply a state of effectiveness in any situation of health or sickness.

HC begins from the basic understanding of who we are, in order to recognize the importance of being in harmony with the environment and to prepare us to develop a sense of what a healthy body, calm mind, and a sharp intellect can do to develop our unrealized potential. It allows us to choose and be an effective participant based on our respective natures and acquired skills in a world of information overload. It heightens our awareness to discriminate and use discretion for actions in life that are conducive to maintain a healthy body and a cool mind that, in turn, may provide feedback to develop awareness of what the body and mind may need for sustained happiness. The sense of well-being is developed through a set of disciplined actions that allow one to activate the body's natural healing processes.

There is no active regimen or therapy, and in that sense, HC is not a prescriptive form of either modern or alternative medicine. It is best described as a collection of disciplinary tools that, with practice, add up to a state of well-being. It draws upon a variety of traditions for the well-being of the total body. For physical well-being, it draws from (1) specific Yoga postures, contributing to muscle toning, and circulation of blood in the body with specific Yoga aerobics, and (2) a vegetarian and wholesome diet from Āyurvedic schools for physical health. For physical and mental well-being, it prescribes Prāṇāyāma (the art of breathing) to stimulate the five vital airs in the body. For mental and causal well-being, it suggests chanting of healing words, listening to healing tunes, practicing *dhyāna* (meditation), and visiting places of natural healing.

Certain Yoga postures for aerobics provide endurance for breathing. *Sūrya Namaskāra* is a cycle of ten Yoga postures repeated in succession. It gives combined benefits of posture and aerobics when repeated in a prescribed sequence. Some other postures regulate and stimulate the endocrine glands. Some postures prepare the physical body for Prāṇāyāma and *dhyāna*. Yoga postures discipline the mind and the intellect, to bring these to a state of equanimity and allow one to be in harmony with one's environment.

Disciplined breathing of air (Prāṇāyāma) is an important principle of HC. This action alone allows one to achieve and maintain a basic level of physical and mental health. It rejuvenates body cells to continue doing what they are supposed to do. The control of breath controls the fluctuations of mind. It brings to the surface the interior wisdom that is dulled through actions born of passion, anger, and delusion. It promotes concentration and focus. The mind is restless and hard to control. However, it can be trained to attain calmness by constant practice and freedom from desire as discussed earlier.

Sound or vibration is the initial object of manifestation. The words we hear are so powerful that they leave permanent impressions on our minds. The chanting of certain words invokes certain cosmic powers that provide harmony with the environment. Listening to certain sounds is conducive to calming the mind and making it ready for meditation. "Sound or vibration is the most powerful force in the universe. Music is a divine art to be used not only for pleasure, but as a path to God realization . . . communion and ecstatic joy and through them healing of body, mind, and soul."[4] Healing sounds and certain mantra chants in concert with certain Yoga postures provide healing of body and mind, and through them, one may experience the very state of bliss.

By consistent *dhyāna* (deep meditation), one can make one's mind free from desires that make it restless and inconsistent, and thus realize the self within, a silent witness of it all. *Dhyāna* is the process of developing awareness of who we are and of our constituent natures. Each one of us can be one with the self within own constitutive natures, which is the same for all. Then there is no distinction between the knower, the knowledge, and the known, just as a red-hot iron ball in a kiln loses its distinction from the heat of the red-hot oven. Visiting places of natural healing brings an awareness of oneness with the environment and our creator.

A specific Āyurvedic diet is palatable as well as suitable for all constituent natures and has a balancing effect. The constitutive elements of the human body as well as food are the same. The food selected must maintain normal functioning of the gastric fire as well as keep the constitutive nature in balance. Cooking for HC emphasizes that the food must be cooked and seasoned to provide taste, digestion, and nutrition. It encompasses healing of body, mind, and spirit through diet, digestion, and rejuvenation.

The purpose of HC is to assist all people in developing a sense of awareness of well-being and thereby attain that state and the resulting happiness. It does so through diet and integration of a variety of techniques that may augment a person's constitutive nature. Continuous practice of HC principles allows one to become aware of one's constituent nature, contributing to and affected by the underlying causes of imbalance in the body or the mind, if any. The body generally possesses self-healing capacities and interior wisdom in responding to emotional and imbalance-causing situations. The HC stimulates and reactivates compromised healing capacity and suppressed wisdom. The HC includes many of the disciplines described above. However, one of the disciplines, Prāṇāyāma is the most important and is described below.

PRĀṆĀYĀMA (SCIENCE OF BREATH REGULATION)

Prāṇā is universal energy, which is the source of all manifestation. It is harnessed as bio-energy in manifested life. It is the very medium through which matter and mind are linked to consciousness and hence pervades as corresponding energy in all manifestations: spiritual, mental, and physical. It acts in unison with consciousness. It moves in the form of vibrations wherever consciousness moves. It stops wherever consciousness is focused. According to Yoga philosophy, when the breath is still, prāṇā is still and consciousness is still. All vibrations come to an end. As the breath moves to any part of the body, so does prāṇā and consciousness. Control of the flow of prāṇā helps control the mind and therefore leads to concentration and awareness about oneself.

In Prāṇāyāma, *āyāma* refers to regulation and control. During Prāṇāyāma, breath is regulated and modified. A well-regulated breath can control the fluctuations of the mind. It brings to the surface the interior wisdom that is dulled from actions born of passion, anger, and delusion. It promotes concentration and focus. Prāṇāyāma is the fourth stage after *yamas* (consisting of the five self-restraints: nonviolence, truth, honesty, sexual control, and non-possessiveness), *niyamas* (consisting of the five rules to observed: physical and mental cleanliness, contentment, austerity, scriptural study, and self-surrender), and *āsanas* (consisting of postures) in the Patañjali's eight limbs of Rāja Yoga, leading to meditation for the spiritual journey. These disciplines are necessary if one really wants to pursue meditation.

Not only is Prāṇāyāma one of the necessary and the most effective tools for meditation, its constant practice promotes the well-being of a person. It is by far the most basic and important discipline for disease-free, healthy living. In addition, some Prāṇāyāma exercises raise and then lower the heart rate and blood pressure, much like aerobic exercises. These exercises relax our muscles and oxygenate the blood, so we think better after Prāṇāyāma. However, a warning must be given: Prāṇāyāma is very powerful. It should never be attempted without expert guidance. There are a variety of benefits achieved by practicing Prāṇāyāma.

There are five manifestations of prāṇā in human body, of which two are important. One is prāṇā that is seated in the heart and is the uplifting prānic current. Prāṇā travels upward along the spine. It causes inhalation and is generated by the process of inhalation. It controls cortical functions. The second is *apāna*, which is seated in the anus and is the descending prānic current. *Apāna* flows down the spine. It causes exhalation and is generated by exhalation. It controls the elimination functions. It is clear then that breathing is a manifestation of the universal energy, prāṇā.

There are specific *āsanas* recommended for Prāṇāyāma. Some of these postures are *siddhāsana, padmāsana,* and *vajrāsana. Siddhāsana* has a calming effect on the nervous system and helps in maintaining spinal steadiness during meditation. *Padmāsana* is the most effective posture for meditation while maintaining physical, mental, and emotional balance. *Vajrāsana* is beneficial posture for those with knee pain and sciatica.

Stages of Prāṇāyāma

Prāṇāyāma is practiced through several breathing exercises, each with its own benefit and effectiveness. In order to carry this out successfully, it is important to know the four stages of breathing:

- *Pūraka* (controlled inhalation): a process of drawing air in a smooth and continuous manner during a single inhalation
- *Antar Kumbhaka* (inner retention): a deliberate stoppage of the flow of air and retention of air in the lungs
- *Recaka* (controlled exhalation): the process of expelling air out in a smooth and continuous manner during a single exhalation
- *Bāhya Kumbhaka* (outer retention): a deliberate pause to keep the air out before a new inhalation begins

Types of Prāṇāyāma

After one begins to have some control on the four stages of breathing, one moves on to the advanced practices of Prāṇāyāma. Some of these are

- *Nāḍī Śodhana Prāṇāyāma* (alternate nostril breathing). Performing *Pūraka* and *Recaka* from alternate nostrils with *Antar Kumbhaka* and *Bāhya Kumbhaka* is *Nāḍī Śodhana.* It is very effective for concentration and meditation.
- *Ujjayī Prāṇāyāma* (throat-snoring breathing). Performing *Recaka* keeping the mouth closed while making a snoring sound at the throat during *Pūraka* is *Ujjayī.* It has a tremendous impact on calming the mind and regulating blood pressure.

- *Bhastrikā Prāṇāyāma* (bellows breathing). Performing *Pūraka* and *Recaka* continuously with full force is called *Bhastrikā*. It is a very good exercise for respiratory and coronary ailments and helps lower blood pressure.
- *Kapālabhāti Prāṇāyāma* (contracting-tummy breathing). Performing only *Recaka* with full force and letting *Pūraka* happen naturally is called *Kapālabhāti*. It is the most effective exercise to bring a natural glow and beauty to the face.
- *Bhrāmarī Prāṇāyāma* (nasal-snoring breathing). Performing *Recaka* (keeping the ears plugged and the mouth closed) while making the buzzing bee sound after *Pūraka* is *Bhrāmarī*. It helps alleviate anger, anxiety, and tension, and correspondingly lowers blood pressure.

In order to illustrate the efficacy of Prāṇāyāma in treating the state of *vikṛti* introduced because of a certain lifestyle, anatomic defects, or environmental impact, two case histories are discussed below.

The first case demonstrates the effect of Prāṇāyāma in treating a chronic case of an anatomic defect. A forty-five-year-old Asian female had suffered[5] from spells of sporadic hypotension, palpitations, typical chest pain, dizziness, weakness, and prostration for ten years. The symptoms were exacerbated in the summer of 2003, involving admission to an emergency room. A complete medical checkup, including cardiac work and a neuroendocrine examination, revealed a prolapsed mitral valve with moderate mitral incontinence. Regular practice of *Nāḍī Śodhana* (heart and lungs) and *Kapālabhāti Prāṇāyāma* had a significant effect on her cardiovascular, respiratory, and neuroendocrine functioning, including reversal of mitral regurgitation.

Another case is an application of Prāṇāyāma at high altitudes.[6] Two test cases were examined to determine the effect of *Nāḍī Śodhana Prāṇāyāma* in avoiding symptoms associated with high altitudes. In one case, regular practice of *Nāḍī Śodhana* (lungs) prevented occurrence of any of the known symptoms associated with High Altitude Sickness (HAS) and Acute Mountain Sickness (AMS) up to an altitude of 18,600 feet. In the other case, only fifteen minutes of *Nāḍī Śodhana Prāṇāyāma* (lungs) alleviated all symptoms associated with HAS at an altitude of approximately 16,000 feet and brought oxygen saturation and heart rate to normal levels.

BENEFITS OF HEALING CONSCIOUSNESS

The benefits of HC are harvested in the development of awareness of one's total well-being. HC prepares the user to explore one's unrealized potential. Its continuous practice maintains a healthy mind by building immunity against disease. In addition, it develops a calm mind by reducing overexcitement, single pointedness of thought, and freedom from unnecessary pursuits; it helps maintain a sharp intellect by intensifying discrimination and discretion; and it heightens spiritual awareness by developing willpower. There are a variety of benefits achieved by practicing HC techniques:

- Raises awareness about one's constitutive nature
- Maintains body's life processes and balance
- Fights laziness and inertia

- Promotes endurance and resistance against fatigue, thereby reducing the impact of stress
- Strengthens metabolism and endocrine gland function
- Alleviates anxiety, calms nerves, and keeps emotional balance, thereby increasing work productivity
- Develops concentration and memory

One begins to develop a good understanding of one's goals based on one's constituent nature and acquired skills so that one can pursue one's ambitions with understanding and ease. Above all, one's mind begins to lessen the evil tendencies such as lust, anger, greed, attachment, jealousy, malice, envy, pride, enmity, pride, and fear. And that provides access to inner powers, leading to spiritual awareness and closeness to the source.

Consistent practice of HC principles connects participants at the level of the spirit. It prepares one to accept thoughts different from one's own, and therefore broadens understanding. It allows one to listen to the other without any bias toward other faiths or traditions. Consequently, teaching and discussion of HC offers one of the most effective methods for the transformation of minds.[7]

* * *

Some preliminary requirements for initiation into Yoga are as follows:

- A healthy and pure body
- Pure and simple food (vegetarian)
- A rational faith, a zeal for knowledge, and purity in thought
- Skill in postures or exercises
- Breath control

Many regard Yoga as nothing more than the last two. But these are only the external means of Yoga conducive to purity of body. It is only after these stages have been realized that Yoga proper begins.

The eight scientific steps of Yoga are these:

1. **Moral Observances.** These consist of five commandments:
   Nonviolence: Let all cease to bear malice to any living being and all animals with no exception to any, let him always love all. Eating of flesh of any kind is most sinful as it leads to the killing of God's innocent creatures.
   Truthfulness: Let all practice truth, discriminating between right and wrong. It consists in acquiring knowledge of the nature, properties, and characteristics of all things from earth to God, in assiduously obeying God's commandments and worshiping him, in never going against his will, and in making nature subservient to oneself.
   Honesty: Let none ever commit theft, and let all be honest in their dealings.
   Self-control: Let all practice self-control; never be lustful.
   Humility: Let all be humble, never vain.

2. **Physical Discipline.** This consists of another five commandments:
   Purification: Renounce all passions and vicious desires, externally by the free use of water, for example.
   Contentment: Work hard righteously but neither rejoice in the resulting profit nor be sorrowful in the case of loss. Renounce sloth and be always cheerful and active.
   Austerity: Keep the mind unruffled whether in happiness or misery, and do righteous deeds.
   Self-Study: Study the books of true knowledge, and teach them as well, and associate with good and pious men, and contemplate on and mentally recite OM (God), which is the highest name of the Supreme Spirit.
   Devotion: Let all resign their souls to the will of God.

   These ten commandments are important not only in Yoga but also in life, providing for the support of life itself. Without them there can be no progress whether individually or socially, for character is built out of them. Whether one believes in God or not, the observance of morals is essential, because without them nobody, not even a scientist or a scholar or a genius, can be called a true human being. Without observing morals, there can be no control of the mind. And, as the aim of Yoga is mind control, morals must be observed.

   Many aspirants have fallen by the wayside because they did not pay sufficient attention to morality. Moral precepts play an important part in concentrating the rays of the mind. For instance, even when a person is established in the practice of nonviolence, will he not become angry even under provocation? Scriptural studies help one in establishing concentration and gradually purify one's mind.
3. **Exercise.** This is a system of making all parts of the body strong, healthy, and supple. Even those not practicing the mystical aspects of Yoga may do exercise to improve health. Exercise regulates breathing, ensures proper digestion of food, and increases longevity. Exercise strengthens the nervous system, having a salutary effect on the brain centers and spinal cord. Exercise relaxes the five systems that make up the physical body:
   The physical system: all the tissues and fluids of the body from bone to skin.
   The vital systems: the vital airs (prāṇas) of the system.
   The mento-motor system: the principle of volition, the principle of individuality, and the five principles of action—articulation, grasp, locomotion, reproduction, and excretion.
   The mento-sensory system: the principle of judgment, the principle of memory, and the five principles of sensation—sight, hearing, taste, smell, and touch.
   The spirituo-emotional system: love, cheerfulness, and happiness (little or much). The elementary matter is the medium through which the soul entertains these feelings. It is only when the physical body is in perfect health that the mind can concentrate.
4. **Deep Breathing.** This includes the vital forces, the media through which the soul acquires all kinds of knowledge, carries on all the mental processes, and performs all its actions:
   Expiratory force: breathing out
   Inspiratory force: breathing in

Solar-sympathetic force: situated in the center parts of the body
Gloss-pharyngeal force: draws food into the stomach, giving the body strength and energy
Motor-muscular force: the cause of motion

Deep breathing is a special method of breath control by which the life force is brought under control and made regular. This is achieved by controlling incoming and outgoing breaths.

It is not the normal way we breathe but something else. It is the subtle life force behind the breathing function. Breath is only a gross manifestation of the subtle energy we call breathing. In fact, all functions of the body have air as their life force. For instance, breathing, flickering of the eyelids, heartbeat, circulation, and digestion all have it as their life force. Breathing is a conscious life force in all living beings and is derived from air, sunlight, water, vegetation, and minerals of the earth. It works together with the soul in all animals.

The correct practice of deep breathing controls the governing powers of the body, which are the nose, mouth, eyes, and ears. In the lower abdominal region, waste materials are expelled via the kidneys and intestines; the region around the navel promotes the proper digestion of food, and its seat is within the heart and in the veins and arteries, which propel the proper circulation of the blood. The blood is the vitalizing force in the nerve centers and in the brain, and it is this force that is responsible for the reincarnation of the soul by serving as a guiding vehicle. Deep breathing stills and steadies the restless mind, thus making concentration and meditation easier to achieve.

5. **Detachment.** This is the ability to withdraw the senses or internal organs from the centers of objects to which they are attached. The natural inclination of the senses toward the objects of enjoyment leads the mind astray. When children in a classroom hear some loud noise outside, they immediately look through the window and do not pay attention to their studies. But if their minds were engaged in their studies, no noise or distraction would have the power to lead them astray. So the ability to withdraw the senses from the objects of attachment is detachment. Just as a tortoise withdraws all its limbs in the face of danger, so must an aspirant completely withdraw his senses from their objects.

   When you have become the master of your mind, the mind is controlled, and simultaneously all senses are under control as well. When heaven is spoken of, it is meant to be a place, whether it is in some location in the sky or here on earth, of perpetual happiness. Therefore, isn't it natural to assume one has to qualify for it? Those who chose to become doctors have to do so in theory and practice. They have to conquer all errors and weaknesses. They know that one mistake can be very fatal. As a matter of fact, they must be qualified before they practice. Likewise, it is reasonable to assume that one has to enjoy perpetual happiness before going to heaven. That means one has to conquer all unhappiness and discomforts in life here on earth before departure. Some of those discomforts are hunger, sleep, heat and cold, sex, anger, and inanition.
6. **Concentration.** When the mind is withdrawn from outside objects and is totally fixed on an idea or a center, it is said to be concentrated. In concentration, all the rays of the mind are collected and fixed on a center or idea. No artist, sculptor, musician, sportsman, or student can hope to succeed if the mind is not engaged in the task on hand. So in Yoga also, concentration is most essential.

7. **Communion.** When the mind is fully engaged in a particular thought or idea without interruption, it is said to be in communion. In this state, a person forgets his surroundings, his body, or anything that is connected with him. Even the pleasures that interest him at other times or his pet fancies, worries, or tensions of his daily life do not trouble him whatsoever at this time. In Yoga, because the object of concentration is God or the Absolute, all the powers of the mind are directed in the contemplation of God.

   The mind of the yogi in the state of meditation is compared to the light of a lamp that burns without flickering. In this state, the mind is calm and enjoys immense bliss, a foretaste of the uninterrupted bliss and boundless joy that is inherent in the very nature of God or the Supreme Consciousness. Concentration should be focused on the characteristics, attributes, and nature of the Supreme Being, and only a deep study of the scriptures (Vedas) can enable us to focus that attention.
8. **Supreme Consciousness or Self-Realization.** The final step in meditation or contemplation brings us to experience the oneness with God. The achievement of Supreme Consciousness is the true meaning of Yoga. This final union with God confers supreme bliss, felicity, and an end to all sorrows. This state transcends all thought, and all logical processes such as thinking, reflecting, and calculating cease to function. It is the final experience in which the yogi attains a state of perfection, the crowning glory of success on the spiritual realm. This is Yoga.

A clean and solitary place is necessary for the engagement of communion. Get comfortably seated and practice breath control, restrain the senses from the pursuit of outward objects, fix the mind on one of the following: the navel, the heart, the throat, eyes, the top of the head (forehead), or the spine. Discriminate between the soul and the Supreme Spirit, get absorbed in contemplation of the latter and commune with God.

When these practices are followed, the mind as well as the soul becomes pure and imbued with righteousness. Knowledge and wisdom advance day by day until salvation is obtained. If one hour of contemplation to the Deity is practiced daily, there will be spiritual advancement.

NOTES

1. L. Mahadevan, *Ayurveda Intensives, Summer 2001* (Saylorsburg, PA: Arsha Vidya Gurukulam, 2001).
2. Laj Utreja, *Who Are We?* (Bloomington, IN: AuthorHouse, 2006).
3. Utreja, *Who Are We?*
4. Yogananda Paramahansa, *Autobiography of a Yogi* (Los Angeles: Self-Realization Fellowship, 1946).
5. Monita Soni and Laj Utreja, "Effect of Praanaayaama and Yoga on Signs and Symptoms Associated with Mitral Valve Prolapse" (Paper presented at International Yoga Conference, Svyasa, Bangalore, India, December 2005).
6. Utreja, "Praanaayaama as an Alternate Method to Avoid Sickness Associated with High Altitudes and Very High Altitudes" (Paper presented at International Yoga Conference, Svyasa, Bangalore, India, December 2005).
7. For more information on Healing Consciousness workshops and camps, visit www.lajutreja.com or www.IshDhaam.com.

About the Editor and Contributors

ARVIND SHARMA is Birks Professor of Comparative Religion in the Faculty of Religious Studies at McGill University in Montreal, Canada, and has published extensively in the fields of Indian religions and comparative religion. He was president of the steering committee for the Global Congress on World's Religions after September 11, which met in Montreal September 11–15, 2006, and is currently engaged in promoting the adoption of A Universal Declaration of Human Rights by the World's Religions.

MABEL ARANHA has an Ed.D. from Columbia University and a certificate in peace and conflict resolution from the European Peace University in Austria. She also has a Ph.D. in alternative medicine from Sri Lanka. She has worked for thirty-one years in the field of education, and was principal of a primary, middle, and high school for twenty-one years in Mumbai, India. She wrote a book titled *Guidelines for Peace Education for Indian Schools,* for which she received a commendation from the National Council for Educational Research and Training from the government of India. Currently retired, she has written two more books, *Guidelines for Parents and Teachers on Loving-Kindness Meditation* and *Religion and Beyond.*

DEBRA BEHRLE's attendance at the Parliament of World Religions in Barcelona, Spain, in 2004 led her to create her presentation for the Global Congress on World's Religions after September 11. Debra, an ordained Science of Mind minister, focused on world religions in her ordination studies. She is passionate about maintaining respect for each other and the earth. She has been on an intentional journey of self-discovery, connection to nature, and dedicates her work to sustaining the earth. She is a landscape designer and master gardener devoted to sustainability using ornamental grasses, especially bamboo and cane. She manages a twelve-acre estate in Asheville, North Carolina, complete with formal gardens.

ODETTE BÉLANGER (ALIAS VEDHYAS DIVYA), having become a hygienist and a teacher of Yoga, decided to enter the discipline of meditation and went to perfect this discipline in the Ashram of Swami Hamsananda in France in the 1970s. She stayed there approximately twelve years as a monk. Thanks to this experience, she had the privilege of being initiated by His Holiness, Lord Hamsah Manarah, Cosmoplanetary Messiah of Synthesis and the founder of Aumism. Upon her return to Canada, Vedhyas Divya founded her own Yoga center and Centrom, where she gives Yoga and meditation classes while occupying a post as legal assistant. She is currently pursuing a master's degree in the science of religions, in preparation for which she obtained a bachelor's degree in arts and letters, languages and communication, and a certificate in the science of religion from UQÀM.

FABRICE BLÉE teaches Christian spirituality and interreligious dialogue as professor in the faculty of theology at Saint Paul University. After his studies in Strasbourg and Montreal, he undertook two postdoctoral research projects on interreligious dialogue, one in the faculty of theology in Delhi (Vidyajyoti) and the other at the Woodstock Theological Center of Georgetown University in Washington, D.C. He successfully defended his doctoral dissertation on monastic interreligious dialogue in North America at the University of Montreal (1999). He is the author of *Le désert de l'altérité: une expérience spirituelle du dialogue interreligieux* (2004). He is director of the series "Spiritualités en dialogue," published by Mediaspaul Publications. His research and publications focus on the significance and relevance of a Christian spirituality of dialogue among religions.

MARY ANN BUCKLEY is a member of the Sisters of the Holy Child Jesus (SHCJ). She holds an M.A. in humanities from New York University and has recently moved to Santiago, Chile, to join Holy Child sisters and associates there.

HUM D. BUI, M.D., from a CaoDai family in Vietnam, came to the United States in 1975 and began sharing the religious unity and oneness of CaoDai teachings with the Western world. He has participated in interfaith activities in Rome; Mt Hiei, Japan; Cape Town, South Africa; Barcelona, Spain; and in the United States. He continues translating CaoDai teachings into English and maintains the CaoDai organization web page, www.caodai.org.

HELEN COSTIGANE has a doctorate in moral theology from Heythrop College, London, where she also teaches. She presents a vision of the incarnate God as present in the everyday business world, addressing the question, Can religion be a force for good in the business world, or is the gulf between God and Mammon too wide even for people of goodwill to build bridges? She is a member of the Sisters of the Holy Child Jesus (SHCJ).

JAGESSAR DAS, currently retired, was a family physician for over forty years in North Delta, British Columbia. His interests include religion and spirituality. He was the host of a thirteen-part television series on world religions and three programs on the Indian mystic saint Kabir. He is often interviewed on religious topics on ethnic television in Vancouver. He is president of the Kabir Association of Canada and produced the association's *Kabir Voice* periodical for several years. He has written four books on the teachings and poems of Kabir. He gives weekly religious talks, and has lectured in Los Angeles, Trinidad, and Toronto. He is a founding member of the Clergy for Compassion and Harmony in Surrey, British Columbia.

LAURA GALLO holds a B.A. in world religions from McGill University. She is currently a graduate student (M.A.) in the history and philosophy of religion at Concordia University in Montreal.

RAVI GANGADHAR is presently working as visiting faculty at M.Arch (Habitat Design) B.M.S. College of Engineering, Bangalore-19. He completed his M.S., in physics (specializing in astrophysics) at Bangalore University in 2000. His project, Humane Physics, has been awarded a fellowship by the Indian Council for Philosophical Research (ICPR), New Delhi.

SHANTILAL G. GORADIA was born and raised in India. He holds a degree from the University of Nebraska and has done postgraduate work at Purdue University–West Lafayette and Kansas State University–Manhattan. He is a registered professional engineer in Ohio, a member and active participant in the American Physical Society, and a life member of the International Society of General Relativity and Gravitation. He has authored many technical publications and lectured at conferences all over the world, sharing his insights regarding nuclear physics, thermodynamics, and gravitation.

MARSHALL GOVINDAN is the author of several acclaimed books and the founder of Canada's and India's largest publishing houses of books related to Classical Yoga, as well as three charitable organizations dedicated to the teaching of Kriya Yoga. His most recent book is titled *The Wisdom of Jesus and the Yoga Siddhas.* He has practiced Kriya Yoga intensively since 1969, and leads seminars and retreats worldwide. He is a graduate of Georgetown University and George Washington University. His website is www.babaji.ca. He may be contacted at satchidananda@babaji.ca.

EMMANUEL J. KARAVOUSANOS retired in 1990 after thirty-three years of service as an insurance investigator. His interest, however, always lay in the realm of consciousness and religion. He has spoken at several conferences on consciousness, most recently at the Society for the Anthropology of Consciousness in April 2007. He has published numerous articles on the New Testament. In 2007 he authored *The Gift of Mystical Insight,* a book containing the basis, evidence, and logic for mystical experiences. His work is based on that of Alfred North Whitehead and others who discuss the analysis of familiar, obvious, and known things.

ISSA KIRARIRA is the executive director at Media for Peace and Religious Tolerance (MPRT) in Uganda.

SAI MAA LAKSHMI DEVI is a dynamic visionary and spiritual master who practices "Divine Will in Action." Dedicated to global enlightenment and eliminating the pain and suffering of humanity, she tirelessly tours the world, inspiring listeners from all walks of life. Her Holiness Sai Maa honors the many paths that awaken people to their true selves. She has been honored by and collaborated with the world's foremost spiritual luminaries. H. H. Sai Maa is the founder of Humanity in Unity, a nonprofit organization based in Boulder, Colorado.

ANDREA D. LOBEL is a Ph.D. student at Concordia University in Montreal, Canada. Her research interests encompass the history of astronomy, cosmology, cosmogony, and celestial mythologies within Judaism; extra-biblical literature and the ancient Near East; and calendar development and its emergence from astronomical observation. Additional interests include Jewish mysticism and magic, astronomy and celestial mythologies within Hinduism, and the history of religions.

VEDHYAS MANDAJA, Ed.D., is a retired professor of French nationality. She lectures internationally even as she continues her comparative researches in education and religions. She is today engaged in the promotion of values of tolerance, brotherhood, and peace as bishop of the Aumist religion, founded by His Holiness, Lord Hamsah Manarah.

JOANNA MANNING is an award-winning writer and teacher. A former Catholic nun who was born in England, she now resides in Toronto, where she is active in outreach to the poor. Once famously referred to as "that bitch" by Cardinal Aloysius Ambrozic, Joanna is also an outspoken advocate for women's equality at all levels of religion and society. She is the author of three books: *Is the Pope Catholic? A Woman Confronts Her Church* (1999), *Take Back the Truth: Confronting Papal Power and the Religious Right* (2002), and *The Magdalene Moment* (2006).

JEAN M. O'MEARA, a member of the Sisters of the Holy Child Jesus (SHCJ), illustrates how Holy Child sisters are collaborating with other religious women to address violations against the dignity and human rights of individuals, specifically through the work of UNANIMA-International (U-I), a UN nongovernmental organization focused on human trafficking. She has an M.A. in religious studies from Manhattan College and is the representative to U-I for the Holy Child sisters.

TOM PICKENS holds a B.A. in zoology from the University of California and an M.S. in systems analysis from the Air Force Institute of Technology. His work experience has been primarily in technology, beginning with communications and electronic systems in the U.S. Air Force and ending in the wind power and semiconductor energy industries in the United States. He moved to Canada in 1997 and is now retired.

B. R. SHANTHA KUMARI is a reader in the department of philosophy at Pondicherry University, India. Her areas of specialization are Advaita, aesthetics, and classical Indian philosophy. A recipient of the UGC Junior & Senior Research Fellowships (1989–92), she completed a minor research project funded by a UGC unassigned grant on "The Philosophy of Professor S. S. Suryanarayana Sastri" in 1997. She is also a member of the Board of Studies in Philosophy. She has delivered many lectures in philosophy, and her articles have been published in journals of philosophy with national and international circulation.

T. N. ACHUTA RAO is a graduate of Mysore University, with a master's in geography and a doctorate in regional development from Utkal University, Orissa. He is presently director of the Aurobindo Centre for the Study of Consciousness, under the auspices of the Divine Grace Foundation, Bharatiya Vida Bhavan, RC Nagar, Belgaum -6. He presented a paper titled "Environmental Compatibility and Human Habitat Development" at the World Congress of the International Union of Anthropological & Ethnological Sciences (IUAES) in 1988 at Zagreb. His spiritual background is also revealed in his other titles: *Ancient Wisdom, Spirit of the Soul, Muktiyoga Rahasya of the Bhagavad-gita,* and *Maha Vishnu—The Poorna Prajnyaa and His Prajnyaadhaaraa—The Eternal Flow of Consciousness.*

VINESH SAXENA is a professional engineer. He also holds an M.B.A. from McGill University and a C.M.A. designation. He has been interested in such fundamental questions as does the soul exist and is there life after death for a long time. He is currently taking care of a registered charitable foundation (www.vsffoundation.ca), which he established a few years ago. The objectives of this foundation are "to help the needy" and also to explore "the unanswered fundamental questions."

ROB SELLERS is Connally Professor of Missions at Logsdon School of Theology, Hardin-Simmons University, in Abilene, Texas. He draws upon his Ph.D. in theological ethics, twenty years working in Java, Indonesia, and travels in thirty-six countries to teach cross-cultural studies, liberation theology, interreligious dialogue, Two-Thirds

World theologies, and various courses in mission theology and methodology. Outside the United States, he has taught seminary classes in Asia, Europe, Africa, and South America. Active in a local interfaith organization, he is helping plan a national Baptist-Muslim dialogue for 2008, and frequently speaks or writes on the world's religions and cultures.

SUBHAS R. TIWARI has been full-time faculty at the Hindu University of America since 2003, teaching courses on Yoga, meditation, and Yoga philosophy. He graduated from Bihar Yoga Bhāratī, a world-class Yoga university, with a master's degree in Yoga philosophy, and taught Yoga for more than ten years in Ontario, Canada, and in the United States before setting out to India to further his Yoga studies. He completed his thesis "*Samādhi within Patañjali Yoga Sūtras.*" Professor Tiwari also holds an honors and a master's degree in political science from Ontario, where he had worked in human resources management. He is also secretary of the Wise Earth School and has many years of active *seva* (service) to spiritual and religious communities.

TOBIE TONDI has a doctorate in theology from Gregorian University, Rome, and teaches religious studies at Rosemont College, Rosemont, PA. Her chapter discusses the Incarnation as a worldview and as a philosophical foundation for both prayer and activity. She is a member of the Sisters of the Holy Child Jesus (SHCJ).

LAJ UTREJA's professional experience covers a wide range of disciplines related to the U.S. space and defense programs. He has worked in various capacities: as a hands-on engineer, a technical leader in people management, and a CEO of a small business in developing a corporate vision. Besides his career in engineering, he has provided counseling at the Huntsville Helpline. He is active at the Interfaith Mission Service, promoting cross-cultural understanding through interfaith dialogs and interfaith forums. He is an ardent student of Sanātana Dharma (Hinduism) and has given a myriad of talks on various aspects of his faith as part of his work on cross-cultural understanding. He conducts workshops and seminars on Prāṇāyāma, meditation, and Āyurvedic cooking.

Index